SPIRIT CHILDREN

AFRICA AND THE DIASPORA
History, Politics, Culture

Spirit Children

ILLNESS, POVERTY, AND INFANTICIDE IN NORTHERN GHANA

Aaron R. Denham

The University of Wisconsin Press

The University of Wisconsin Press
1930 Monroe Street, 3rd Floor
Madison, Wisconsin 53711-2059
uwpress.wisc.edu

Gray's Inn House, 127 Cleerkenwell Road
London EC1R 5DB, United Kingdom
eurospanbookstore.com

Printed in the United States of America

This book may be available in a digital edition.

Library of Congress Cataloging-in-Publication Data

Names: Denham, Aaron R., author.
Title: Spirit children: illness, poverty, and infanticide in northern Ghana /
Aaron R. Denham.
Other titles: Africa and the diaspora.
Description: Madison, Wisconsin: The University of Wisconsin Press, [2017]
| Series: Africa and the diaspora: history, politics, culture
| Includes bibliographical references and index.
Identifiers: LCCN 2016041575 | ISBN 9780299311209 (cloth: alk. paper)
Subjects: LCSH: Infanticide—Ghana. | Children—Ghana—Death—Religious aspects.
| Frafra (African people)—Ghana—Religion.
| Frafra (African people)—Ghana—Social life and customs.
| Frafra (African people)—Ghana—Social conditions.
Classification: LCC DT510.43.F73 D464 2017 | DDC 364.152/308309667—dc23
LC record available at https://lccn.loc.gov/2016041575

ISBN 9780299311247 (pbk.: alk. paper)

For
THE SPIRIT CHILDREN
everywhere

CONTENTS

ILLUSTRATIONS

ACKNOWLEDGMENTS

The work of the ethnographer involves inhabiting the spaces in between, the intersections among people, places, institutions, and cultures. Hence, any ethnographic endeavor encompasses contributions from many people who directly and indirectly impart their experiences, insights, and practices. This book is the outcome of nearly ten years of being in the presence of others and is a result of an expansive horizon of interactions and contributions from countless generous people.

I wish to express my deep appreciation to the Nankani people throughout the Kassena-Nankana East and West Districts for their hospitality and tolerance of my endless questions and requests. This book would not exist without the families with spirit children, which opened their homes to me and shared their experiences. I am particularly thankful to elders Asingiya, Asorigiya, and Ayanobasiya for taking the time to regularly sit with me and talk about their lives. I am deeply indebted to Joe Asakibeem, Elijah Agongo, and Matthew Abagna, my teachers, colleagues, and friends. They were always giving and always patient. This book embodies their significant contributions.

This research would not have been possible without the support of and collaboration with AfriKids, a child rights nongovernmental organization working in northern Ghana, and the Navrongo Health Research Centre operated by the Ghanaian Ministry of Health. I also thank the Department of Anthropology at the University of Alberta, Northern Arizona University, which granted me the time and the funding to pursue further fieldwork, and the Department of Anthropology at Macquarie University for providing me with significant blocks of time to write.

While I cannot acknowledge them individually by name, I thank the concoction men. I would not have been able to grasp the breadth and depth of their experiences and the meanings associated with holding the *dongo* without their openness and generosity. I am appreciative of members of the staff of the Sirigu Women's Organization of Pottery and Art (SWOPA), who often fed me, housed me, and answered my questions. I also thank the various women's organizations and youth groups and the Ghana Health Service nurses, midwives, and medical assistants throughout the Kassena-Nankana Districts for their assistance.

The staff of AfriKids Ghana was instrumental in the success of this project. I thank Cletus Anaaya, Mamma Laadi Awuni, Sebastian Ayaaba, Raymond Ayinne, Dramani Isiah, Nicholas Kumah, and Linda Marfoh. I am extremely appreciative of your support, tolerance, and insight. This research would not have been possible without the unending support of Georgie Fienberg, founder and former director of AfriKids. I also thank Sarah Devine, Andy Thornton, Sally Vivyan, and other past and present AfriKids United Kingdom staff.

I wish to express my gratitude to Rodney Frey, who immersed me in the fundamentals of ethnographic research, ethics, and representation. This book rests on that foundation. I thank Chris Fletcher and Philip Adongo, who provided support and advising during my fieldwork. I cannot offer enough thanks to my other mentors and friends, in particular, David Lancy, who helped me frame infanticide and childhood from a broader perspective and offered numerous insights; Jim Wilce, a friend and intellectual mentor who was always available to listen to my ideas and share his thoughts; and Jim Phillips, who offered many useful suggestions during the formative phases of this project, helped me establish it, and linked me to a network of other scholars. I also want to acknowledge the influence of John Hendee, who encouraged some of my early research interests many years before this project began.

While at Northern Arizona University, I benefited from the contributions and help of Jessica Lum—who conducted the research for her master's degree in Sirigu—and the research assistance of Mercedes Douglass, Danielle Shafer, and Brooke Weber. I extend a special thanks to Stephen Fisher and Ananda Robie for their photographic talent while in Ghana and the contributions that appear in this book.

I could not research and write this without the intellectual stimulus, encouragement, advice, and support from my many mentors, students, colleagues, collaborators, and friends, including Emmanuel Akayeti, Anthony Akunzule, Patricia Akweongo, Thompson Apempale, Kerry and Tom Bruce, John Campbell, Alison Clough, Greg Downey, Jónína Einarsdóttir, Catherine Ellis, Connie Geekie, Nancy Gibson, Lisa Hardy, Abraham Hodgson, Janet Dixon Keller, Corina Kellner, Pamela Lamb, Murray Last, Ben and Jaina Moan, Naomi Linzer Indexing Services, Kathleen Lowrey, Carly McLafferty-Dokis, Andie Palmer, Mindy Pitre, Daisy Purdy, Payel Ray, Florence Rosiello, David Schlosberg, Christine Schreyer, Jason Shea, Denise Stippick, Kerry Thompson, Paulina Tindana, Paul Trotta, Danielle Varnes, Clint Westman, Lisa Wynn, John Yatsko, and the many others who provided assistance and are not listed here. The writing process is a solitary endeavor. Kevin Groark made it much easier through our innumerable conversations and by offering his unique insights into this project over pints of beer in Chinatown. The copyediting assistance of Jan Opdyke was instrumental in smoothing out the rough edges. I also thank Gwen Walker and the University of Wisconsin Press for their helpful suggestions.

Parts of this book have appeared, in altered form, in an article and two chapters published elsewhere. Some material in chapter 4 appeared in "Shifting Maternal Responsibilities and the Trajectory of Blame in Northern Ghana," in *Risk Reproduction and Narratives of Experience*, edited by Lauren Fordyce and Aminata Marasea, copyright © 2012 by Vanderbilt University Press. Material in the introduction concerning the representation of infanticide appeared in "Misconceptions and the Mystification of Infanticide in Northern Ghana: Ethnographic Insights," in *Medical Anthropology in Global Africa*, edited by Kathryn Rhine, John Janzen, Glenn Adams, and Heather Aldersey, copyright © 2014 by the University of Kansas Department of Anthropology. Some material in chapter 6 appeared in "Psychodynamic Phenomenology of Nankani Interpretive Divination and the Formation of Meaning," *Ethos* 43 (2) (2015).

Finally, my research and this book would not have happened without the support of my family. Nicole introduced me to the spirit child topic and played a role in the research, from my initial musings to its conclusion. She sustained me through the difficult periods and read and commented on my drafts. Her ideas, compassion, and presence permeate this work. I extend profound and heartfelt thanks to my sister, Jamie Knott, and my parents, Mike and Marty Denham. They have always offered unfailing encouragement and understanding. They have always championed my pursuits and are responsible for inspiring my curiosity and encouraging me to look at the bigger picture.

SPIRIT CHILDREN

Introduction

After a long day spent at the rural home of a local Nankani family, I returned to Sirigu, a small village in the Upper East Region of Ghana. Two of my assistants, Matthew, a primary school teacher, and Elijah, a local nongovernmental organization (NGO) social worker, abruptly stopped me in the market as I was passing through. Somehow, they had already heard of my encounter with N'ma, a chronically ill and disabled three-year-old girl believed to be a "spirit child" and thus at risk for infanticide because her family felt she was intent on instigating misfortune and killing family members.

They approached me smiling. "So, Aaron," Elijah said, shaking my hand, "now you've seen some of our wonderful things!" Since we had had many conversations about spirit children and the two of them had participated in countless interviews with me, I was a little perplexed by their newfound enthusiasm for my experience with another spirit child. I had been studying the spirit child phenomenon for several months already, working closely with Matthew, Elijah, and other community members on coming to a more accurate and holistic understanding of what it means when a family suspects that its infant or child is "nonhuman."

I shrugged. "I may have. Actually, I'm not sure what I saw."

Matthew said, "Tell us exactly what you saw." I was tired, overwhelmed, and still recovering from a lingering illness. I hesitated, wondering how I could explain my unsettling experience with N'ma. I felt too caught up within my own disjointed thoughts, too tired to place what I had witnessed within much if any framework, biomedical, spiritual, or otherwise. I paused for a moment before cobbling together a fragmented and pressured summary of the day.

I began by describing N'ma's slight body, her erratic movements, and her family's interpretation of her illness and behaviors as being spiritual in origin. I detailed her uncanny response to the assessment of a visiting "concoction man"—a ritual practitioner who specialized in sending spirit children back to the bush to rejoin the spirit world. I remarked on the way N'ma's family, laughing nervously, had narrated the unfolding of the "spiritual battle" occurring before us as N'ma resisted the concoction man's attempts to engage her. I noted how later that day the family had definitively agreed that N'ma was trying hard to prove to us that she was indeed a spirit wanting to return to the bush.

Matthew and Elijah nodded with unusual attention, taking it all in, and encouraged me to continue. I explained how unnerved I had felt later that day when an elder confronted me before I left, convinced that I comprehended the seriousness of the situation, and asked if I would ever go to sleep at night knowing that a deadly snake was loose in the house. I concluded that there was little we could do for N'ma; her condition was permanent. When I finished, I was surprised to see that Elijah and Matthew were satisfied with my explanation, even excited.

"Yes!" they exclaimed. "Yes, finally you see! It is true. These things exist! You've seen the spirit with your own eyes. Now you know."

I was at a loss for words, still trying to put together what I had just experienced. "I . . . I honestly don't know what to say or how to describe it all," I said.

"Some things here," Matthew replied, "cannot be explained."

Although preventable diseases and, ultimately, the effects of poverty constitute the primary causes of mortality throughout the Upper East Region of Ghana, local discourse suggests that a number of infant and child deaths are facilitated through poisoning by family members and concoction men. In these cases, deformed or ailing infants, those whose births were concurrent with tragic events, or children displaying unusual abilities may be regarded as spirits sent "from the bush" to cause misfortune and destroy the family. From the Nankani people's perspective, spirit children are not human but are bush spirits masquerading as such. From a biological perspective, many of these children have disabilities or are chronically ill. Community members, population health researchers, and development workers have interpreted the spirit child phenomenon as ritualistic murder, a way to cope with unwanted or sick children, and a "primitive" infanticide practice grounded in ignorance and needing, in the words of one development worker, "complete eradication." Despite the sensational nature of infanticide and the significant amount of attention the idea of the spirit child has attracted, the phenomenon has not been subject to direct study even in the Upper East Region where child and maternal health research and interventions have been successful.

Moreover, the spirit child and infanticide accounts in general rarely represent families' experiences and regularly employ reductionist models, such as sociobiological and rational choice or other economic paradigms, to account for infanticide practices. They explain that it makes sense as an adaptive strategy to eliminate nonviable infants perceived as "high cost." I argue that these perspectives are not necessarily inaccurate—they are often obvious within my own ethnographic experiences and this book—yet these are limiting accounts, relatively easy to apply to nearly any infanticide case. More important, they miss the experiences and ways of knowing central to what Matthew and Elijah described as the reality and truth of the spirit child's existence.

In a commentary on essentialism and reductionism, Webb Keane remarked that, despite how irritating it is to others, "We need to complicate the story" (2003, 222). In other words, particularly within the study of disabilities and culture, anthropologists especially need to be wary of practices that "distance and decontextualize persons, ideas, and practices" (Ingstad and Renyolds-Whyte 1995, 139). This also holds true for studies concerning forms of maternal neglect, which, according to Ruthbeth Finerman, "appear strikingly reductionistic" in their inattention to predisposing variables, value systems, actions, and outcomes (1995, 11). Indeed, to contend that infanticide or any form of complex decision-making expresses only rational goals is "to pretend that the iceberg exists only above water" (Appel 2011, 64).

In *Spirit Children*, I offer a comprehensive ethnographic account of the spirit child phenomenon, situating infanticide and the spirit child as forms of discourse and practice within the Nankani society of Ghana and its surrounding region, as well as within the larger global context. My encounters with spirit children and their families bring to the fore more significant diversity in decision-making, interpretation of abnormalities, and sentiments associated with fragile infants and children than commonly depicted in the infanticide literature. What is currently missing from infanticide accounts is people. *Spirit Children* fills this gap by depicting the vicissitudes of human experience around infanticide and offering closer comprehension of local meanings, moral worlds, and what is at stake for families when they confront a spirit child. I want to explore the possibility that in pushing past shallow descriptions of infanticide—or any other so-called harmful traditional practice—toward an experience-near and interconnected interpretation, one creates opportunities for a richer vocabulary with which to describe, critically question, and understand what many people regard as incomprehensible.

Essentially, I am arguing for what anthropology claims it is best at achieving: an integrative or holistic perspective. I am not aiming at the simultaneous practice of diverse anthropological subfields or a holism fixed to a biocultural synthesis. Rather, I seek that familiar methodological and interpretive holism fundamental to anthropology in its ability to demonstrate the Geertzian-like web of interconnections of nearly any cultural practice with other parts of society (Parkin 2007, 4) while also acknowledging that any holistic interpretation is itself a part (Sahlins 2010). I do not want to confuse my approach with a totalizing or structural-functionalist form of holism concerned with deconstructing a phenomenon only to reassemble it under a new guise. Attending to the unfolding of events over time, I present an open-ended perspective that focuses on the spirit child phenomenon and infanticide as an interconnected and temporal process of becoming (Ingold 2007). This approach permits, for example, insight into the trajectory of families' sentiments, a consideration of what mediates families' understandings of suspected spirit children, an engagement with the structural forces shaping their experiences, and attention to the way their interpretations of children change as suspicions arise and are resolved.

Interpreting and Representing Infanticide

Why is a closer insight into infanticide important? For now, I offer an initial argument. Representations, or, more importantly, misrepresentations, matter. In particular, media and academic depictions—or spectacles—of so-called harmful traditional practices inevitably result in a reactionary rallying cry for intervention, moral reform, or eradication. Too often these accounts are divorced or extracted from their dependent contextual factors and are represented, as Charles Briggs observes, "as products of pathological subjectivities and defective domesticities, and made to represent entire populations" (2007, 331). When considered at the individual level, observers too often focus on parental responsibility and assigning blame regardless of the social and economic context (Tobin 1997, 77).

Infanticide is not a value-neutral term protected by the presumed neutrality of science. It is often associated with pathology, illegal activity, or immoral behaviors. There is, in fact, too much stigma and diversity attached to the term to render it of much use at all. *Infanticide* tends to obscure and confuse more than it reveals. Since *infanticide* is such an ideologically laden term, it remains difficult to identify, for example, the differences between discourse and practice through the veneer of condemnation and bias. Can anthropologists offer neutral accounts free of moral judgment? Completely value free representations are unlikely, particularly those that focus solely on the act of infanticide itself. Holistic accounts are ideal, however, particularly ones that attend to "the social, economic, and political context in which high infant mortality and the discourse of infanticide co-exist" (Tobin 1997, 68).

Despite the significance of infanticide in most societies through human history and its prominent position within theory, it remains rare to find detailed ethnographic accounts of infanticide practices, particularly representations that transcend deterministic and often one-dimensional considerations of context and causative factors. Moreover, in those cases in which anthropologists have observed and written about infanticide practices, their discussions are often limited to a few paragraphs noting that it is unproblematic, routine, or expected because of economic and environmental conditions.

The difficulty in studying infanticide is perhaps understandable. Research efforts are not made easier by the fact that it is a sensitive topic about which it is often difficult for people to talk, and these factors may help account for the small number of detailed ethnographic descriptions concerning it (Scheper-Hughes 1992). Carolyn Sargent, in her research with the Bariba people, demonstrated that it was difficult to get direct information on infanticide practices and that the best information only came indirectly (1988, 87). The difficulty in talking to people about child mortality and the complex process of gathering first-hand accounts of infanticide may compel scholars to rely on anecdotal, dated, or inaccurate ethnographic information—often treated as the ethnographic present—that with each use has the potential to be inappropriately applied and transformed. Such problematic accounts risk being recycled and their ethnographic inaccuracies propagated within scholarly and popular discourses. For instance, literature reviews on infanticide often extract or extrapolate information, removing accounts of practices from their sources and reductionistically framing them into a table, for example, of ethnic groups that practice infanticide.[1] The resulting black-and-white depictions not only leave little indication of the contemporary status of practices but also offer no suggestion of the context within which families make such decisions. While authors may not intend it to be so, these dated depictions risk leaving readers with inaccurate, generalized understandings about others, resulting in blanket assumptions.

Researching and representing a sensitive topic like infanticide is fraught with challenges. Many anthropologists have been reluctant to study or discuss the phenomenon. This is hardly surprising since various organizations and media characterize the people involved as moral inferiors (Hrdy 1999, 294). Sensitive to these concerns, some anthropologists have hesitated to publish data that could be used to justify intervention, support racist agendas, or be called upon to emphasize a "primal nature" or "backwardness" that might constitute or justify barriers to progress or development (Hrdy 1999; Olivier de Sardan 2005, 76).

Indigenous groups worldwide are often subject to stereotypical and faulty research. Considering the perpetuation of stereotypes about aboriginal North America, James Waldram's (2004) critical examination of culture-bound syndromes, such as windigo psychosis, demonstrated that the construction and perpetuation of these syndromes within the literature are based on continued use of assumptions and dated, inaccurate, or questionable research. In another example, John Steckley critically examined "arctic hysteria," revealing that the construction of this disorder is a reflection of European-Inuit relations and the power imbalance embodied in specific contexts (2008, 18). A close examination of the literature on exotic culture-bound disorders exposes often biased and erroneous ethnographic materials that may "have their origins in the imaginations of scholars rather than the cultures" at issue (Waldram 2004, 190). One can learn critical lessons from these examples.

Other scholars have similarly critiqued research and the perpetuation of inaccurate representations throughout Africa. Achille Mbembe notes, "Instead of patient, careful, in-depth research, there are off-the-cuff representations possessed and accumulated without anyone's knowing how, notions that everyone uses but of origin quite unknown" (2001, 7–8). Repetition within the literature does not mean something is true; rather, the repetition of supposed truths risks eventual transformation and acceptance as truth. This repetition of stories and assumptions, particularly those of the exotic or fantastic, risks becoming what Jean Baudrillard described as "hyperreal"—that is, according to Steckly, "more real than concrete evidence-based constructions of reality in a culture" (2008, 26). Additionally, lurking within the shadow of development and public health practice is the history of using images of African people as inferior, primitive, or living close to the earth and subject to the primal urges associated with nature in an effort to legitimize intervention (Mudimbe 1988).

Indeed, infanticide practices have historically been regarded by missionaries and the Euro-American public as quintessential acts of savagery particularly worthy of a Christian godly intervention. Perceptions that people throughout Africa despise twins, for example, while in some cases factual, are largely a product of missionary narratives of twin murder and heroic twin salvation (Bastian 2001, 14). Closely researched ethnographic accounts can help set the record straight. Anthropologists, however, remain wary. Several years ago I spoke with a prominent anthropologist who had written a handful of carefully worded paragraphs about an infanticide practice similar to that of the spirit child in her ethnographies. When I asked her why she had never developed any of her observations on infanticide, she emphasized that the ethical and representational concerns were too significant—people could use the information against the community and fuel stereotypes. Similarly, another anthropologist described how his supervisor had told him to remove a chapter on an infanticide practice in South America from his doctoral dissertation—the chapter was dismissed as unnecessary. Similarly, Nelson Graburn (1987) stated that he did not publish on cases of severe child abuse in an Inuit community due to the sensitive nature of the material. Cases like these abound.

Could this hesitation be appropriate? Even attempts to offer experience-near accounts or attend to the sentiments of family members are fraught with other issues, such as the author's own projections and pretheoretical assumptions, which can cloud other explanations. For example, Katherine Dettwyler (1994), in her book *Dancing Skeletons*, describes infanticide data as "exotic" and offers a set of rhetorical questions that presume maternal attachment while commenting that westerners cannot truly understand what it is like to abandon one's child. After a Malian elder described to her the practice of abandoning "snake children," she remarked:

> "Yes, I understand now." . . . Of course, I didn't really understand. How can anyone understand what it feels like to give up on a child who is hopelessly "developmentally delayed"—to take the child of your body, the child of your heart, and abandon him or her to the universe? How can anyone who hasn't experienced it understand the heartache of losing a child? (86)

Indeed, how can outsiders understand? What choices are available? While it is positive to humanize infanticide and construct a link between mothers and readers, care is needed when projecting outside sentiments onto mothers' experiences of snake children. We cannot assume that all mothers in these circumstances experience heartache. Might some encourage abandonment?[22] My point is that one must be wary of imposing one's own conceptual categories or emotional world onto others and perpetuating incomplete and possibly inaccurate suppositions, particularly when speaking of sensitive practices.

Finally, the subject itself can provoke anxiety. For many readers and scholars, the act of infanticide is incomprehensible. Perhaps in this vein, readers' attempts to understand the vulnerability of others and engage in imaginative sympathy, or place themselves in the different circumstances, result in the defensive projection of their own desires, responses to traumatic situations, or safe assumptions onto the situation. Researchers' emotional responses to child mortality can result in methodologies and defenses that distance them from the affective and lived realities of infanticide practices—potentially resulting in reductionistic accounts. That is, a preference for experience-distant perspectives on infanticide can "domesticate reality"—sanitize complex human experiences into manageable objects that exist far from the realities of those experiencing them (Devereux 1967, 97). George Devereux's work is instructive here in identifying the importance of confronting distortions and illusions that arise within fieldwork and the role of countertransference, defense reactions, and blind spots. Attending to one's own responses to infanticide, or any other topic for that matter, can help minimize the possibility of isolating culture from its affective repercussions, limit an anxious clinging to rigid theory, and prevent what Devereux describes as the defense of interpretive "undercomprehension"—a process of considering data "sound" only because the scholar cannot tolerate other interpretations (46).

It is apparent that a variety of factors can cloud our understanding of infanticide. What would it take to make these practices more comprehensible? Can anthropology's commitment to complexity and a methodological and interpretive holism assist in capturing the reality and truths of the spirit child that Matthew and Elijah affirm? Can one reach a balance by moving between paradigms that offer breadth (evolutionary and economic theories) as well as depth (experience-based and person-centered approaches)? By offering rich accounts, more importantly, one can begin to build an interpretive bridge, address representational issues, and offer a way for the reader to connect with the experiences of families, understand their circumstances, and, ultimately, recognize that the experiences and decisions around spirit children might not be as distant as they seem.

Constructing the Spirit Child

Some of the first ethnographic accounts of northern Ghana reference spirit children. Meyer Fortes's early ethnographic work among the Tallensi describes unusual births as a result of *kɔlkpaaris*, or "malicious bush sprites" (1949, 271). He remarks that these spirits "sometimes quite wantonly enter a woman's womb and are born as twins or triplets, masquerading as incipient humans" (1987, 260). Fortes also suggests that what appears to be a normal adult human could actually be a spirit impersonating a human, only to reveal itself upon its death (1949, 329).

Among the Nankani people living in the eastern sections of the Kassena-Nankana East and West Districts, spirit children are referred to as *sisigo* (sing.: *sisito*) or "dwarves." Also recognizable is the term *kinkito* (sing.: *kinkiriko*), which is used farther east toward the regional capital of Bolgatanga. The neighboring Kasena refer to spirit children as *chuchuru* or *chichirru*.

Several scholars working in the Kassena-Nankana Districts (KND) have mentioned spirit children in their research.[3] They describe spirit children as a having a prominent physical abnormality or illness and characterize it as a nonhuman visitor intent on leaving the family when it is finished playing or causing misfortune. According to the literature, families identify spirit children by means of a wide range of signs and symptoms. They may exhibit physical anomalies at birth, including an unusually large or small head, spina bifida, premature teeth, or broken limbs. Spirit children may cry constantly and become upset if someone stares at them. Families are certain that if spirit children are allowed to live they will plague the lineage with bad luck and misfortune and can ruin the family's economic prospects. Spirit children are often framed as a way for families to understand abnormalities. A spirit child's mother may have had a difficult pregnancy or have died during or after childbirth. There is concern that spirit children dislike other siblings and can render their parents infertile. Families also worry that a spirit child will kill other family members.

While most general descriptions of spirit children are accurate, misunderstandings and problems arise when authors attempt to push past descriptions to explain or interpret, for example, how families confirm the presence of a spirit child and how deaths occur. Further confusion results when the myths and discourses about spirits are confused with what happens in practice when a family confronts a spirit child.

Research based on speculation, popular discourse, and problematic demographic data fuels the misunderstandings surrounding the practice (Denham et al. 2010). Previous studies speculated that the spirit child is an "important risk factor for infant mortality" and that up to 15 percent of deaths of infants under three months of age in the district could be due to the practice (Allotey and Reidpath 2001, 1010). Others conclude that significant reductions in infant mortality could be made with the elimination of infanticide in the districts (Baiden et al. 2006). The discourse circulating among health researchers in the region also identifies infanticide as a significant public health issue. Despite the attention it has received, there have been no complete ethnographic accounts of the spirit child phenomenon in Ghana, minimal direct contact with families with spirit children, and few considerations of what mediates families' experiences of misfortune and abnormality.

Media efforts have been misguided. An investigatory news segment appearing on Al Jazeera in January 2013 depicted the spirit child as a major problem in need of punitive law enforcement measures to eliminate the practice. Using hidden cameras and an investigative journalist posing as the father of a spirit child, the network recorded discussions with concoction men and agreements to treat a fictitious spirit child. Entrapped while preparing a concoction, police rushed in and arrested a concoction man. A diviner alleged to have "declared" the child a spirit was also arrested. The documentary inadequately considered the local culture, causes, and realities behind the practice. It did little but fuel a moral agenda and criminalize issues that are more closely connected to poverty and lack of adequate medical care than to law enforcement. While many outsiders praised the punitive approach and moral entrepreneurs called for change, the local community was outraged.

When I first learned of the spirit child it was under the rubric of ritual infanticide. As I began to learn more about them, people offered numerous accounts of children displaying extraordinary levels of human and nonhuman agency. I most often encountered narratives of three-month-old infants, for example, walking and talking like adults or vanishing at will. As my ethnographic research progressed, I found tremendous variation in the way families perceive and respond to spirit children and the role the phenomenon plays in accentuating the larger sociocultural processes and issues at stake for a family and community. As my awareness of the largely fantastic and dubious spirit child discourse grew, I began to question whether "infanticide" was occurring and if it was a public health issue at all.

During my fieldwork, I was interested not only in the local narratives and myths about spirit children but also how development workers, researchers, and scholars uncritically accepted and employed the spirit child discourse within research, education, and intervention programs. At the Navrongo Health Research Centre (NHRC), where local health researchers and fieldworkers encountered a variety of spirit child stories and indications of infanticide within demographic data, the spirit child reached legendary proportions and became active in the imaginations of many. Nearly all the local and international staff members had fantastic accounts of nefarious nighttime gatherings of spirit children and stories of infants destroying livestock, consuming adult foods, or killing family members.

For example, the discursive dimensions of the spirit child phenomenon reached their utmost apocryphal and symbolic expression during a spirit child drinking ritual held at the research center. Traditionally, researchers visiting from overseas bring a bottle of liquor to share with other researchers or project members, local and international. On the designated evening, staff members meet at a local drinking spot. At a midpoint in the evening, a senior researcher, a symbolic "concoction man," stands, thanks everyone for attending, offers words of appreciation to the powers that be, and explains the ritual at hand: the need to kill the bottle of spirits—the spirit child—standing in the middle of the table. As the bottle is passed carefully around the table, cradled in people's arms as though it's a baby, the speaker remarks that the spirit has been causing problems for the "family" and must be dealt with in the traditional manner. He exclaims that the spirit child must be sent to the bush, since that is the only way to liberate us from our misfortunes. When he has finished, the "concoction man" takes the bottle of spirits and in one swift motion twists its neck, breaking the seal. All present emit a sigh of relief and chuckle. A small libation is poured for the ancestors (the researchers that came before us), the bottle is passed around the table, and the spirits are, in effect, "killed." As the bottle circulates, the metaphor of sending the spirit child back to the bush becomes one of making the participants "go bush"—the local term for becoming intoxicated.

This prefieldwork experience was my first glimpse into one particular type of spirit child ceremony, one worthy of its own analysis and comparison. Throughout the next year, I would observe several other vastly different enactments, most necessitating a critical eye. A colleague's comment about the spirit child discourse during my fieldwork preparations motivated this critical turn. She sternly stated that she did not believe spirit children even exist, that people's stories about spirit children were really about something else entirely, and that it was unlikely that I would encounter an actual case of infanticide. While her argument was rhetorical in part, it forced me to step outside preexisting assumptions and encouraged me to think differently about the diverse forms the spirit child may assume within community discourse and consider the roles it may fill. What if it did not exist? Would I simply spend my time in the field chasing spirits, or was there something else occurring?

The consideration of Nankani spirits and the social and mythical world in which they reside is central to answering questions about the existence of spirit children and the possible forms they take. Alma Gottlieb remarked that folklore and myth ultimately contain "truths and issues of explicitly cosmological significance" (1992, 98). Indeed, stories and rumors, no matter how fantastic, can contain multiple debates about what is "real" and often are not only involved in *speaking* a truth but also *seeking* the truth (Kapferer 1987, 3; White 2000, 66). Thus, if one takes the position that the spirit child is speaking of and seeking multiple truths, then what are they and what is their significance?

Perhaps the best approach is not to dwell too deeply on the truth of the spirit child in objective terms (does it exist?), or as a distinction between what is "real" and what is "illusory," but to attend to the ontological underpinnings, experiences, and relationships between spirit child discourse, practice, and their social world, for example, as a way to facilitate an understanding of the kind of lifeworld that Nankani people "make and engage" through stories and accusations (West 2007, 47). The best way to analyze and understand spirit child accounts is to contextualize them, show their interconnectivity, and

communicate how they make sense to the people without removing them from
the intensity of lived experiences and the meanings and details they reference,
no matter how fantastic the narratives might appear (White 2000, 5).

Despite my colleague's doubts, it was not long before I encountered actual
spirit child cases and witnessed the way families interpreted children's bodies
and their closely intertwined circumstances and relational worlds. The following
vignette concerns one of these cases. I now return to the case of N'ma to introduce a Nankani family's experience of a spirit child.

The Case of N'ma

Outside his office one morning, Joe was urgently awaiting my arrival. With a
notebook and mobile phone in hand, he quickly jumped into my truck and directed me to pick up Ayisoba, a concoction man with whom I had been closely
working.[4] Earlier that morning, Ayisoba informed Joe, a local Nankani NGO
worker, that a family with a spirit child wanted him to "test" the child. On our
way to the family's house, Ayisoba explained that she was a very powerful spirit
child. Two concoction men had previously tried but failed to kill her.

On arriving at the family's home, we exchanged greetings with the eight or
so men and women present and positioned our benches in the shade. Ayisoba
explained to the family that he had brought us along because I was interested
in learning more about spirit children and because the NGO I was observing
might have other choices for N'ma, the suspected spirit child. N'ma, meaning
"my mother," is a generic name given to newborn girls before a more permanent name is determined, usually before the child's first birthday. Although
N'ma hardly appeared to have reached her first birthday, she was actually close
to three years old. She looked fragile and malnourished; indeed, at age two, the
last time she was weighed, she was, according to her medical card, 7.4 kilograms
(16 pounds).

The World Health Organization's fiftieth percentile weight-for-age guide-
lines for a two-year-old girl are 11.5 kilograms (25 pounds). N'ma was below the
first percentile. She could not stand, crawl, or talk and had experienced several
episodes of malaria in addition to the primary cause of her current state, a serious case of meningitis contracted when she was six months old. When I asked
about the meningitis, N'ma's mother, Atipoka, described how within an hour
after coming down with a fever, N'ma went into convulsions and even stopped
breathing for a short time. The family took her to the clinic, where she was
treated and survived. However, since that illness she had stopped developing.
Family members described her as being far behind other children her age.
"This is her age mate," they said, dragging a much larger and unwilling child

A nurse weighing babies at a mobile children's health clinic (Stephen Fisher)

A typical child's medical record held above a nurse's records of clinic vaccinations (Stephen Fisher)

over next to her. "Look at how big he is and all the things that he can do. Why is this one not like that?"

N'ma was similar to the other spirit children I encountered. Many suffered from a severe illness or congenital disability. When I asked people what a spirit child was, the common response was "a child that does not possess the right qualities of a normal human being." In addition to recognizing physical differences, families scrutinize a child's behavior and are wary of delays or early onset in the normal developmental patterns for such events as talking or walking. Most of the families with spirit children were poor, relied primarily on subsistence agriculture, and had limited access to health services. Childhood abnormality alone, however, is rarely enough to confirm a spirit child case. Other circumstances and misfortunes associated with the child, such as illness or death, contagious epidemics, crop failure, drought and abnormal climatic events, death of livestock, or a period of conflict or bad luck in the family, must be present to generate suspicion that a child is the source of these problems.

I asked Atinga, the family head, how he had discovered N'ma was a spirit child. He replied that two years ago, when her sickness began, he and N'ma's father went to consult the diviner numerous times and discovered that the child was trying to find a way to kill everyone in the family. At that point, he said, "We knew she was a spirit child."

The diviner facilitates communication with the ancestors, who are consulted on important issues related to the family, including determining illness causation. All families will go to the diviner when verifying their suspicions concerning a child.

In this case, a concern arose that N'ma was planning to kill family members. This issue took on importance as those of us present discussed the situation openly in front of her. Atinga feared that since N'ma knew what he was trying to do, she would kill him first. "We are fighting," he said. "The child has to go away."

The discourse and limited amount of literature on the spirit child describes decisions progressing quickly from detection to death. However, my evidence indicates that there is commonly a period of help-seeking activity before a concoction man is summoned. In the case of N'ma, family members described how they had taken her to a hospital and clinic several times over the past two years with little success. Even an herbalist they consulted concluded that she could not be helped. The family was running out of choices. "It has been making me suffer a lot," Atipoka said, "always being indoors and having to watch her. She just sits on the ground and cries all the time. That tells me she is not a normal human being."

Joe cut in with a joking and teasing tone of voice, possibly trying to break the tension. "Does the crying prevent you from sleeping with your husband?" he asked. Atipoka looked down. Ayisoba noted, in a more serious tone, that perhaps N'ma just wanted a younger brother, which is why she stopped breast-feeding.

"Yes," Joe said. "That means her husband will have to have intercourse with her!" Everyone laughed.

Ayisoba shook his head. "Yes, but how can you have something like this and go in and have sex with a woman?"

Issues concerning sexuality and reproduction surfaced frequently. Families also articulate these concerns through taboos that surround women's behavior and in myths about spirits. This discourse reciprocally shapes and reinforces interpretations of a suspicious child's body and behavior. Explanations of how a spirit child enters a woman's womb highlight these themes as well. Fundamentally, the goal of the spirit is to pass from the wild and undomesticated bush into a domestic space by any means possible. The easiest way for a spirit to accomplish this is to enter a woman through a taboo violation such as illicit sexual activity, take human form, and be born into a family.

Earlier that morning, elder family members had accused Atipoka of secretly continuing to breast-feed to prevent pregnancy, a claim she denied. Nankani families traditionally expect women to have another child soon after the previous child is weaned. The child, Atipoka said, refused to eat properly altogether. Refusing to eat—a "failure to thrive," as biomedical health care workers might describe it—is another defining characteristic of a spirit child. Families note that such children obtain their food from the bush during clandestine visits at night. Families also describe suspected spirit children with voracious appetites who would suckle their mothers dry, consume adult foods, and drink milk from lactating cattle.

As we continued to chat with the family, Ayisoba made repeated attempts to engage N'ma. She refused to look at him, although she did look at and turn toward everyone else. We all watched closely and suspiciously noted this inconsistency. Ayisoba took his goatskin medicine bag and repeatedly held it near N'ma; each time she would recoil and look away with a pained expression on her face. Everyone was intrigued and a bit unsettled.

N'ma was purposefully handed to Ayisoba. He gently held her and talked to her in a soft voice, but N'ma remained motionless, her eyes closed. "Pretending to sleep," someone said, although she had been wide awake just moments before. Ayisoba raised his voice but was unable to rouse her. Her motionless body was quite rigid. She looked uncomfortable; in fact, she looked dead.

Sensing our apprehension, Joe took N'ma from Ayisoba's arms. N'ma quickly opened her eyes, looked intently at Joe, and defecated on him.

"Look at what Ayisoba made her do," someone remarked as others laughed nervously. "This is a very powerful child."

This sparked a flurry of discussion that reinforced everyone's suspicions.

"Their spirits [those of N'ma and Ayisoba] are battling," another man exclaimed.

Even Joe, who aids families with ill or disabled children, suspected that N'ma was really a spirit child. "She wants to return to the bush," he said. "That's why she's behaving that way." Another person remarked that she was doing these things to demonstrate her power. Ayisoba agreed, saying, "I normally have to treat children like this. The child has shown you it is a spirit child for sure and now wants to prove it. Look. I haven't given the child anything and she's behaving like that. Why?"

Joe handed N'ma to her mother and cleaned himself. Family members continued to make jokes and laugh nervously. From the family's perspective, N'ma was exercising an unusual and uncanny level of agency. While families do not usually diaper infants and these sorts of accidents are common, it was the context and the timing in which it occurred that increased the family's suspicions and put them on edge.

My own perspective shifted. The previous months of listening to families recount myths and experiences of spirit children began to take on a new significance. I began to see the family's interpretive process, particularly how the social and cultural context and discourse dialectically influenced interpretations of her embodied status and behavior. While I was able to see how N'ma's existence threatened reproductive continuity and resources, what was more pressing was how her family interpreted and condensed the meanings of her body and existence into danger.

After everyone calmed down, Ayisoba asked for some water, indicating that he wanted to "test" N'ma to see what would happen.

I spoke up. "You're not going to give her the concoction, are you?"

"No," Ayisoba replied, "just some groundnuts from my bag."

"Specially treated groundnuts," Joe clarified. "I don't know if he should do it."

I asked Ayisoba what he put on the groundnuts and he said nothing, but Joe pointed out that the nuts came from inside his goatskin bag. I frequently joked with Ayisoba that we should trade bags sometime, my messenger bag, with its various ethnographic tools, for his, which contained substances of power, items for medicinal protection, and mobile representations or proxies for particular sorcery and ancestral shrines. I was only able to explore it years later. The bag never left his side, and he frequently clutched it across his belly when approaching an unfamiliar situation or feeling uncomfortable. He adamantly refused my halfhearted offers of a temporary exchange, saying that if his bag left his side he would be attacked and surely die.

Ayisoba, with his bag resting across his lap, shrugged his shoulders and assured us that the nuts were not poisonous, but everyone recognized that they were spiritually enhanced. He told the family that they could bring their own nuts so he could give them to the child. Convinced, they allowed Ayisoba to break his nuts into pieces and give them to her with water. N'ma refused to eat them, spitting the nuts and the water out. Ayisoba tried again, but still she refused, her mouth and eyes tightly clenched as she turned her head to the side, desperately avoiding Ayisoba's hands and gaze. The meaning of her refusal was obvious to every family member present, and if they needed additional confirmation, it came when N'ma urinated on Atipoka after spitting out the final pieces of groundnut. From the local perspective, N'ma was doing everything in her power to show that she was a spirit child.

Joe turned to me. "There's nothing we can do," he said. "There are a lot of reasons why the child is this way. But they have to do away with it because of the tradition."

As we were saying our good-byes and arranging to visit again later in the day, the family head aggressively confronted me. "It is a snake!" he exclaimed. "Tell me, would you go to sleep at night knowing there was a poisonous snake in your house?"

Hesitating, I replied, "Only a fool would."

Joe and I slowly walked away from N'ma's home in the stifling midday heat. Back at his office, we discussed that fact that the family was committed to killing the child, as evidenced by the two concoction men who had visited the family before Ayisoba and by the scene we had just witnessed. Joe believed that the only thing we could do was step away and recommend that the family wait to let the child die naturally.

We discussed the issues involved in imposing outside moral frameworks on what the family should do while being unable to also provide an adequate solution. Despite my recognition of our different notions of what constitutes a human being, it remained difficult for me not to see the decision to step away as a death sentence for N'ma. From the family's perspective, however, she wasn't a child; she was a spirit. The moral dilemma was not in the act of killing the child but in determining what had caused her to enter the family in the first place.

Later that afternoon, Joe and I returned to the house. Joe explained to the family that he could not do anything to help and that further trips to the hospital would change nothing. The family head agreed and remarked that he had suspected this to be the case. Joe encouraged the family to wait even a week to see what might happen. The family agreed to wait a week but no longer, since this was a serious case. Ayisoba also agreed not to do anything right away, although he added that sometimes these things are real and must be taken care of before they become a larger problem. A few days later I learned that N'ma's mother had fled to the urban center of Kumasi six hundred kilometers away. Apparently, she was afraid that N'ma was trying to kill her.

In N'ma's case, we can move easily from the family's descriptions regarding parental burdens and reproductive imperatives to applying sociobiologically oriented interpretations, which are almost obvious and go without saying. If a child cannot go off with the other children soon after she is weaned so the mother can work and have another child, problems arise. While considering these interpretations, I prefer to focus on offering additional layers of analysis throughout this book. For example, from another perspective, I recognize, quoting Rayna Rapp and Faye Ginsburg, that "the birth of anomalous children is an occasion for meaning-making" (2001, 536). Thus, I ask what a suspected spirit child means to a community and families. What concerns does it foreground? Examining the wider meanings of *normality* and *abnormality* are central to this work, as the human body is not only a profoundly historical site but a moral site as well; with certain forms of illness and disability, particular bodily states can problematize or threaten the balance of social and domestic relations (Livingston 2005, 2–9; Rapp and Ginsburg 2001).

Four days after our visit, Ayisoba came to Sirigu to let us know that the family had been pressuring him to come and "finish the child." He told us that even if an NGO could help N'ma, the family was now refusing to give her up. The family feared that N'ma was spiritually powerful enough to continue to disturb them and cause misfortunes as long as she was living, no matter where she might be. When Ayisoba left soon after, we both understood what he was going to do.

1

Contextualizing Infanticide and Northern Ghana

Infanticide is more common than people imagine. Studies indicate that roughly 80 percent of societies have practiced infanticide at some point in time (Lancy 2008, 86). A survey of sixty societies indicated that infanticide is present in thirty-nine (Daly and Wilson 1984, 490), although the numbers are likely higher due to imperatives to hide practices or the fact that ethnographers have not observed or recorded the incident (Lancy 2008, 86).

For a practice that has been a part of nearly every society at some point in its history (Williamson 1978), it is surprising that no agreed-upon definition of *infanticide* exists (Bechtold and Graves 2010, v). Definitions tend to differ across disciplines and remain flexible to fit specific aims. Strictly defined, infanticide is the killing of a child under one year of age (Miller 1987, 96). Scholars and the media, however, generally refer to infanticide as the willful death of newborns, young children, and older children without reference to age (Scrimshaw 1984, 440). For example, Samuel Kimball offers a broad definition of *infanticide* as fatal violence against infants and children by a preceding generation (2007, 15). Other terms provide greater specificity based on age, such as *neonaticide* (the killing of an infant within twenty-four hours of its birth), *foeticide* (the killing of a fetus), and *filicide* (including the intentional death of a dependent older than one year and broader definitions that reference children from one day old to middle childhood) (Schwartz 2000, 1; Shaw 2006, 256).

Some infanticide definitions evoke further questions. For example, does specifying "fatal violence," as above, include passive forms of neglect or obscured but equally brutal forms of structural violence? Definitions also conjure the moral category of murder,[1] yet are all infanticide cases murderous and, if so, how do we account for cultures that have different moral conceptions of what constitutes murder, who is a person, and when life begins? With critical scrutiny, it becomes apparent that infanticide is not necessarily a "transparent or natural category" (Tobin 1997, 67); rather, infanticide and its definitions are contextually shaped and culturally bound.

Infanticide can be further delineated according to the actions of the responsible agent and the agent's degree of intention. Active infanticide involves behaviors completed with the goal of deliberately killing the child. The means for active infanticide are, in Robert Weir's words, "limited only by the human imagination and the available technology of particular times and places," for instance, poisoning, exposure, drowning, the use of weapons, and, with technological advances, lethal overdoses of sedatives or intentional exposure to pathogens, as demonstrated in some contemporary neonatal euthanasia cases (1984, 5). Passive forms of infanticide involve intentional and unconscious forms of underinvestment, neglect, and other forms of "lowered biological support" (Scrimshaw 1984, 444). In these cases, for example, a caretaker might unconsciously give a sick child less food in order to speed its death.

The attribution of individual responsibility is not far from contemporary Euro-American discourses on infanticide, whether they are identifying murderous and narcissistic fathers, neglectful mothers, or natural impulses. These discourses of individual blame overshadow the contextual and structural factors that can accentuate and shift responsibility to political-economy, inequality, exploitative class relations, and cultural practices (Scheper-Hughes 1987, 2–5). Rarely can one identify incidents of infanticide that exhibit a narrow cause-and-effect relationship. The causes are often complex, interactive, and extend beyond individuals.

I define *infanticide* as a set of intentional or unconscious behaviors and contextual circumstances that contribute to the death of a dependent of a succeeding generation.[2] This definition includes both active and passive forms, and it places equal attention on the role of context in shaping practices. Like Kimball (2007), I use "dependent of a succeeding generation" rather than specifying toddler, child, or other age categories, as in other definitions.[3] I also omit the use of *parent* to reflect the variability present in family arrangements and caretaking or dependency patterns. As is demonstrated in the spirit child cases, this broad formulation of infanticide is necessary due to the diverse causes of death, the close involvement of family members outside the parental dyad, and the contributing contextual factors, such as poverty or access to medical care, that closely shape the space of vulnerability wherein spirit child deaths occur.

Infanticide across Cultures

Cultural and historical accounts have indicated that infanticide is widely distributed culturally, historically, and geographically: "rather than being the exception, it has been the rule" (Williamson 1978, 61). For example, the ethnographic literature indicates that in parts of Nigeria twins were previously regarded as bad omens and promptly killed at birth (Bastian 2001). The Yaudapa Enga of New Guinea abandoned selected children to be whisked off and reared by supernatural beings (Scrimshaw 1984). The Yanomamo practiced infanticide in cases in which the mother already had an infant (Scott 2001, 4). It has been reported that the Netsilik Eskimo historically would abandon female neonates in favor of boys (Scott 2001). There are extensive accounts of how unwanted or undesirable infants in Europe before and during the industrial revolution were abandoned (Piers 1978) or given to overburdened wet nurses with full knowledge that the infant would not survive (Hrdy 1999).

In West Africa, the cultural models for infants and children subject to rejection and infanticide are frequently described as spirit, witch, or snake children. For the Bariba people of Benin, physically stigmatized infants and those not conforming to social and behavioral expectations are rejected as malevolent witch-babies. The loss of such children is not to be grieved due to the misfortune and harm that such a child can cause the family (Sargent 1982, 1988). Solitary birth practices give the mother flexibility in determining the fate of the child. Sargent also describes how poison is commonly used and that exposure, lack of feeding, and, less often, physical violence are practiced. In Mali, Katherine Dettwyler (1994) describes how children with developmental delays or disabilities are seen as "snake children." In these cases, evil spirits are seen as taking over one's child, resulting in stillbirth, deformity, or a child that never grows. These children are usually abandoned in the bush, though not without a period of help seeking (85–86). Among the Beng people of Cote d'Ivoire, Anna Gottlieb describes how a spirit can switch places with a fetus. In these cases, children with physical and behavioral delays are interpreted as having snakelike behaviors and are regarded as nonpersons (Gottlieb 1992, 2000a; Gottlieb and Graham 1993). Gottlieb also describes how in precolonial times a child born with a tooth was killed immediately and quickly buried in the bush, for if it were allowed to live an adult relative would die (2004, 224–25). The Papel people of Guinea-Bissau identify *iran*, or spirit children, which are regarded as nonhuman and dangerous. Some of these children have a range of abnormalities and impairments. Suspected *iran* children are taken to the sea, where they disappear into the water (Einarsdóttir 2004, 2005).

Why practice infanticide? From a cultural evolutionary perspective, Lloyd deMause (1974) claims that infanticide and forms of neglect of children were quite common early in history and were a reflection of parental ambivalence and widespread attitudes of hostility toward children. Most explanations for infanticide, however, fall into a broad range of economic rationales. This expansive category includes evolutionary, sociobiological, rational choice, and other perspectives that describe conscious or unconscious choices as economizing, utility-maximizing responses to a perceived economic burden of birthing and rearing (Kimball 2007, 11–12). These perspectives explain infanticide as an investment strategy for privileging some offspring over others (Ginsburg and Rapp 1991, 326) and an adaptive mechanism for regulating population size, contributing to group survival, or increasing inclusive fitness (Hrdy and Hausfater 1984, xiii).

I organized the various scholarly explanations for infanticide into a set of common rationales used to explain why people practice it. The domains are not mutually exclusive and often overlap, since infanticide rationales frequently involve more than one causative factor and are dependent on intersecting circumstances.

The most frequent explanation for infanticide is as a family planning strategy or a way to ensure reproductive success. In this case, infanticide is practiced to regulate family numbers, to ensure adequate birth spacing, or as a response to the birth of twins in situations in which a family cannot care for both infants (Peek 2011, 2).

Sex preferences are also a common reason. Families' preference for boys in parts of Asia coupled with strict family-planning programs, for example, can result in significant gender imbalances (Sen 1990). High female infanticide rates have also been debated as an adaptive response to higher male mortality rates in Arctic communities or as a form of population control (Balikci 1967). However, Carmel Schrire and William Steiger contend that female infanticide in Arctic communities is likely not a "natural" response but is influenced by increasing contact with outsiders impacting their way of life (1974, 163).

Occasionally, infants and children with physical disabilities, chronic illnesses, or other abnormalities are subject to infanticide. Physical abnormalities may be indicative of poor phenotypic quality (Daly and Wilson 1984), require disproportionate levels of care (Hill and Ball 1996, 857), subject the family to sigma or shame (Bechtold and Graves 2006, 19), or symbolically index other problems occurring within the family (Denham 2012).

With or without an abnormality, a child can be subject to infanticide due to internal and external disruptions, including marriage instability and conflict

(Bugos and McCarthy 1984, 518–19), the unavailability of a partner or lack of a partner's support (Porter and Gavin 2010), spousal revenge (Corti 1998), and the consequences of forms of domination and subjugation such as war, colonialism, and dislocation (Devereux 1948; Schrire and Steiger 1974, 162; Swain 2006).

Mental illness, or explanations that conceive of the mother as temporarily or permanently psychotic or suffering from a severe postpartum condition, are often described in Euro-American contexts. These conditions are rare, however, and the majority of infanticides are not a direct consequence of a women's mental health (Porter and Gavin 2010, 103).

Finally, structural violence and a lack of social support shift the focus from individual mental health or fitness and decision-making models to describing how scarce resources, policies, inequality, and structural barriers play a significant role in infanticide practices (Scheper-Hughes 1992).

Economic paradigms have wide degrees of applicability, and many types of infanticide fit within explanations for resource competition (Hrdy and Hausfater 1984, xvii). Still, care and a critical perspective are needed when working with these theories. Robert Sussman and his colleagues caution that it is not difficult to generate explanations and hypotheses from attractive evolutionary perspectives (Sussman, Cheverud, and Bartlett 1994, 150). Furthermore, much of the support for these theories uses comparative data from other mammals. Sara Hrdy warns that humans are much more complex and, unlike animals, "are able to consciously make choices counter to their self-interest" (1999, 460). I bring attention to this not to discredit the value of evolutionary explanations but to temper enthusiasm to uncritically apply them to all data when in fact greater complexity is present.

Hence, in working toward complex accounts of infanticide, it is important to understand the local cultural models and experiences, the rationale or triggers, and the potential similarities or differences between these levels of interpretation. For example, Kim Hill and Magdalena Hurtado's (1996) account of Aché infanticide offers greater explanatory range. They present infanticide as a reproductive strategy alongside Aché people's accounts of their grave dislike of orphans and their explanation that children make good companions for the deceased.

Nankani infanticide explanations fit many of these rationales (excluding mental illness and sex preferences). It is not my intention to gather evidence to support them or to develop a new theory. Rather, I find it important to acknowledge the enduring power of these paradigms while moving closer to lived experiences, local interpretations and moral worlds, and ultimately a more contextualized depiction of spirit children.

Methods

While my research was focused on infanticide and the spirit child phenomenon, much of my time was spent learning about a range of common ethnographic themes in the Nankani lifeworld, including child rearing, social structure, history, myths, ancestors, the management of misfortune, and conceptions of deviance, illness, and well-being. The spirit child phenomenon is intermeshed within the Nankani material, relational, and discursive worlds. My attempts to understand infanticide and spirit children required at times more attention to what was occurring around the phenomena than to the practices themselves.

Critical and phenomenological research paradigms directed my attention toward the complexities of people's lifeworlds and experiences of illness, misfortune, and healing situated within their broader political-economic, biological, and historical contexts. I was particularly interested in the relationships and interplay between domains, such as the social and psychological, as an analytic method intended to avoid reducing experience, sickness, and decision-making to purely internal essences or external circumstances.[4] Throughout my analysis, I often adopt a symbolic and interpretive approach (Turner 1967) to elucidate meanings, interpret what metaphors condense and articulate, and demonstrate the interconnections.

I position this research in part at the intersections of the anthropology of childhood and the anthropology of reproduction. In some respects, the intersections between childhood and reproduction encompass a set of topics that can be cast as an anthropology of infancy or even a pre- or perinatal anthropology.[5] My framing of infancy in this project is quite loose. To understand infancy (and childhood) among the Nankani requires considering a broader trajectory encompassing the pre- and perinatal periods and the ideologies and practices associated throughout each. In my expanded approach to an anthropology of infancy, important areas of inquiry include, for example, people's understanding of conception and the roles of the parents and other entities, the impact of cultural and structural forces on fetal and infant development, beliefs and practices around abortion or infanticide, understandings of risk, and the timing and determinants of the acquisition of humanness and personhood. Another area of inquiry within this project, for instance, involved attending to the relationships between a coming or recently born infant and family members, spiritual entities, and ancestors and how these relations change throughout the pregnancy and the child's development.

I carried out ethnographic fieldwork in the Upper East Region of Ghana in 2006–7, with three shorter one- to two-month visits between 2008 and 2010. I worked primarily within Nankani ethnic communities in the eastern portions of what are currently the Kassena-Nankana East and Kassena-Nankana West districts. While the village of Sirigu was a focal point, I spent time in other rural areas within and surrounding Zoko to the east, Kandiga to the south, Mirigu and Manyoro to the west, and Yua and rural areas in Burkina Faso to the north. I also spent significant time in the cities of Navrongo and Bolgatanga.

I conducted a wide range of individual and group interviews with Nankani community members, focusing in particular on families with spirit children, concoction men, diviners, NGO workers, biomedical health professionals, and key community leaders and representatives. I also used a person-centered ethnographic approach to enable a closer understanding of the everyday lives, self-processes, and cultural practices of several individuals within the community (Levy and Hollan 1998). I adopted an in-depth case study approach with four families suspected to have spirit children, following some for up to five years. As with any ethnographic approach, participant observation was immersive and continuous, ranging from acquiring basic living skills and spending time socializing to administering vaccinations, weighing babies, and keeping records at child and maternal health clinics. I learned how to participate in divination, eventually taking legitimate issues to the diviner. I worked closely with a group of sixteen concoction men to learn about elements related to the spirit child ritual in detail.

The NHRC, run by the Ghana Health Service, was instrumental in assisting with the research, providing local ethical approval, and offering access to verbal postmortem autopsy data collected as part of the Navrongo Demographic Surveillance System. These data offered narrative accounts of infanticide deaths and enumerated the frequency of which infanticide was reported as the cause of death.

I worked closely with fieldworkers in the Sirigu office of the children's rights NGO AfriKids. AfriKids represents the convergence of several people's efforts to address social problems throughout the Upper East Region. Conceived in 1997 as a way to support the Mother of Mercy Babies Home in Sirigu—established to help unwanted spirit children—the Ghanaian-run NGO, supported in part by a UK charity, has grown to over forty projects focused on child protection, health care, education, advocacy, and social enterprise. Operation Sirigu, now part of the Kassena-Nankana Area Program, was formally established in 2002 to assist children identified as spirits while also addressing the root causes of spirit child practice. The program is closely involved in maternal and child health services and programming, health and disability awareness and education, women's groups, and livelihood programs for vulnerable families. AfriKids was vital to establishing my contact with families of spirit children and my presence in Sirigu and the surrounding communities. Much of my time was spent observing and working alongside Joe, Elijah, and Matthew, the latter a schoolteacher and field assistant who was later employed by AfriKids. They frequently appear throughout the book. It is not my goal to critically engage or formally evaluate AfriKids' approach or NGO politics in the region. Rather than positioning AfriKids as the subject of inquiry, I view it as one of many forces that shape the spirit child phenomenon and family experiences.

Many interviews and discussions were audio-recorded and later transcribed. Therefore, much of the dialogue and people's accounts herein are direct rather than reconstructed from field notes. In many cases, this enabled me to preserve local speech patterns and rhythms, such as repetition of important points in a discussion.

The research was conducted in both the Nankani and English languages. I worked closely with assistants to ensure my understanding of Nankani discussions and later subjected all recorded material and notes to a close translation with a Nankani speaker. Nankani is a dialect within the larger language group referred to as Gurene, which is also described as Frafra. I attempt to follow the Nankani terms and pronunciations specified by my interlocutors and language teachers. When relevant I use the spellings outlined in the Gurene-French dictionary compiled by Mary Esther Kropp-Dakubu (2009).

Imagining the North

The Upper East Region of Ghana is primarily comprised of sub-Sahelian guinea savanna, a semiarid scrubland with limited and widely spaced trees and shrubs, which resembles the topography north into Burkina Faso more than the rainforests of the south (Mensch et al. 1999). The same might be said of the cultural characteristics of this region, since its inhabitants are more culturally akin to those living in Burkina Faso. Early migration evidence and oral histories support the supposition that many ethnic groups in the Upper East Region originally migrated from northern regions. A significant portion of the Upper East and other regions constituting northern Ghana remains extremely rural, remote, and isolated from the rest of the country.

The primary occupation in the district is subsistence farming (90 percent) and livestock rearing (Tonah 1994). Even individuals with nonagricultural full-time jobs maintain farms and rely on their food in addition to market-purchased goods. Common crops include early and late forms of millet, sorghum, and groundnuts. Livestock such as goats, sheep, cattle, and fowls are primarily used for social, religious, and market exchange purposes. Agriculture is limited to the one annual rainy season (*sio*), which averages thirty-three inches of precipitation per month from May through October. The dry season (*une*) is very dry, hot, and subject to Harmattan winds and dust. Due to the dependence on a single growing season, food insecurity, periods of famine, and seasonal malnutrition are a persistent threat (Binka, Nazzar, and Phillips 1995; Mensch et al. 1999). Community members remarked that over the past decade the rains had become unpredictable and storms more intense.

Limited irrigation permits the sale of some cash crops, such as tomatoes, but poor soil quality, the cost of accessing water and fertilizer, and increasingly unpredictable weather conditions make farming difficult. Farmers rely mainly on rain-fed irrigation, and less than 1 percent of subsistence farmers have access to modern farm machinery and irrigation (Adongo et al. 1997). The transportation of crops and other goods between markets or urban areas is via privately owned trucks. Traveling by foot and bicycle is the most common mode of transportation within and outside the district. Small motorbikes are also common. Taxis or small buses provide transportation between the nearby cities (Navrongo and Bolgatanga) and major markets. Larger buses link the district capitals with urban areas in the south. In rural areas, finding affordable and fast transportation is difficult, and transportation issues become paramount during medical emergencies. The decision to take a family member to the hospital, which in some cases is a life-or-death decision, is dictated largely by the cost and hardship it imposes on the family.

Unlike the cocoa farms and gold mines in the southern sectors, northern Ghana has little in the way of large cash crops or industry. The lack of economic development in the north combined with seasonal agriculture patterns results in migration to the south (Adongo et al. 1997; Tonah 1994). Presently, wage-labor migration to the south, particularly during the dry season, is a source of family income, although these workers often find that they are unable to support themselves and their families. In some cases, men are unable to return home to farm.

Data from the 2010 Population and Housing Census indicates a poverty rate, defined as 1,314 Ghanaian cedis per year (in 2010 the equivalent of around 900 US dollars), of 45.9 percent in the Upper East Region, compared to 6.6 percent in the Greater Accra Region and around 25 percent for all of Ghana (Ghana Statistical Service 2015).

Historically, aid programs have tended to channel more money and resources to the southern sectors of the country, purportedly due to differences in population and additional geographic and economic challenges facing projects in northern Ghana. Since I first visited the region in 2006, however, the number of NGOs and other development organizations and initiatives has increased, and Bolgatanga, like the Northern Region capital Tamale, is becoming a center of development activity.

While people in northern Ghana often say "We are all one people," the cultural, ecological, economic, and rural geographic differences emphasize their economically and politically marginal status. The north-south or forest-savanna political-economic distinctions are immediately apparent. Northerners often compare themselves to their southern neighbors, who they see as having much easier lives. People describe how there are fewer income opportunities, services, and material goods in the north. Rural people also note that local food is not as good or nutritious as that of the south and weather conditions are more difficult. One primary school teacher described the disparity among teachers. Rather than differences in salary, he said, teachers in the south are able to find a greater number of alternative moneymaking schemes. "When we go to teachers' meetings," he noted, "I can see the difference. We are always thin." In the north, teachers continue to farm, as wages are rarely sufficient to purchase food and support a family. Many southern employees view work assignments in the north as punishment.

Early European accounts of Ghana made sharp distinctions between the dispersed, stateless societies in the north—or "the tribes of the Ashanti hinterland," according to Robert Rattray (1932)—and the centralized kingdoms in the south (Allman and Parker 2005, 27). The colonial observers saw in the north a stereotype of primitive isolation, which persists today. Southerners and outsiders view northern practices involving the spirit child, a history of female genital cutting, and the patriarchal structure and marginalized status of women as evidence of backwardness (Eguavoen 2008, 74) and often fail to consider the larger political-economic, historical, and ecological reasons for the north's underdevelopment.

When I visited the urban areas of southern Ghana, I was frequently asked why I was living in the north. No person would choose to live there, southerners told me. The discourse concerning the north revealed a great deal about people's assumptions and the north-south dichotomy. One typical exchange occurred in a taxi in Accra.

"Where are you from?" asked the driver.

"I'm from America, but I live up in the north near Navrongo," I replied.

"Ahh!" he responded, "the North! How do you do it? What do you eat?"

"Oh, it's a wonderful place," I said, evading his question. "It's very peaceful. I like it better than Accra. Have you been there?"

"Oh no, no," he said.

"Why not?" I asked. "You should visit sometime."

"No, no, I can't," he replied gravely. "If I did, I would surely die."

For many outsiders, the north, because of its marginal and ambiguous status, also functions as an imaginary space of the other, where mysterious and fantastic occurrences and powers are envisioned. It is a place tangibly unknown to many. In its otherness lies the source of both peoples' aversion and perceptions of inherent power.

Jean Allman and John Parker write that northern savanna people are viewed with a degree of ambivalence because their cultural and ecological otherness is recognized as a powerful source of ritual power (2005, 127). Gabriel Bannerman-Richter (1987) provides several examples of the spiritual powers of the north in his quasi-fictional account, which describes mysterious "little people," or powerful spirit beings originating in northern Ghana, that have the ability to grant people's wishes.[6] He also describes a type of deity or fetish used in the south that originally came from the north. "The spirits inhabiting these objects," he explains, "are Northerners, so they may often communicate in the language of Mossi . . . or dress in a northern fashion" (73, 94). He describes a journey he undertook to the north to find and speak with specialists, indicating, "If I really wanted to know more about the supernatural entities which were pivotal in traditional African religions, northern Ghana was a treasure-house for such information" (94).

Allman and Parker explain that during colonial times a degree of "ritual potency" associated with the liminal frontier zones was "mapped onto the arbitrary boundaries created just a few decades before by colonial conquest" (2005, 137). They continue, noting, "The Gurunsi, Frafra, and others were generally regarded as primitive barbarians, who as slaves or subsequently as migrant wage laborers were fit only to perform the most menial of tasks. On the other hand, these uncivilized aliens possessed the esoteric knowledge to access a range of deities that could combat witchcraft, the greatest single threat to the civilized order. The ambiguity of ethnic otherness therefore intersected with a further ambivalence, that of the historical battle against witchcraft" (141).

Before moving on, I address two additional themes that shape the way the north is imagined: the assumption of homogeneity and the characterization of tradition.

When describing the social and cultural characteristics of northern Ghana, many scholars and other observers assume homogeneity across its numerous ethnic groups. Meyer Fortes, noted for his work with the Tallensi, remarked that there are no real linguistic, cultural, political, or structural boundaries between the Nankani and the Tallensi since "they overlap in every way" (1945, 16). I asked several Nankani people if they regard themselves as similar to the Tallensi. Respondents would reply that there are many similarities, such as parts of the language and social and religious structures, but the Nankani are not Tallensi and they would hesitate to say that they overlapped entirely. While Fortes asserted homogeneity and isolation, Allan Wolsey Cardinall (1920), nearly two decades before Fortes's fieldwork, noted the differences between northern ethnic groups. He remarked that, aside from similar religious practices, he wanted to "make clear how intensely individualistic [different from each other] all these people are." He continued, observing, "Before the arrival of the white man each compound formed practically a community apart, and being of mixed origin the customs observed by each community differed" (ix).

Cardinall's observation is important and remains relevant. In addition to noting the colonial impact and the movement of people between ethnic groups, he recognized the differences that exist between families within similar groups. While the larger structural configurations—such as kinship and ancestor veneration—may be similar, there are important differences in the details and the ways in which these are practiced. This diversity is particularly apparent in the spirit child phenomenon, wherein, for example, two neighboring families can have opposing interpretations.

Assumptions of homogeneity between clans and ethnic groups can falsely create a discrete sense of boundedness (Abu-Lughod 1991). Thus, I attempt to qualify and contextualize my comparisons to emphasize specific forms of discourse and practice over a unified notion of culture in the region. In this way, one can glimpse the overall patterns while also appreciating the clear variations between families. This approach is essential to understanding the diversity present in the spirit child phenomenon.

Finally, I frequently refer to *tradition*, although it is a fraught term. Following Charles Piot, I do not position tradition as opposing modernity, being "non-modern," or "failing to embrace modernity" (1999, 2). I recognize that the traditional, while grounded within the past, is malleable and complex. I thus draw on local definitions of who or what is traditional within this project. For many Nankani, a traditional person's lifeworld consists of beliefs, a social structure, and practices that are historical or continuous with what came before and, in most cases, are seen as having originated within the community. People commonly characterize a person living within the traditional family structure and practicing ancestrally focused religion and rituals as traditional. If tradition is a selection of practices and forms of discourse identified as such, one can be both traditional and modern. Hence, a person can be educated and attend Christian church services—both symbolic of modernity—yet live in a traditional compound, visit a diviner, and support accusations that a child is a spirit, particularly during a period of crisis.

Illness and Healing

Nankani community members characterize a state of health (*ema'asum*) in a manner similar to biomedical definitions: the absence of disease or infirmity. While the 1990s brought increased access to biomedical services and public health campaigns, there is some indication that their perception of health as the absence of disease and pain is long-standing. When speaking of health, people describe being free of headaches or stomachaches and reference a person's appearance, noting that health is, for example, "when a person has not grown lean." It is also a state of "coolness" and sleeping well.

Health is also understood in much broader terms. People describe health in terms of social stability and cohesion, associations that are common throughout sub-Saharan Africa. A community health nurse remarked that health could only be achieved when there is "peace and harmony" (*nuyeene*) in the family. "If there is no peace in the family," he stated, "health will never be promoted. So, the family members must have peace. They must have love for one another." A healthy person, an elder noted, is happy (*pupeelum*) and "not mean to others."

Some people stated that health necessitates access to resources. Healthy people have nothing to worry about, an elder remarked. A person is healthy when "everything is available in abundance."

A variety of forces can result in illness: seasonal changes or extremes of hot and cold, wetness, or the wind, such as the Harmattan; witchcraft, sorcery, and spiritual or ancestral forces, which can point to disturbances in the person's social world and networks; the absence of ancestral protection; and biomedical notions of contagion and infectious disease. Some people, due to their backgrounds, might be predisposed to particular conditions.[7] Conditions and afflictions can be passed intergenerationally. A child is susceptible to the afflictions or diseases present in its parent's body, even if the parent is asymptomatic.

Medicines (*tiim*) are a broad category that includes agents that reduce symptoms and heal as well as harm. Medicines can be pharmaceutical (*nasaara tiim*, "modern medicine"), herbal, symbolic, or ritual based. Medicines are valued for their empirical qualities but are also used to protect or defend against attacks. "Juju," or sorcery medicines, can be used to enact revenge or harm another person.

The origins and social contexts of medicines and treatments are important, and medicines cannot be divorced from their symbolic powers and associated rituals, which can promote symptom relief or behavioral change. For example, after the onset of a headache one afternoon, I removed a bottle of ibuprofen from my bag. The bottle was from an American brand, but I had refilled it with locally available ibuprofen. On seeing the bottle, two others complained of a headache and asked for some of the "American ibuprofen." I pointed to a file cabinet and remarked that they should use their own as my ibuprofen was exactly the same; I had just refilled the old bottle from a local blister pack. They were not convinced. The symbolic associations of the bottle itself, regardless of its contents, rendered the medicine more powerful by virtue of its unique form, owner, and origin. Additionally, concerns over the quality of local medications and the possibility of counterfeit drugs likely contributed to their desire for outside medications.

Health Context

Infancy and childhood in the Upper East Region are precarious in terms of both encountering illness and being in the presence of spiritual dangers. The challenges begin long before birth, as political-economic constraints, maternal difficulties, malnutrition, inadequate prenatal care, and delivery complications place the fetus and infant at risk. The primary causes of infant and child mortality in the Kassena-Nankana Districts (KND) at the time of my research included malaria, diarrheal diseases, acute respiratory infections, and meningitis (Baiden et al. 2006).

Since the mid-1990s, the KND has seen significant improvements in child and maternal health. Due to the targeted health campaigns of the Ministry of Health and NHRC, launched in the mid-1990s, maternal mortality in the KND was reduced from 636 deaths per 100,000 in 1995–96 to 373 in 2002–4 (Mills et al. 2008). Similarly, infant and child mortality rates, while still excessive, also fell. Prior to the health campaigns, it was estimated that one in nine children did not make it to age five (Binka et al. 1999). In 1988 under-five mortality was 155 deaths per 1,000 births (Binka et al. 2007, 579). For historical comparison, a 1919 estimate for the Northern Territories of Ghana showed that only 33 percent of children reaching five years of age lived until they were ten (Howell 1997, 80).

In 2004 statistics collected nearest the start of my research, infant mortality (0 to <1 year) was 84.6 deaths per 1,000 births and under-five mortality (0 to <5 years) was 82.9 deaths per 1,000 births (Binka et al. 2007). The more recent 2011 statistics indicate that infant mortality was 32.1 deaths per 1,000 births and under-five mortality was 60.8 deaths per 1,000 births (Oduro et al. 2012, 972).[8] These ongoing improvements are not due to rapid economic growth or social change (Binka et al. 2007, 579); rather, they reflect an increase in community health nurses in rural areas, the increasing availability of maternal health care, and infant and childhood vaccination programs.

Despite these gains, health inequities remain. A study examining such inequities in the KND found that children of the poorest families are more frequently underweight, stunted, and anemic and have greater rates of diarrhea. Poor women are also more likely to be underweight and anemic, to use fewer contraceptives, and to deliver at home (Zere et al. 2012).

Community members frequently commented on the improvements in health witnessed over the previous decades. According to one grandmother:

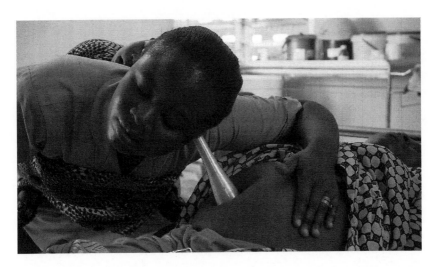

A midwife listening to a fetal heartbeat (Stephen Fisher)

> People no longer die as they used to die in the olden days. With children,
> we were afraid of measles attacking them. Measles can come and easily kill
> or if it does not kill it will cause blindness. So, as you see blind people these
> days, the children today will not be like that. Because of the vaccinations
> and health facilities, when people are sick they go there and get medicine
> and antenatal care.

While health statistics are valuable for program planning and evaluation
and depict the larger landscape of health challenges and uncertainties, they
miss the experiences, stories, and complexity of how families actually experience
their livelihood and health challenges. The larger contextual and epidemiologi-
cal picture is best seen when it is positioned alongside specific cases and insights
into how such statistical and structural realities are lived and shape health
decisions.

Illness Decision-Making:
The Case of Leah

Throughout my research, I maintained an interest in families' health care
decision-making and the options available to families with children with serious
medical conditions. Specifically, I was interested in how and why some families
interpreted child disability or sickness as a spiritual danger and why others did
not. I was also interested in situations in which families prioritized a child's care
despite the economic and social costs and when decision-making was not "in

the family's best interests" from a utilitarian perspective. Leah's story introduces the region's health context and demonstrates a family's care seeking and decision-making for a severely ill infant.

While making his weekly rounds through a rural area, Elijah, an AfriKids fieldworker, heard rumors about an infant with hydrocephalus and a "skeletal body." Neighbors said it surely was a spirit child. Elijah visited Leah, the sick infant, and her family to learn more about her condition and to see if it was possible for the NGO to assist.

Elijah and I arrived at the family compound in the middle of the dry season heat. While commenting on the heat, which easily exceeded 41°C (105°F), Elijah casually remarked that people were really starting to suffer.

"The famine season," I acknowledged in a low voice as we walked across an open field that during the wet season would be filled with millet all the way to the family's compound entrance. "Some families are starting to run out of food."

"Yes," he replied. "The poorer families are having a hard time now. This time of year is always hard. Wait until you get to May and June. Once you survive that, you'll be eating again."

"Would you say this family we are visiting is poor?"

Elijah nodded his head and we soon ducked under the sun shelter outside the entrance to the compound.

Several visible signs can offer insight into a family's economic status, for example, the physical appearance and condition of the home, the number of animals, the number of dependents, the presence of a bicycle, and even the activity levels and presence of children around the house. Other, less visible factors include the family's health, the presence of conflict, and the extent of its social and kinship network. As Elijah and I sat down on the logs positioned in the shade, I glanced around the outside of the compound. It was in a state of disrepair, and few animals were present. It was strangely silent—even the children that usually gather around to listen were missing.

We exchanged customary greetings with Akoka, who was in his mid to late twenties. He explained that his wife Ayampoka was fetching water. Their daughter Leah was with her, and they would return soon. When Ayampoka returned, she unwrapped the 3 kilogram (6.5 pound) three-month-old infant from her back and sat in the shade with us. When she uncovered the baby for us to see, it was difficult to conceal my shock. The child appeared to have hydrocephalus, was extremely malnourished, and lay motionless. Her body was stiff. I asked Ayampoka to tell me about her condition.

"Every day she has a hot body," the mother told me. "And once every day for the past two months she shakes and cries out when she does that."

"The child also had diarrhea," the father stated. "But it's been some time since she has passed feces."

"Is she able to breast-feed?" I asked the mother.

"Yes, she sucks well, but I do not produce much milk anymore."

It was obvious that the child needed to go to the hospital soon. I asked a few more questions and, aware of the rumors in the community, asked if they thought Leah was a spirit child.

"No," replied the mother. "It's not a spirit child."

"Why not?"

"The family does not believe in those things," she responded.

"Some families do not have the spirit child in their family," Elijah added. Either families do not believe spirit children exist or believe that because they have never had a spirit child in previous generations, they are not susceptible to them.

"Have you taken Leah to the health clinic?" I asked Akoka.

"Yes," he said. "We saw a nurse, and he advised that we take Leah to the hospital as soon as possible. Ayampoka walked to the Navrongo hospital [more than ten miles]. But she arrived at the hospital with only 12,000 cedis [US$1.30 at the time], not the 22,000 cedis required to get the medical card and see a doctor. So she brought Leah home."

I nodded my head in silence, frustrated that she had walked so far with such a sick child and that the hospital turned them away. Later I found that Ayampoka did not know how to navigate the hospital system or advocate for herself and Leah in this unfamiliar place.

We continued to chat about Leah's condition and said that we would return to take her to the hospital. Formal biomedical health care options in the area include the district's Navrongo War Memorial Hospital and several smaller community health stations staffed by nurses, midwives, and medical assistants. The Ghana Health Service provides primary health care at these satellite clinics, as well as outreach services throughout the district, with teams of nurses on motorbikes divided among the communities.

On leaving, I found myself considering Leah's father's resigned appearance. I wrote in my field notes that evening, "They made one trip [to the hospital], and it appears inconceivable that they would try to go again. I am troubled by the fact that the father appeared so detached as he looked at the child. He seemed like he didn't care if the child lived or died. The father was strangely silent."

When thinking about Leah's situation and reflecting on Akoka's short responses, I found myself in frustration, blaming him for failing to pursue further treatment. Couldn't he just sell some animals or make another attempt to get Leah help? Why did he appear so fatalistic?

The archetype of the reluctant or neglectful father commonly circulates throughout the medical and development discourse in the region. It describes how fathers can be hesitant to invest in children and prefer to spend money on alcohol rather than health or education. Additionally, the practice of gatekeeping in many families, wherein mothers must ask for money or seek the support of men in the household, complicates the perceptions of the uninvested father and contributes to care-seeking delays.

I reviewed my notes later and recognized their narrowness. I realized that even if Akoka sold a fowl to get the extra money for admission to the hospital, family members would still be unable to pay for the necessary medications or feed themselves as they attended to Leah at the hospital. I began to wonder if their decision not to return to the hospital was due to their recognition of the grim reality of the situation. Had I encountered them at a point when they realized that there was nothing more they could do? Had they already spent everything they had?

Elijah and I returned to take Ayampoka and Leah to the hospital. While we were waiting for them, I spoke further with Akoka. "We went to the health center and to many herbalists," he told me. "Even my in-laws came and saw the condition of the child. They sent another herbalist here to treat her. After the treatments, I did see some small improvement and I continued to send fowls to the herbalists [as payment]."

Families use a range of biomedical and traditional treatments and preventative methods simultaneously. Deciding who to visit depends on the type of illness, its seriousness, and recommendations from family or friends. For example, a person may visit a diviner to determine the cause of an illness and offer the necessary sacrifices to his ancestor while also visiting an herbalist and the community health clinic for medications, sometimes all in the same day.

Undoubtedly, it is costly to attend a clinic, purchase health insurance and medications, and pay for transportation and one's living and food requirements while caring for a family member in the hospital. Local herbalists and healers can also be expensive. During this fieldwork, the Ghana Health Service initiated the National Health Insurance Scheme, which provides health insurance for individuals and families for a fee and free services for children, pregnant women, the elderly, and the poor. Many families living in rural areas and with limited access to cash resources could not afford the health insurance fee, which does not include drug coverage. The Ministry of Health does provide free maternal and infant health clinics, which offer related instruction and vaccinations.

"Did you have any animals to sell to pay for treatment at the hospital?" I asked.

"I already used or sold most of my fowls to pay for Leah's treatment," he said. "Last year I had a sore on my leg and couldn't farm enough food. We are currently suffering from lack of food. I want to travel to Kumasi to visit my younger brother to ask if he could help out with money or food."

Family and social connections can work as insurance, and when one is in need, appeals are made. A family's financial resources strongly influence its help-seeking choices and can pose the most significant barrier to accessing bio-medical care.

"When I realized I had nothing left that I could do, I stopped and sat down," Leah's father quietly remarked, indicating that when a person "sits," he or she is contemplating something serious, making a decision, or discussing a family situation with others. "I sat and said that if the child should live that is fine, if she is to die then that is fine. I have done all I can, and now I am stopping. This is now in the child's hands."

I nodded again. "How many children are you supporting?"

"Six. I live in this compound with my brother, but he died recently. His wife and child farm a different area, and I'm not able to feed them."

"Was it difficult," I asked, "knowing there was nothing more you could do for Leah?"

"Yes," he replied, glancing down. "There's nothing left. That is why I now have to go to my relatives in Kumasi."

Presently Ayampoka came out of the house with Leah. We drove to the regional hospital in Bolgatanga, completed the paperwork, paid the fees, and had Leah examined by a physician. I accompanied Ayampoka and Leah into the exam room. The Russian-trained Cuban doctor, one of several that rotate through the region on humanitarian missions, examined Leah and asked her mother what was wrong. Ayampoka stated that the child had diarrhea and a hot body but offered little additional information.

My fieldwork indicated that people often place a great deal of trust in doctors and expect them to be able to determine, usually with medical instruments, what the problem is with little input on their part. The examination continued with little dialogue or discussion. Just before Leah was sent to the lab for tests, I added that she had been having convulsions on a daily basis and that the mother was unable to produce enough breast milk. The doctor took note of the convulsions while the nurse questioned the mother about feeding. "What? Have you been eating enough? You need to be sure to eat more!" she instructed. Ayampoka remained silent.

The doctor admitted Leah to the hospital, though not without some misunderstandings. Ayampoka refused to let the nurses take Leah away to begin treatment. She remarked that she did not want the child to have all the drugs we had just purchased, nor did she want so many people touching or caring for her child. The nurses repeatedly explained why they had to take Leah, but the mother continued to refuse and threatened to run away with the child. At one point, at the peak of the argument, Elijah physically blocked her attempted exit. It was the other mothers in the adjacent neonatal room, when they heard the commotion, who came to comfort Ayampoka, told her their stories, and convinced her to stay.

I present this case to bring a more human face to the health statistics of rural families, as well as their care-seeking and decision-making processes, and to highlight the reality of the related economic and transportation barriers. Solutions are frequently more complicated than eating more to induce lactation, as the nurse instructed.

This story presents a different perspective on the economic expectations of low parental investment and detachment in regions with high infant mortality and limited resources.[9] Additionally, it is important to critically examine assumptions that cast family members as detached, fatalistic, or defensive without taking time to understand the trajectory of decisions that bring families to their current positions. When we come to a closer understanding of families' lived experiences and their contextual circumstances, a picture emerges that can demonstrate greater complexity and variation in the way families respond to sick or disabled children.

At the time of Leah's birth and the recognition of her condition, which occurred during the first weeks of the dry season, the family was already facing a grim reality. Despite the poor harvest of the previous season and the family's limited means, it invested considerable resources as it searched for treatments and attempted to access the hospital with whatever resources remained. Throughout this book, we will see similar cases in which families continue to engage in help seeking knowing there is a strong possibility that they will be unsuccessful or, in the case of spirit children, that the administration of a costly and sometimes fatal concoction will be inevitable.

Families in the region know that children with Leah's condition rarely survive, but Leah's family, like others I encountered, maintained the hope that she would improve. Her family took a significant risk and expended every resource despite the odds.

Leah died soon after her admission to the hospital.

2

For the House

The use of *house* to refer to one's family and clan is common through Africa (Gottlieb 1992, 50). The Nankani house is symbolic of greater family social relations. The "house" (*yire*) is not only the physical space of several rooms enclosed by a compound wall wherein the family lives, but it also signifies its immediate and extended patrilineal family system. Thus, family and house are inseparable constructs. This is reflected during the greeting process when it is customary to ask, *Yire ani ŋwani?* (lit. "House/Family it is how?").

The number of people living in a compound varies from six to thirty or more depending on the number of sons, the size of the family, and the extent to which family members migrate for work. Each extended family compound consists of one or more patrilocal groups organized according to marriage relationships. For example, within a large compound a man could live with his wife and children, his brothers and their families, his unmarried sisters, his father, his mother, his father's cowife, and possibly his father's brother. The grouping of each nuclear family unit is reflected in the design of the house, wherein each family unit is situated in separate sections. Despite such physical separation, family members cooperate in a variety of tasks, such as farming and child care. These close relationships are also reflected in broad classificatory kin terms and accompanying responsibilities, which identify, for example, one's mothers (including one's father's cowives and one's aunts) and brothers (including half brothers and cousins) within the house.

Family compounds are spaced throughout the savanna, separated by farms and smaller garden plots and linked by means of a network of paths and roads etched into the landscape leading to the market, water sources, relatives, and friends. With use the size and depth of the paths come to represent the depth of social ties and relationships between families. During the wet season—when the millet reaches above one's head—paths tunnel and snake between farms and eventually open onto compounds in small clearings.

Earthen walls form the perimeter of a compound by spanning the spaces between several individual structures or rooms positioned in a semicircular arrangement around a central yard. When approaching a compound, the path and wall of the compound gently direct visitors to the main entrance, aligned in a west to southwesterly direction. Compounds should face away from the prevailing direction of storms.

When approaching a compound, a large shade tree and a sun shelter made of old logs, millet stalks, or scraps of metal roofing are often found near the entrance, although the entrance must never directly face the tree. Logs, stones, and occasionally a bench are positioned as sitting areas outside the entrance, often within the shelter. This is primarily a male space and the place where the senior male of the house is usually found. He will visit with others, supervise work projects, eat, watch the coming and going of family members and live-stock, and facilitate discussions or debates. Women often sit and visit within this area but will depart when men conduct official business or hold discussions that do not require their input. Since the spaces inside a compound can become quite hot in the dry season, women sometimes have their own shaded areas outside where they sit and visit or work.

The main entrance is the public representation of the house, what Ann Cassiman describes as its "face" or a "visiting card," indicative of its size, wealth, and quality (2006, 105). The entrance is also the primary "appropriate" gateway that family members will use when going about their daily business. If someone does not want to be seen, she or he uses the unofficial exits, for example, by climbing over the wall or using a section of wall in disrepair toward the back of the compound. Such unmonitored entrances and exits are a cause for concern and may be indicative of hidden or antisocial activities.

Entrances are a vulnerable transitional boundary between the domestic, the threats associated with the bush, and the liminal paths and spaces that link these domains. The compound is a physical, as well as moral, space that defines the boundaries between the domestic areas of safety and security (things that are "for the house") and the external threats of disruption and disorder (things that are "for the bush").[1] Spirits and other intruders may cross these boundaries. While it is possible for spirits to transgress the boundaries of the house alone,

A family compound late in the wet season (Aaron Denham)

A large family compound (Stephen Fisher)

Ancestral shrines in front of a family compound (Stephen Fisher)

more often human behaviors violate the moral and physical boundaries of the house and create vulnerabilities that invite spirits into the family's midst. Consequently, elder men and deceased ancestors (*yaaba*) are responsible for watching over the physical and moral boundaries of the house.

Conical adobe shrines, often bearing the blood and feather remains of previous sacrifices, are located near the main entrance to the compound. The ancestors, who are represented by and dwell near these shrines, protect the entrance to the house and watch over family members. In exchange, the ancestors require sacrifices and other offerings to feed and support them in the afterlife. Due to their proximity, they are able to intercede if someone, or some spiritual being, is sneaking into the house. "If a thief is coming," Elijah said, "he must pass through the gateway. Because the ancestors are lying there, they know the man is coming and they can warn the owner."

The enshrinement of the ancestors at the gateway to the house is part of the integrative process that visibly maintains the ancestral presence within the family and bridges the ancestral world with the living while providing a protective screen against the unwelcome wilds of the bush. Entering or exiting the house and passing by the ancestral shrines are reminders that the ancestors are always watching, always vigilant of one's missteps, and, ideally, extending their protection over one's journey.

After passing through the main entrance to the compound, one enters the cattle yard, a foyerlike space where the animals are kept in the evening. The yard may contain chicken coops embedded in walls and one or more "barns" or granaries (*baare*)—large mud, conical structures up to ten feet in height. The phalluslike barn is a man's private space used primarily to store grain and other important items. The largest barn in the yard is reserved for the eldest man of the family, and access to it is usually restricted. Sometimes the eldest wife may enter the barn to retrieve grain, but generally women are prohibited. The eldest son, who is destined to take over the house upon the death of his father, is also prohibited from looking inside the barn, as there is concern that he will covet his father's belongings and will his death.[2] A woman's equivalent private storage space is the area within her room where she keeps her pots and valuables. Her eldest daughter is similarly prohibited from looking inside this space.

The house is shaped by and dialectically reproduces gendered ascriptions of space, labor, and movement in its contours and the social practices emplaced within. Proceeding from the cattle yard into the courtyard of the compound, one must step or slide over a waist-high wall, its top surface worn smooth from generations of passage. While the front of the house and the cattle yard are male-oriented spaces, this wall represents a formal transition into the women's space. Positioned throughout the courtyard are numerous one- and two-room (*deo*) structures where family members reside. As I learned more about the ebbs and flows of the house as a living object, I came to understand how certain locations within the home affect one's expected behaviors and increase or diminish one's authority and freedom according to gender and age. The juxtaposition between the social norms governing behavior and interactions inside and outside the compound are significant. For example, within the compound women can act with authority toward men or tell them what to do, behavior that is often uncharacteristic in public settings or outside in front of the house. Cassiman's (2006) ethnographic work among a neighboring Kasena community offers an intimate examination of the house, gender, and domestic spaces within the region.

Daily compound activities vary according to the season and one's age and gender. Typically, people awake just before or as the sun rises. Women and children will gather water for bathing and daily needs from boreholes, wells, and dams. Often family members walk considerable distances to fetch water, particularly during the dry season. During the wet season, families will work their various farm plots, weeding or harvesting. The dry season is the time for repairs to homes or the construction of new buildings. Most festivals, funerals, and increased socialization also occur during the dry season. Some days may require a trip to the local market, which in major villages occur every third day. Animals, vegetables, grain, and other supplies may be sold and news and gossip shared at the market. In addition to child care and their responsibilities around the house, many women will sell goods at the local market to earn extra money to supplement the family diet and pay medical expenses or school fees. Generally, men farm, occasionally sell animals, tobacco, and other items at the market, and are in control of religious, political, and public life.

Identification and social positioning of an individual occurs according to clan membership, gender, and age-relative role within the clan. Although locations throughout the family compound are associated with male and female genders, children have significant flexibility in their ability to navigate between these spaces. A young boy may spend time inside the compound with his mother but may also be encouraged to sit and observe or play outside near the men. As children age, there is the expectation that they will spend more time in their respective gendered spaces, learning the tasks associated with that role. A man explained, "When you are a boy and you are fond of sitting inside it means that you are a woman. You have to come and sit and listen to the men speak. It is only the women who are supposed to be there."

Around two years of age, a child begins spending more time away from his or her mother and joins other children in playgroups. These playgroups are frequently composed of children of various ages. A seven- or eight-year-old girl may be charged with caring for a younger sibling. Older children (age eight and above) often have playgroups separate from those of the younger children. The younger children will follow behind these groups and mimic the older children's behaviors and games, dancing or playing on the periphery. Once a child is able to roam with the other children with minimal adult supervision—behavior expected when a child is around three years of age—the parents consider having another child.

Kinship and the Family

The family and kinship system is the foundation of all social, cultural, and religious dimensions of Nankani life. When asked why a family is significant, people describe the vital role of supporting others, particularly when people are ill, poor, or elderly and in need of assistance. A large family is very desirable and a source of prestige. Having an abundance of children is also a joy. A grandmother stated that life is meaningless without a child and noted, "It does not speak well for a family when you go to sacrifice a fowl and you have to pluck it yourself." Just as vital is the sense of belonging and the honor associated with belonging to a particular family. An elder said, "What is more important is the name that you are called, because you come from a certain family. That alone is a great thing." One's social identity and belonging are set along the continuity of the agnatic line and the centrality of one's deceased ancestors (see Fortes 1945, 26). Relatedness is not only a matter of descent but also of one's moral values and behaviors, such as engaging in forms of reciprocity expected within specific relationships.

People also cite the historically high infant and child mortality rates as a reason to have large numbers of children. Despite the desire and imperatives for having a large family, the district's fertility rate has fallen in conjunction with community health and family-planning projects and other regional demographic changes (Debpuur et al. 2002, 141). Between 1995 and 2011 the total fertility rate in the KND declined from 5.1 to 3.8 (Badien et al. 2006; Oduro et al. 2012, 972). This is not only due to health improvements and family-planning services; families also note that, compared to their parents' time, it is now more expensive to have and raise children.

Large numbers of children ensure the growth of the clan and its continuation. It is also essential to leave behind many children, particularly male children, who can sacrifice. This is to ensure that the deceased will make it to the ancestral world by means of a properly performed funeral and that the ancestors will be cared for. Due to ongoing social and religious changes in the region, elders today express serious concern that their children will not perform the final funeral rites required to send them to the ancestral world or that no one will perform the necessary sacrifices to support them in the afterlife, forcing them into the humiliating position of having to beg from others.

The veneration of ancestors is the bedrock of the traditional family structure, and family and clan ancestors participate in all domains of individual and family life. Even before birth, the expected child is under the influence and watchful eye of the ancestors. During the pregnancy or after the child is born, the family head will visit a diviner to determine whether the child is "for the family." These divination sessions help the family determine the child's identity and what role the ancestors will play in its life.

Throughout the life of a traditional Nankani person, the ancestors are implicated in many if not all events, from sickness to good fortune. Ancestors reward individuals and families with good fortune or punish them for a wide range of possible transgressions. Ancestors are also able to protect family members from potential threats or actions taken against them. Divination is the primary way to communicate with the ancestors and to determine the sacrifices required to thank or placate them.[3] Sacrifices range from water or alcohol libations to small or, more rarely, large animal sacrifices. A man described the purpose of communicating with the ancestors through divination.

> You will not be able to tell what is causing any of the problems that you
> are having. But when you go to the soothsayer's [diviner's] house, it is

through the soothsaying that the ancestors will be able to communicate what has happened. Or, if you are doing something that is in the wrong direction, or if someone is trying to do something to harm you, it is through soothsaying that the ancestor will speak to you and tell you this is what is happening.

Ancestors make their presence and needs known by causing misfortunes, and they can be particularly persecutory and vindictive. Misfortunes are a result of a family member's intentional and unintentional transgressions or may occur as a notification to individuals or families that they need to attend to the ancestor's specific desires. A grandmother described the cause of misfortune in a house.

> When people are sick in the family, or when other bad things happen in the family, it means that the head or someone else in the house has not obeyed the ancestors. The ancestors asked for something and maybe they did not give. That's why the ancestors cause sickness in the family. You then go to the soothsayer's house and identify the ancestor that did it. Maybe you didn't do this for the ancestor, that is why he is making you sick. If you are able to do those things, provide those necessary things for the ancestor, the sickness will go away.

To become an ancestor, one must achieve personhood, described below, and often have reached elder status before one dies. Personhood and ancestral status are confirmed through divination, which occurs during the funeral. If the man has lived a long or important life, his children or grandchildren may create an ancestral shrine for him and offer sacrifices in his honor. The smaller or genealogically immediate ancestors are represented by the shrines located in front of the house. Maternal shrines are often found incorporated into the wall of the traditional women's room inside the compound. Larger male clan ancestors, those that are genealogically distant, are represented at the *tingane*, or tree shrines, a sacred cluster of trees away from the compound where offerings to clan ancestors (of the maximal lineage) are made.

The head of the home (*yidaana*) is responsible for overall resources, jural affairs, and the house's public engagement with the larger clan and community. The female head (*deodaana*) is responsible for much of the functioning inside the boundaries of the home, which include running the house and ensuring that things are done smoothly. Each *yidaana* is responsible for minor issues, decision-making, and sacrifices and other matters related to the family's direct ancestors. He might also sacrifice to the more significant and distant clan ancestors. Each

A child pouring a libation for the ancestors under the guidance of family members (Stephen Fisher)

yire is part of a maximal lineage or clan that is united by a *yi-zuo* (household head) and referred to by the name of the founding ancestor ending in *büsi* (children of). The head of the clan is responsible for any issues or problems that arise within the clan and for major sacrifices. "The clan elder's house is always there," a man explained. "If there's a problem, or even if it is something good, like after a bountiful harvest, we will go to the house of the eldest clan member to pour libations and sacrifice." The land (*teŋa*) that each house farms is managed and ritually administered by each section's *teŋdanna* (custodian of the land). Each family head has control over his farming plots, but the *teŋdanna* manages the clan's larger landholdings and is responsible for the rituals needed to maintain the productivity of the land.

While much of the visible and jural authority is vested in the patrilineal side of the family, which is associated with the visible, public front of the house, one's matrilateral side, associated with the more hidden areas inside the house, confers its own equally important set of social roles, privileges, and responsibilities. One's matrilateral side also can bestow mystical powers. Divination ancestors are passed through one's mother's side, as are some sorcery shrines and, most concerning, witchcraft (sɔa) powers, which threaten to disrupt or destroy the family.

The mother's family, or one's matrilateral connections, comprises a significant network of relationships and social connections that extend laterally beyond one's patrilineal line, with women thus symbolizing, according to Victor Turner, the broader community network and its ethical system (1969, 117). Matrilateral relationships allow a man to expand his networking opportunities and "extend a widely cast net of less formal contacts" outside the structure and confines of his agnatic lineage, which tends to be more rigid and limited (Shaw 2000, 31).

The importance and strength of a Nankani person's matrilateral kin is expressed in the avuncular relationship. The Nankani have strong relationships with their mother's brother (aseba). During my fieldwork, the importance of this relationship was highlighted when people were not surprised that my uncle came to visit me while my parents did not. An elder remarked that his visit was the correct thing for an uncle to do and that God placed us in this world in such pairs to watch out for and remember each other. After his visit, a man asked about him and rhetorically inquired, "What would we do without our uncles?"

Matthew stated that one goes to the uncle's house whenever something is wrong. "Your strength lies in your uncle's house," he said. "That's where your mother comes from. A man has power in his uncle's house; any power you have comes from there. You can go to your uncle's house and do anything. Within your father's house you don't have that power."

"My uncle taught me how to make a good argument," Elijah added, "and how I can win in family disputes. When others escalate the argument, don't you escalate it too. Stay silent. When it comes time for them to ask your opinion, you bring up one point that will bring their argument down and they all come down together to this one level." If there is a dispute or other problem within the house, a man or a woman has the right to leave without explanation by simply stating that he or she is going to their uncle's house. The uncle is outside of and not bound by the patrilineal jural structure. Yet, despite the power represented by one's avuncular and matrilateral ties, such relationships cannot override the agnatic ties and do not extend beyond the personal level.

Marriage

Marriages are exogamous, and residence is patrilocal: the new wife goes to live with her husband in his father's compound. Historically, polygyny was common and dependent on a man's ability to support multiple wives and children. Polygyny is still practiced, though to a much lesser extent. A man brings gifts to the woman's home as the first step in courting and establishing a conjugal union. However, according to one origin story, things were not always this way. A Sirigu elder recalled the story of the first family.

God [Yini] created man and all the things on earth. Before making man, however, he first made the spirit beings. The woman was the next one he created, and later that same day he made man. God made the woman at one place in the forest and made the man in another. They didn't know each other. Where the woman was living, God later made a young girl and a dog. The woman, girl, and dog lived together.

After some time, the spirits were able to locate the woman and the young girl. Many spirits came to court the young girl. Some of them decided that they wanted to marry her and asked the woman for the hand of the girl in marriage. The woman didn't know what to do about the girl's suitors. Until then, she thought that she and the girl were alone on earth and that there were no other living beings. When the woman first saw the spirits, she didn't even know that such things existed.

The dog advised the woman that she should tell the spirits that if they wanted to marry the girl, they should court her by bringing guinea fowl each time they visited. The woman told the spirits this and they began bringing fowl.

One day the woman devised a plan to trick the spirits. She decided to cut the dog into two parts. One part would be the side with the head, and the other would be the side with the rear legs. When the woman cut the dog in half both parts turned into a woman. Now there were three girls: the proper girl and two from the dog cut in half. When the spirits returned to visit, they saw that there were now four females on earth. The woman gave them the two girls cut from the dog.

Later on, the man was roaming about the forest looking for honey. That is how he found where the woman lived. The man was looking for honey up in the trees. Upon finding a hive, he climbed into the tree to get closer. That is when the woman saw the man. At the time the woman was the chief of all the land; she was very powerful, more powerful than the man. When the man saw the woman, he was afraid of her, afraid that she would harm him. She approached the tree and asked the man what he was doing. The man replied that he was trying to find honey. The woman had never had honey before and asked if she could taste it. The man dropped some honey down for her to try, and she said it was good.

The woman asked what the honey was called, and the man said it was *puga ba panbarige*, meaning you take a stick to go inside the hole and move it around [stirring]. He said he had called the honey after that. He came down from the tree and told her that she should let him show her what he meant by *puga ba panbarige*, and she did.

When the man slept with her, the woman said that it was a very good thing. Because of that, she decided that the man should stay with her. He

agreed. The woman built a house for the man so that they had a place to
sleep. As she was building the house and the mud was still not dry, a goat
walked by, stepping in the mud. The woman asked God what was this
thing that stepped in her mud. God told the woman that it was a kid goat
[*butila*]. Soon after, the woman gave birth to a son, and she named it *budigla*,
the "male child."

One day the women lost their power [*panŋa*] over the men. It was the
men who were coming to marry the women, not the women marrying the
men. When you marry a woman, you have to send fowls and other things
to her family. It's not proper that I, the one sending these things to a
woman, should allow the woman to come and rule over me. The men
could not allow the women to rule them. That is why the women have lost
their control over men.

The narrative presents several interesting themes concerning the first relationship between humans, the involvement of spirits, and the making of the first
home and child, all of which provide important background for subsequent
chapters. First, it tells us that the relationship between humans and spirit beings
was present from the beginning. Other Nankani myths about spirits describe
how God used them to help form the world. This narrative depicts the first
people's relationship with the spirits as ambivalent at best. Spirits have a great
deal they can offer humans, but they are also dangerous and unpredictable,
and any knowledge gained from a spirit comes at a cost. Accounts also depict
spirits as desirous of women and eager to breach family boundaries and gain
access to domestic life.[4]

Second, the dog plays an important intermediary role between humans
and spirits, since it is able to see into and occupy both human and spiritual
realms. I detail the characteristics of dogs, particularly their role in catching
spirit children, in subsequent chapters. Here the dog offers important advice
about how to deal with spirits and, in its liminal role, acts as a substitute human
to be given away like a daughter.

Third, the narrative offers a glimpse of a time when women had greater
power. In it the woman is managing the spirits and taking charge of the relationship with the man by deciding, for example, that he should stay at her house—
the opposite of contemporary practices. The narrative describes how a reversal
of power resulted from the system of exchange leading to marriage. It incorpo-
rates issues related to the patrilineal system and patriarchal dominance and
informs us that the system resulted from, and is justified by, the bride price.
Finally, the goat stepping into the mud symbolically links the mud used to build
the house with the formation and birth of the first descendant, establishing and

affirming the human link to the land and the house as the physical manifestation of the family.

Marriages today are commonly based on choice. Historically, arranged marriages or betrothals and marriage by elopement or "capture" were more common. I asked the elder Asingiya when a person is ready for marriage. He said that a girl around sixteen years of age is marriageable, but a man, even at nineteen, is not "fully grown." If he has a child at that age, it will be weak. On average, men tend to be older than women when they marry. This is partly due to the longer transition to adulthood for men, often involving migratory work, schooling or apprenticeships, the need to gather resources, and the preference for assuming greater family responsibilities before marriage takes place.

A man enters adult status upon marriage, which is strengthened if he has children and a large family. The transition to womanhood, however, was historically more abrupt and tied to common household skills and female genital cutting. The ritual of female circumcision—involving both excision and a period of education—marked a specific change that situated women's connection to the ancestral world and rendered her ready for marriage. The incidence of genital cutting, which was widespread before it was outlawed in 1994, was quickly reduced by means of several health campaigns primarily designed to stigmatize the practice. Consequently, the rapid disappearance of the transitional rituals without a replacement has resulted in an unclear transition period for girls. Female adolescence has now become a prolonged phenomenon largely as a result of health campaigns, religious institutions, and increased access to educational opportunities (Eguavoen 2008, 90–91; Mensch et al. 1999).

The processes around courtship and marriage vary according to family and community. Generally, after a period of courtship, the man will approach his father and speak of his interest in the woman. In some instances, the man's father will inform the woman's father. When a woman is interested in a man, she might determine if any people she knows have married into his family and begin to ask about him. An elder woman explained to me how she looks first to see if a man has a good work ethic and is able to farm. "If the man is not good," she explained, "they will sit their daughter down and tell her, advise her to get a different man." She described how love could come first in a relationship, but if a woman fails to study the man carefully, problems can later develop. If problems do arise, a woman can return to her father's house, depending on how much of the bride price (*sulɛ*) has been given, or she can go to a new husband, who will be required to reimburse her previous husband for what he has lost.

In the past, girls were often betrothed. A girl's family might place pressure on her to marry a friend of the family; in most cases these men were significantly older and might already have one or more wives. A grandmother remarked that in these circumstances the girl's family "doesn't want a disgrace; maybe the man has done something for them, so they also want to do something that will please their friend." She noted that in some cases women who refused were beaten for their defiance.

In many cases, if a woman wants to marry someone else, she can "dodge out, pass through the rooftop [out of the compound], not the main gate, and go marry. And her parents will not be aware of it." The process of taking up residence in the man's house is the first of many steps that establish the conjugal union.

There is no specific act or ritual that clearly marks the exact moment when the couple is officially married. The closest is when the woman moves into her new husband's compound, but even then, her ties to that man remain tenuous. Before this occurs, the man will bring a series of gifts to the woman's family—drinks, guinea fowls, or tobacco. The family might refuse the gifts if they are not interested in him or in losing their daughter. A couple might elope if the parents do not approve. An elopement, however, does not preclude the later exchange of bride price.

When her family agrees, the man will then bring a hen to her home, and they will perform a ritual that shifts their daughter's residence to the man's house. After this ceremony, the man will continue to bring gifts to the family and will also be obligated to assist the family with farming or other bride service. "You have to be very submissive to the in-laws," a man remarked. "You have to do whatever they say. Going to marry a woman is not easy."

The man has some time to gather the necessary bride price. Bride price can be negotiable and involve an intermediary to help broker the arrangement. A common exchange traditionally consists of all the items and fowls given before the daughter changed residence; two cows, one of which must be a bull; seven sheep; some hoes for farming; additional guinea fowls; and—if it is the eldest daughter—an additional sheep, which will be sacrificed to her house. Many of these items have locally recognized symbolic significance surrounding fertility (hoes) and womanhood (guinea fowls). There is significant variation in gifts and the timing of the exchanges. Christian families might still engage in the courtship process, but the church wedding becomes the focal point and the exchanges are emphasized less. Overall, it is only through this lengthy sequence of gifts that the marriage is solidified and that the children born are recognized as legitimate and for the patriline.

The institution of and practices surrounding conjugal unions have been subject to significant change throughout the pre- to postcolonial periods, and they continue to change alongside regional demographic and religious shifts. Sean Hawkins (2002) describes how British colonial governance and jural systems transformed marriage practices in northern Ghana and how colonial government processes and ethnocentric representations demonstrated a lack of commensurability between colonial categories and understandings of marriage and local practices and meanings. Notably, even translating *marriage* and what it encodes is misleading. Several languages in northern Ghana, including Nankani, do not have a noun that describes marriage as it is understood in English. Rather, the symbolism of eating or consuming is often used to describe unions, and the closest equivalents to marriage are the statements that "men eat women" while "women enter men."[5] These phrases describe not the entire process of solidifying the union but primarily the act of the woman changing residence.

Most marriages, at least historically, are more informal, fluid, and complex. In addition to the historical and ethnographic evidence, elders say that women had significant flexibility and control over conjugal unions. While men today, as well as in the past, may take lovers while married, historically it was also common for women to have "one or two favourite lovers to whom her husband has no objection" (Cardinall 1920, 79). According to descriptions of conjugal unions by early colonial administrators, women enjoyed significant autonomy before the colonial period, making unions uncertain and fueling rivalry between men (Hawkins 2002, 233). The instability of unions, which was related to competition for women, was often a source of conflict between families and communities. Much like an unmarried woman, married women might elope or be "stolen," often with her complicity, which could result in fighting and violence. Seduction and eventual abduction of another man's wife, even of one's own clansman, occurred with greater frequency in the past (Hawkins 2002). I raise these historical details because the anxieties around controlling the movements of women and new wives are, as described in chapter 4, central to understanding the cause of spirit children.

Children born into a conjugal union legitimated by the agreed exchange are, as many women described, "for the man." If a woman leaves a union or is sent home to her father's house, the children will stay with the patriline. Today, this ideal is not always practiced, particularly with the increasing costs of raising children; a child can be sent with its mother if the family cannot care for it. If a woman permanently leaves her husband for another man, that man must make conjugal payments to compensate the former husband and legitimate the union. Children born of unions for which the payments have not been made can be considered property of the first man. In the 1970s, the courts began applying blood relation as the basis of paternity, but previous to this, conjugal payments were the primary determinant of a child's family membership (Hawkins 2002, 278).

Unions can be dissolved for a variety of reasons. A man might return his wife to her father's house if she engages in witchcraft or theft. Frequent gossip about one's husband or family can result in problems, as can frequent disregard of a husband's wishes when the woman is outside the home or in male-oriented spaces. A woman can leave a man if he is not providing for her or if she is abused or neglected. It is easier for a woman to leave if the bride price has not been paid. If it has been paid, the husband may ask for its return, although it is unlikely that the woman's father will do so. Consequently, fathers are not likely to support the dissolution of their daughters' unions. The option of leaving becomes less likely if a woman has children. However, it is possible that a younger wife's outsider status and her children's membership within the patriline make it easier for some women to move into another relationship.

Being Born into the House

The arrival of a newborn child is an exciting but also ambivalent time for family members. The preparations and concerns surrounding the infant's arrival demonstrate that families are often unsure of the child's intentions and its status as a member of the house. A new child could be from God and the ancestors, but it could also be a spirit from the bush. When a newborn comes, a man explained, "The first thing the family does is consult a soothsayer to determine whether the new baby is for the family and if it is a normal human being or not." Consultations with diviners, which often occur before, during, and after the coming of a child, help determine the intentions and destiny (*paala*) of the child, the ancestral desires for the child, and if the child will be good for the family. When and how often these consultations occur vary within each family; some will consult the diviner several times before the birth and others directly after the birth. A man explained the process.

> When you marry, you have to go to the soothsayer's house to find out whether the woman is able to give birth. When she gives birth, it is through soothsaying that you find out if the child is coming from God. You can also soothsay to see what the child will do on earth. You can find out that maybe the child will be a great person in the family. That means that he will live long or be a great ancestor. Sometimes, they can say that the child that is coming is not good. If so, you have to ask further to know what you can do to prevent that. You have to ask so you can perform certain sacrifices and ceremonies to prevent the bad children from coming.

Nankani infants and young children are assigned a considerable ability to make choices, have preferences, and consciously impose themselves on the world. By virtue of their proximity to the spirit world, children can have closer contact with spirits than do adults. I observed family members recounting infants' behaviors and imbuing them with higher-level adult awareness and problem-solving skills. The attribution to infants of decision-making powers and knowledge of not only this world but the previous one is found in other parts of West Africa (Gottlieb 2004). With this agency, however, comes families' concern that the child might not be for the house. As in the case of N'ma, family members will closely read and interpret a child's behavior and intentions within the family's context for signs that the child is not as it appears. The ambivalence associated with childhood is given significant symbolic association, and its power is linked to what is hidden and unknown (Ferme 2001, 197–98). Much like its mother, the family considers the infant a stranger or outsider. As it ages and its identity emerges, it is slowly brought more fully into the folds of social membership.

When a child is born, many families will not immediately bestow on it a permanent name.[6] A child may simply be called "my father" (N'so) or "my mother" (N'ma), reflecting its connection to the ancestral world. The child or ancestor eventually chooses the permanent name. When a child is ready to be named, it will communicate its desire by excessive crying or becoming sick, often with a fever. Community members describe an infant's ill body as a battleground for ancestral dominance, with the ancestor spirits struggling over the infant to determine who it will represent or embody on earth. The family will go to a diviner to determine the cause of the sickness and which ancestor "wants" the child. A child might have many names before the correct one is eventually identified.

Naming is a formal recognition of the child's relationship with those who came before and of its attachment to the larger family and social group. For the Nankani, the receipt of a name is one of the first steps in the lifelong process of acquiring personhood. While a child is not necessarily a strict reincarnation of an ancestor, it does act as an extension of the ancestor in the world of the living, and in this process it can possess the simultaneous dual qualities of a new individual and one linked to someone who came before.[7] The individual has day-to-day agency, but the ancestor is ultimately responsible for many significant events in that person's life.[8] If a child or adult prospers and is healthy, it is because the ancestor is watching over that person. In return for good fortune, individuals honor the ancestor by sacrificing and pouring libations. People say that some individuals have a personality similar to that of the ancestor after which they were named. In this sense, being named after an ancestor intergenerationally maintains the memory of the ancestor and links it to the larger moral community, both living and deceased.

Subjunctive Personhood

Elijah and I sat chatting with three elder men outside a compound. Earlier we were discussing spirits, but the postlunch conversation soon switched to more mundane topics. There was a brief lull in the conversation before Akolbire declared, to our astonishment, "I am a spirit child."

"What are you talking about? You shouldn't be revealing this," admonished a second, more vocal elder sitting with us.

"These things are not to be shared. You should leave these things behind," the third man added.

Akolbire ignored their reproaches and described the circumstances surrounding his childhood. "They went to the soothsayer and even brought the concoction man and gave me the medicine, but I didn't die. Soon my mother was able to teach me how to walk. Now I am alive and strong. But if I die today, what will my family say? Am I still a spirit child to the community? People will still condemn me, so I wanted to reveal myself. [When I die] they will know that I am a spirit child."

I was intrigued. Why would an adult willingly disclose that he is a spirit? While Akolbire's disclosure would not result in immediate ostracization, his declaration nullified his status as a legitimate member of his lineage and the possibility that he would be regarded as an ancestor. To better understand spirit children and Akolbire's circumstances necessitates an examination of Nankani personhood.

Marcel Mauss (1938) described personhood as a social fact rather than an individual phenomenon. For Fortes (1987), personhood is socially generated, culturally defined, and experienced in relation to the "fiat of society" and the rights and responsibilities associated with one's social role. Personhood is relationally generated; that is, it is rooted in relationships with others and engendered through one's morally acceptable behaviors. Personhood also encompasses one's embodied status and intercorporeal relations. Abnormality and debility, and their moral implications, can thus challenge definitions of personhood.

Personhood in a Euro-American sense follows an ideology of individualism that ascribes family membership and personhood to the moment of one's birth or, within some communities, conception. This pattern of instant and assumed personhood is not universal. Across societies, people delay conferring personhood due to a range of cultural models and attachment strategies that shape the way infants are understood (Lancy 2014). Personhood among the Nankani is not immediately guaranteed, and one's full status as a person is not known or bestowed until one dies. Hence, it is possible for an individual like Akolbire, despite his age, to not achieve personhood.

I liken personhood among the Nankani as a potentiality that dynamically accumulates throughout one's life and can be questioned or withheld if one does not fit the necessary social expectations and characteristics. Similarly, practices of personhood in an Ecuadorian village, observed Lynn Morgan, are not an either/or demarcation or a "uniform or monolithic abstraction" but a gradual acquisition that occurs through a series of socializing actions (1998, 70). John and Jean Comaroff (2001) offer a description of an "African personhood" involving the continuous and active practice of self-construction—or a cumulative gathering and exchange rather than passive accumulation—emphasizing one's social position.

Expectations for personhood among the Nankani include reaching an old age, having children and a family, contributing to the household economy, participating in the sociopolitical system, and fulfilling other normative age- and gender-related social expectations and achievements. Personhood is also an outcome of one's fate and the intercession of the ancestors. Divination during the final funeral rites determines the identity of the deceased and determines whether he or she was a true person for the family or, for example, a bush spirit masquerading as a person. After death, the ancestor spirit may retain his or her status as a person and is engaged with, as a person may be, through divination and sacrifices.

I characterize this tentative accumulation of the traits of personhood throughout the life course as subjunctive personhood—a form of personhood that is a contingent, potential, or prospective attribution. Subjunctive personhood is a state of possibility rather than inevitability. As individuals age, they accumulate the social and moral markers of personhood and enact a subjunctive form of "as if" that socially situates them in relation to others until it is rendered indicative after their death.

Inquiries concerning the status of future family members begin early. As family members determine if the new child is for the house, they inquire, through divination, whether the child is a normal human being (nirisaale vua, lit. "human alive"). This notion of humanness is the first prerequisite on the path to attaining personhood. The determination of whether an infant is a normal human being is dependent on its relationship with the ancestral world and the ancestors' declarations obtained through divination, the infant's physical and behavioral characteristics, and the circumstances surrounding its birth. Misfortunes such as the death of livestock, crop failure, or the sickness and death of family members might increase uncertainty and indicate that the child is not a human being.

Spiritual entities are not normal human beings, are not for the house, and cannot become persons. Children identified as evil spirits do not have the potential to enter into meaningful relations and take on appropriate responsi-bilities within the domestic sphere and the larger social environment (although good spirits might be seen as offering the family good fortune and are thus entitled to closer family relations). While families are vigilant over infants, some spirits can be quite deceptive, appearing normal and feigning appropriate social relations into adulthood.

The assignment of humanness and the initial kernel of subjunctive person-hood to infants and children is a dynamic process fraught with uncertainty. In the case of spirit children, interpretations are variable and families remain open to alternatives and consider new evidence, ranging from changes in health to shifts in ancestral sentiment. In these cases, families sometimes determine the child to be a neutral or good spirit and no action is taken.[9] This is likely what occurred in Akolbire's case after he survived the concoction and reached a developmental milestone. However, the suspicions surrounding his identity remained. Ultimately, one can never be too sure about the status of others, even family members, their intentions, and their statuses as members of the house.

Akolbire's disclosure gives some insight into the construction of personhood and spirit—family relations. Akolbire openly declared his nonpersonhood and, by extension, his ineligibility to be an ancestor. Why would he condemn himself? It is likely that the divination session following his death would have revealed the truth anyway. His case was intriguing because he knew he was not a person, whereas other individuals might go through life unaware that they are spirits.

Personhood is a distinctive part of morality that characterizes who is socially recognized within the community. Personhood is not necessarily an either/or proposition but a subjunctive state of becoming that is, in the Nankani case, intersubjective and intercorporeal. Personhood is subject to one's membership and contributions to the family, embodied status, behaviors, and forms of ex-change and reciprocity expected of a family and community member. While an individual might appear to be a person, his or her true identity, like a person's true intentions, might never be known until it is revealed after death. This results in an interesting paradox. One can appear and act as one is if a person through-out life, building a case for personhood, but it is not until death that this status is ultimately achieved.

3

For the Bush

The bush (*mu'o*) is at once a physical location, an imaginative space, and a state of being. Connotations common to the bush include notions of power, disorder, or pollution, rendering it at once a dangerous, disorienting, and an often-potent space of transformation. The Nankani are generally interested in keeping the bush and its associations separate from the social word of the house. Although it is possibly risky, some people look to the bush as a source of power or medicine and as a place for the discovery of innovations and new forms of knowledge or practice. The meanings and experiences associated with the bush and its denizen spirits play a central role in the Nankani moral imagination and discourse, shaping their subjectivity and interpretations of children.

God created the house and village for humans and designated the bush as the dwelling space for the spirits. While conceived of as distinct spaces, the boundaries separating the two are easily crossed. Just as humans can easily cross into bush spaces, spirits, too, find ways to enter domesticated places.

The size and physical location of the bush vary considerably. The bush may be a small, familiar cluster of trees only meters from one's compound or a distant expanse of uninhabited, uncultivated, and infrequently visited land. People identify features such as the upper reaches of hillsides or rock outcroppings and other unusual geographic spaces as bush. While the bush is associated with the wild, it is not synonymous with the North American notion of wilderness as an expanse of untouched land. Since the bush can be of any size and contain a range of characteristics, it is best understood as a space that lacks or resists social inscription, particularly links to an ancestral history and network of social meanings. The ambiguity and power associated with the bush result from its distinction from the house and its connection to the natural world and supernatural forces.

Elements of daily life are often associated with domestic places or bush spaces, and such categorizations frequently appear in speech. Animals may be categorized as for the house, for the bush, or, as in the case of dogs, somewhere in between. This distinction is also applied to food. Other binaries, such as male-female and dry-wet, are important. A man also explained that "everything that lives on this earth has a bad quality and a good quality, even rocks." Opposing conceptual categories, binary distinctions, or "contrasts," as Michael Jackson (1989) describes them, are central to shaping Nankani experience. These distinctions, chiefly those between the house and the bush, are useful symbolic realms through which experiences—especially misfortune, illness, and healing—are given meaning (Janzen 1978, 203). Africanist scholars have described the significance of binary oppositions present in kinship, gender, aesthetics, and symbolism, for example, as well as the importance of maintaining balanced oppositions between contrasts.[1] Care is needed in working with binary distinctions to ensure that they are not an artifact of Euro-American thinking, confused with Claude Lévi-Strauss's nature-culture dichotomy, or duplicate the problematic primitive-civilized distinctions present in forms of colonial discourse (Gottlieb 1992, 17–18).

People only enter the bush if necessary, either to relieve themselves—most people defecate in the bush—or to gather ever diminishing supplies of firewood or bush foods. People have sex in the bush, particularly if they are engaging in premarital or adulterous relations. Sex is supposed to occur within the safety of the house, and traditionally having sex in the bush is a dangerous and forbidden activity. People can also embody the chaotic, wild, and unpredictable characteristics of the bush; they can "go bush," signifying going wild or becoming drunk. For example, one afternoon Elijah turned down a second cup of instant coffee because it would make him "go bush." He demonstrated this mental state of losing control, which would cause him to run energetically and speak in a rapid, uncontrolled manner.

The bush is associated with elements that are counter to the interests of the family system. Illnesses come from the bush, as do spirit children and other disruptions. The bush is associated with the antisocial actions and nefarious activities of witches, sorcerers, and spirits; at night, for instance, witches meet in the bush to sell or consume captured souls. The bush is also the stage where antisocial behaviors unfold. In discourse, people evoke the bush as a physical and imaginary space where humans and spirits interact and human desires, intentions, and dispositions are seized, articulated, and personified (Jackson 2007, 133).

The Nankani World of Spirits

The Nankani identify a general category of bush spirits referred to as *kulkariga* (pl. *kulkarsi*). People differentiate the *kulkarsi* according to the actions or contexts in which they appear. Variations of the *kulkarsi* include tree spirits and spirit children. There are also less common spiritual beings, the *koko*, *seto*, and *ken-ensigire*, which are more closely related to ghosts or deceased witches, monsters, and zombies, respectively.

Not all people can see the *kulkarsi*. They are generally invisible when in their spiritual form. They are nonetheless able to show themselves if they desire it or if someone has the power or "eyes" to see them. If one happens to see a spirit, it usually vanishes quickly. A man described them as being "just like air. They're maybe even listening to what we are saying right now." People commented that spirits could be walking by your side and you would never know.

When spotted, the spirits appear short or "dwarfish." Spirits often have long and generous amounts of hair, and occasionally some are described as having white skin. They often appear as a small adult or child, which walks "like a child that is just learning how," one man explained. Most people remarked that spirits can run and move quickly, faster than the eye can see. Spirits are impulsive, wise, sneaky, and mischievous. They can cause serious misfortune, such as killing a family member. More often, however, they annoy or play jokes on humans for their own amusement. Spirits can also steal food, fowls, and other animals to share with their friends and kin in the bush.

There are several taboos associated with spirits and the bush. People, particularly women, should avoid bush locations where spirits dwell—usually treed areas or hillsides—as this increases the likelihood that they will encounter a dangerous spirit. I was warned that if you follow a *kulkariga* and step in its footprints, you could easily vanish. "When you go to the trees out there," the elder Asingiya said, gesturing to the south of Sirigu, "if you go and look within those trees, you will see a place that is very clean with no plastic bags or any trash. You should go there and step to see what will happen! It's a *kulkarsi* grave. If you step on it, it will easily harm you or you might disappear." Large bodies of water can also be dangerous. If swimming alone, a spirit can capture a person and take him or her to a spirit world underwater. If lucky, that person might return several years later with new medicines and power.

There is a close relationship between spirits and trees. Some trees are spirits or can become inhabited and animated by spirits. In general people understand that some objects, such as selected rocks and trees, have a spirit or soul, have humanlike needs and social organization, and engage in human activities. "Trees," Asingiya said, "can do all the things that human beings can do." I gave him a curious look. "Seriously, if you think that I'm lying you can come and sleep at my house tonight! There's a tree over there that even soothsays. It does all the soothsaying things. Even the rattle, you can hear it. They can even fetch water."

Spirits, trees, and people are similar in many ways. Spirits live within families, have similar political and kinship organizations, sacrifice to their ancestors, and farm, sing, suffer, desire, and hunger much like people do. Looking toward a high hill in Burkina Faso, a man said that in the evening there is always fire on the mountain. "There are spirit children living there," he said. "And they are cooking. They live together as a family." Spirits are drawn to and enjoy living around trees and the bush. God made them this way, Asingiya assured me, because spirits cannot live with people or in domestic places. In some accounts, spirits will take noteworthy measures to avoid human contact. However, as we will see, despite the similarities between the human and spirit worlds, spirits at times desire and will pursue the benefits of living within human families.

The narrative presented in chapter 2 situated spirits with the first humans and their family. A separate origin narrative states that before the arrival of humans, spirits carried out labor for God when he was building the world, moving rocks and earth. After the arrival of the first humans, spirits came to occupy ambivalent roles, which vacillate between being helpful and harmful to humans. Spirits are often simultaneously purveyors of knowledge and agents of destruction.

Narratives depict the human hunter as an intrepid explorer that risks entering the bush to bring back not only game or medicines but also stories and innovations. A great deal of what humans know, from farming techniques to healing methods, has been learned from hunters entering the bush and encountering spirits. Attracting and catching a spirit can result in new forms of knowledge or secrets that help humans prosper. However, spirits are reluctant to share their knowledge with humans. The following account details an early contact between humans and spirits and tells listeners how to outwit spirits and gain access to their specialized knowledge or techniques. It also demonstrates how a spirit will attempt to fool the hunter and convince him it is a human being.

> We are told that spirit children normally play beneath a tree in the bush. Every day they gather under that particular tree and clean the entire place of leaves and other debris. Normally hunters go into the bush. The hunters would pass beneath that tree and wonder, "How come every day, under this particular tree, it is swept clean? Are there other hunters that converge and clean under this tree?"

The hunters investigated and found that the spirits go there in groups to tell stories, sing, and dance. Just like we human beings sit at a gathering and someone sings before the commencement of whatever we have to do, the spirits do the same beneath that tree over there. The hunters hid and observed the singing and dancing taking place. However, you know the spirit child. It can smell the scent of a human being. The spirits suddenly stopped dancing. They smelled human beings around and decided to search for them, but the hunters left in time. This is how hunters discovered how spirits live in the bush.

Normally, the spirit is a very small child, but it has very long hair and plenty of it. By watching the spirits, the hunters learned how the spirits grow *bambara* beans in the wild. When the hunters go into the bush they can see the mounds where they planted. They would wait until the spirits dispersed, then remove all that the spirits had hidden and tell everyone what they had learned. All the groundnuts and *bambara* beans we have came from the wild because of the spirits.

One day a hunter went into the bush and happened to meet one of the spirit children. The hunter caught it, sat it down, and questioned it. "Who are you?" the hunter asked.

The spirit child replied, "I am a human being."

"A human being from where?"

"A human being in the forest, and a king in the forest. I am the bush's elder. There is no creature in the forest that I do not know."

"Even human beings, or just wild creatures?" the hunter inquired.

"Any creature, including human beings."

The hunter, still skeptical, asked again. "As of now, what are you?"

"I am a human being."

"Then tell me," the hunter inquired, "what is my purpose in the forest?"

"You are a human being here to kill wild animals, you are a hunter," the spirit child responded. "Do you want me to tell you things?"

"Yes," the hunter replied.

"OK. Come with me, if you wish. I will take you to where we live in the forest and show you that we know every creature in the wild and what it eats." When they arrived at the place where the spirit children live, the other spirits were not there, so the spirit took the hunter into his house. The hunter noticed that the house was round and did not have an entrance. But the spirit child chanted, the house opened, and they entered.

Inside there were small pots, a horn containing medicines, a short stick, a gourd that diviners shake to produce a rhythm, and a goatskin bag [containing the tools of divination] hanging. The spirit commenced to teach the hunter how to use these things, one after the other. After showing him, he told the hunter that he had the power to see what was happening at his house. While the hunter was still holding the items, the spirit asked, "Now that I have told you these things, will you let me go?" The hunter said no. The spirit child, wanting to be released, said, "Anything that you want in this forest, I can get it for you."

The hunter was enthralled. "What does *anything* mean? These things you use to know what is happening, if I want them, where would I get them?"

"If you are interested in acquiring them," the spirit responded, "I will show you. You will have to dig certain roots. You will have to get all the herbs I describe. Once you arrive home with all these things, I will come and help you get what you wish." The spirit explained that he would meet him the next day at the house. "You will not see me," the spirit said, "but I will speak to you. If you follow what I say, you will have all you wish for."

"But wait," the hunter said. "What if I don't want you to come to my house?"

"It's no problem," the spirit replied, "but being outside your house it will be difficult for you to remember everything. If you can remember, you can have all that you wish for."

The next day, after the spirit arrived, he again remarked that the hunter must be smart and listen carefully. The spirit narrated the steps. But the secret of the spirit child is that he can tell you what to do to get what you wish for, but at the end, when you let him go, he will stand next to you and say, "Forget everything right now!" and you will not remember a single thing. However, the hunter was smart and aware of this secret, so he immediately killed the spirit child and was able to remember everything.

Ayanobasiya, a grandmother I frequently visited, described a spirit living in a well that her uncle knew. One day he was able to grab it by the hair and pull it out. It cried to be set free, but her uncle held on until the spirit began to tell him how to grow crops and do other things to make himself prosperous. Unfortunately, he forgot to kill it afterward and promptly forgot all the secrets.

Others had similar encounters. "When there are cows in the family," a man said, "and the cow has a calf, sometimes at night a *kulkariga* will come and suck the cow's milk. The following day, because the *kulkariga* came to suck, the calf will not suck again [as no milk is available]." To counter the spirit, he related that his ancestors would place a gluelike substance on the teat of the cow so that when it came again they could capture the spirit. "Actually they would see it, just like a child. They would tie it up and ask it to tell them all the things." The *kulkariga* would then describe the treatment for various illnesses, even snakebite.

He noted, "Sometimes they would grab hold of the *kulkariga* and take it to the bush so it would show them which herbs to use."

Some humans have the power to interact with and control spirits for their own means. Diviners sometimes will work with a spirit and combine its powers with those of their divining shrine and ancestors to identify problems. Sorcerers and herbalists will also use the spirits to heal clients or entertain people.

Spirits may simply be playful or mischievous and for their own enjoyment may frighten humans or make them "lose their senses," particularly those who find themselves in an unfamiliar place. For instance, spirits are prone to untying and even riding horses or donkeys. "You will see the horse running all over the place, but you won't see anybody on it," a man described. Tree spirits commonly throw stones at people at night, attempting to frighten them. "When we were shepherd boys," the elder Asorigiya described, "any time you passed by their abodes in the night, we would be stoned. As the spirits were throwing stones, they would be laughing, although I would never see them [chuckling]. There are real spirits in the wild. In those days, you could hear them crying, shouting, all sorts of noise."

Fewer spirits exist now than in the past. Elders describe how modernity, deforestation and environmental changes, unfamiliar foods, and the coming of white people scared many of the spirits away. "People are also no longer learning about or observing nature," Asorigiya explained. "The spirits and the old ways of doing things are disappearing." Reflections on the declining role of spirits and the bush as a source of knowledge and change also emerged during discussions around development activities.

While spirits can offer helpful knowledge, they are also aggressive and can become hostile if slighted or denied what they desire. In this typical hunter and spirit narrative, the hunter learns how to make *pito* (*daam*), an important fermented sorghum beer, from a foolish spirit that vows revenge.

> There was a hunter who went to the bush and climbed to the top of a tree to look around. He saw some spirit children. He could see them physically, and they were very short. The hunter was able to watch the spirits making the malt and brewing *pito*; they could not see him. He had never had *pito* before, so when the spirits left he got down from the tree and drank the *pito* and found it was very good. He returned to the tree to continue watching. When one spirit came back, he said "Ahh! Who has come here and taken my drink?" This spirit said to himself, "This fellow doesn't know how to make it!" The spirit then spoke aloud, describing all the steps involved in preparing *pito*. The hunter was silent as he listened. It wasn't hard to hear, since the spirit was shouting loudly. When the spirit left, the hunter quickly

returned to his house and instructed his wife on how to make *pito*. When the people began to enjoy *pito*, the spirit children became angry and vowed they would come into people's houses to attack them because the hunter had taken their knowledge.

Humans have an ambivalent relationship with the spirits, as the distinctions between good and bad spirits are not always clear. Knowledge or objects acquired from the bush and its spirits can have strings attached and bring danger as well as value. The narrative about the origins of *pito* exemplifies the danger involved in taking knowledge from the spirits: they might cause misfortune or attack families from within as spirit children. I will soon come to examples of destructive cases.

The discourse on the relationship between spirits and knowledge acquisition and change opens ways for people to talk about and assimilate the possibilities that new encounters, innovations, strategies, and changes engender, for good or bad. Outside agents, processes, or objects of change, like spirits themselves, might be seductive or appear good, but they inevitably are slippery if not approached with caution. Entering the bush or looking to the outside and the unknown, beyond the safety of the domestic sphere, to acquire something new is generally positive. However, people are aware that the new, despite its benefits, can introduce disorder and disrupt the family.

The dangers associated with spirits become more tangible when they take human form. When a spirit appears as a child or an adult, it gains the same destructive potential as a normal human being. The following section describes the narratives associated with spirit children and tree spirits in human form and as agents in the Nankani moral imagination.

The Spirit Child and the Moral Imagination

Moral violations and ruptures in the social world of humans bring spirits into direct contact with families. People also use spirits to talk about these disruptions and issues of moral significance, as well as one's desires. That is, spirit narratives are emplotted to speak of anxieties and concerns, to imagine possibilities for action, and to consider the consequences of antisocial and immoral behavior. Stories about spirits and the bush engage an imaginary space where the speaker and listener are able to envision and discern a variety of possibilities for thought and action, socially acceptable or unacceptable.

Everyone, regardless of education and age, has heard spirit child stories. Accounts are typically mythical narratives heard as children or friend-of-a-friend stories. Quite often people recount their own experiences with spirit children. These spirit child narratives usually consist of recollections of a child performing inconceivable feats that are often framed in a supernatural context. Most narratives depict infants as walking or talking and performing actions beyond their developmental stage. These spirit children steal adult food to eat and share with other spirits; kill livestock; suddenly develop teeth, pubic hair, or other secondary sexual characteristics; and, as a man describes in the following account, kill family members.

> I witnessed a spirit child. My younger brother had a child. When it was very small and could not walk or do anything, it started to cause problems for the family. It killed both the mother and the father. A family member that lived away from the house came to visit. When he walked into the house he saw the child, who could not walk, standing on top of the building and walking around. When the child knew the man had seen him, he just fell down. That means that the man *really* saw the child, he'd seen what it was. The following day that man died.

Spirit narratives and interpretations are emplotted from an intersection of three domains: the Nankani ontological understandings of spirits and the cultural model for spirit children (see chapter 8), the circulation of discourse about mythical spirits and their behaviors, and the lived experience and interpretations of events such as misfortune and childhood abnormalities. The ambivalence surrounding infants and children, which is partly a result of their close proximity to the spirit world, also renders a child's motivations and liminal status a focal point for interpreting strange occurrences. In this example, a mother describes a series of bizarre events associated with a neighbor's child.

> Sometimes when you take your child to the bush or out to the farm, you leave it with its elder sister while you go and weed. If the child is a spirit child, other spirit children nearby can take it away. When they take the child away, you can roam and search for the child, but you won't find it. This even happened to a woman near my house. They searched for the child and couldn't find it for many days. They finally found the child on a nearby hill. The child was alive, sitting on top of some rocks. The women brought the child back to the house, but it was acting strange and misbehaving, just laughing all the time. It died soon after they found it.

Narratives depict spirit children as conflicted, pulled between worlds. They desire the benefits of the human world, but they also yearn to be with their own kind and are susceptible to fellow spirits tempting them to return. This aspect of the Nankani spirit child appears to be similar to that of the Yoruba spirit child, or *abiku*, which is drawn to the afterlife in a cycle of early death and rebirth, tormenting its family. While its desire to return is similar, unlike the Nankani spirit child, the *abiku* is not subject to infanticide, and families do not implicate it in a similar range of behaviors and misfortunes. The Nankani have a separate understanding of *abiku*-type children, who repeatedly depart from and return to this world. These children are referred to as *atule* (lit. "to return," or "to go and come").

The Nankani refer to the spirit child as a snake, a description common in other West African cultures, as illustrated by the case of N'ma.[2] People refer to spirit children as snakes because many cannot walk; are perceived as elusive, cunning, and deceptive; and are as deadly as snakes. The snake is not only a metaphor for spirit children; it is their embodiment. A concoction man describes his experience with a spirit child and the child's transformation into a snake.

> After I had treated one child, I gathered an old mat and put the *dongo* against the child.[3] I exited the room, but something told me to take the *dongo* with me. So, I went back in to get the *dongo* and saw a snake sleeping with the child. When I tried to take the *dongo*, the snake tried to bite me, so I ran out. The child wanted to fight me! I found a stick and went back into the room but did not see the snake. It was hiding. It wasn't until I determined that the treatment had worked on the child—it was dead— that I was able to see the snake again. It was in the corner, so I used the stick to kill it. I went outside to the child's father and said, "Look at how your child behaves," and I showed him the snake. So, we knew that the child was really a spirit child. That's why we sometimes call them snakes.

The narratives of concoction men, some having experienced more than fifty spirit child cases, frequently engaged the hunter motif to describe their battles. Their narratives emphasized the agency of the child and their struggles to send it back to the bush. I often asked concoction men to describe the most powerful spirit child they had encountered. Consider this example.

> The most powerful one I encountered was in Burkina Faso. I came and discovered that the child wanted so many things [sacrifices], even Burkina Faso *pito*. We managed to get all those things for the child, but when I treated it with the *dongo* it refused to go. So, I left the *dongo* there and returned home. The following morning [members of] the family came to get me on a motorbike to bring me back to their house. The place where they left the child, it was not there. The child had vanished! The *dongo* was gone as well. This child can't walk, how did it go out? It was very

powerful. I consulted a soothsayer to determine where the child was and
found out that it was on the hill. I went searching on the hill and saw the
child between two rocks lying there. I asked it, "Even though I have not
killed you with the *dongo*, you have just come to bury yourself here? You
must go back to the house and pass the rite before you can come here." I
went to hold the child, and it tried to bite me, so I had to carry it by its legs
like a goat back to the house to treat it.

The Nankani lived experience of spirit children is not necessarily compart-
mentalized in a real versus a supernatural dichotomy. While some observers
might categorize or make a clear distinction between the world of myth, spirits,
and reality, many Nankani people experience these domains in a more unified
manner. From the Nankani position, the spirit child is simultaneously a set of
narratives or discourses and a real, tangible threat to families.

Following Harry West (2007), I interpret spirit idioms and discourse not
only as representations of experience but also as creative and transformative
forces. This form of discourse, rather than functioning as a group of signs,
becomes a set of "practices that systematically form the objects of which they
speak" (Foucault 1972, 49). Greg Urban describes this as discourse's thinglike
quality (1996, xiii). The reality of the spirit child rests in its multiplicity; it exists
as an embodied being, as a way to explain events and concerns, and as a means
of seeking out the truth and meaning of those events (Evans-Pritchard 1976).
The reality that the spirit child discourse communicates or enacts is often the
reality that carries the values and meanings important to the speaker at that
time (White 2000, 30).

Death and the destruction of the family are the most significant areas of
meaning making present around the spirit child. People express concerns that
once a spirit crosses into the house, it will kill family members, often starting
with the same-sex parent and the head of the house before proceeding to the
others. Narratives warn of cases in which people were unable to stop the spirit
soon enough.

There is one house where the child killed the mother. After they buried
the mother, the following day it went after the father. The father also died.
The older brother of the spirit child then went to the soothsayer. Even
when his father was alive, they went soothsaying and found out that the
child was a spirit child, but they didn't agree with the divination. After the
deaths transpired, the brother left the soothsayer, knowing that the child
was about to kill another in the house. So he ran to the house and told the
family members that if they did not take care, there would be a problem

again. They immediately brought a concoction man to the house. The child could not walk; it was just sitting on the laps of the women in the courtyard. When the concoction man approached, the child left the women, started crawling, and entered a room. The concoction man just threw the *dongo*, and it hit the child. The child died immediately.

Some spirits remain hidden within a family and reach adult status. Evil adult spirits cause significant worry and are particularly destructive. Narratives not only concern the death of family members but also detail anxieties around the disruption of family leadership, order, and succession. In this example, told by a middle-aged man, an "abnormal" adult was identified and confessed to being responsible for the deaths of family heads and misfortune in the family.

There was something strange happening in this house. In the family, the eldest family member inherits the house; he is the family head. In this one house, however, if anyone became that elder, he would always die. They went to the soothsayer and found out that there was an abnormal person in the family causing that. The family called a very powerful concoction man that also had a lot of juju. When he walked to the house, you could hear him coming, as there were so many things hanging on his body. As he approached, the abnormal man responsible for the deaths went into a room and started crying. When the concoction man arrived, he went straight to the room with the *dongo*. By the time he took out the *dongo* where the man was lying, the man began confessing that he had killed many people, that he had done all the bad things in the family. The man said that if they were coming to kill him they were supposed to kill five cows to send his spirit away. If they did not, the family would never have peace. The concoction man added the water to the black medicine and gave it to the man. The man just laid there and died. Later some family members came to dump his body in the bush. When they went to consult the sooth-sayer three days later, they discovered that the spirit wanted to kill the next eldest person in the house and that they must give him all the necessary things—those five cows—to make it stop. They didn't want to give. The family brought a concoction man and a sorcerer to the house to intercede, and the spirit child did not harm them again.

Elements of this example are similar to witchcraft accusations, particularly since it involved an adult identified as marginal who admitted his guilt. Like witchcraft, the spirit child is embedded within local moral systems and is a cultural model that expresses a particular experience of crisis (Stroeken 2004,

46). Both embody chaos, are attempts to manage uncertainty and ambiguity, and are a result of people anxious about their control of the social world (Jackson 2005, 139; Stroeken 2004, 46). In this case, the man is identified as being predatory though not for his own gain, something often associated with witchcraft. The meaning ascribed to his embodied state is aggression and destruction for its own sake. His actions are incomprehensible. Witchcraft usually has a rationale, such as hunger, envy, or cravings for wealth or power. These unexplainable deaths can only be understood in reference to the unquestionable evil associated with spirits and their ultimate desire to disrupt the family and its continuation.

The discourse concerning the spirit child's antisocial actions can also work as a warning that morally unacceptable behaviors or impulses have consequences. People will reference the spirit child to help make sense of behaviors and to better understand and identify the origin of antisocial acts. Tales across a variety of cultures frequently speak of incomprehensible deviant behavior. Such narratives illustrate the importance of controlling impulsive behaviors and other harmful actions that could shatter the family or larger social units (Johnson and Price-Williams 1996, 103). As an example:

> One day a woman was walking with her child and came to a tree with fruit. The child wanted some of the fruit, but the mother said those things were not for her. At that time, there was a spirit child standing on top of the tree. When it heard the woman, it told her she should pluck some of the fruit for the child. "They are for everyone," it said. When the woman plucked the fruit and gave it to her child to eat, the spirit started complaining that she should put it back or else there might be a problem. The mother didn't know what to do. That's why some people say these days, if you really give something to somebody you can't tell the person to give it back again. If you do they will ask, "Are you a spirit child?"

Forms of the spirit discourse can offer a space in which to imagine, fantasize, and express desires and possibilities for action. I draw on the notion of the moral imagination to frame and interpret spirit discourse.[4] The moral imagination is both a process and a space where agents are able to envision or discern a range of possibilities for thought or action in relation to, but not limited by, the social and moral constraints that shape behavior (Livingston 2005, 19). It is a space where people are able to free themselves from the "snares and ambiguities of the immediate lifeworld" and apprehend possibilities that would otherwise be inaccessible (Jackson 1998, 47). I explain my understanding of each of its components—the moral and the imagination—separately.

Moral broadly refers to the values that people express and enact and the things that matter the most to them (Kleinman 2006, 1–2). This conception of morality extends beyond the explicit rules or principles of what is right and wrong or good and bad behavior (Zigon 2008, 16). While the spirit child discourse does imply what are acceptable or unacceptable behaviors, I am also interested in the meaning-based questions central to local moral worlds, questions that ask, for instance, how we should live and make sense of our experience (Fesmire 2003, 2). Jackson (2005) frames this inquiry in terms of what is at stake in people's lifeworlds. Questions about morality can be conceived in terms of social practices and, as Jarret Zigon notes, visible and embodied ways of being in the world (2008, 17, 41). This visible quality of morality is relevant to understanding the meanings of physical disability, for example, and the moral associations it indexes.

My use of *imagination* is not meant to evoke a "made-up" or false world subject to external validation. Rather, the imaginary is a space in which to present perceptible and, more often, imperceptible objects and constructs to consciousness. It is central to our ability to "conjure" objects—spirits, medicines, and extraordinary events—that may not exist in a strict sense but have a durable bearing on lifeworlds (Jackson 2007, 132). We use the imaginary in our efforts to confront and resolve ambiguity, opacity, and conflict; to envision opportunities, solutions, and outcomes; and to make moral judgments and inform social practices. Rather than being illusory, Dewey described the imagination as constructed "of the hard stuff of the world of physical and social experience" (1934, 49). In Weberian terms, it is a bridge between the world of facts and values and the world of practices and meanings (Zigon 2008, 17, 41).

The intermediary and transformative power of the imagination is apparent. Beidelman characterizes the use of the imagination as "an art by which individuals struggle to transform their social baggage into gear that suits urgent situational needs in terms of meanings and moral judgments" (1993, 203). The imagination is "in the service of the new" and is present in the re-creation, revision, and renewal of social and cultural practices (Elliot 2004, 7–8). Indeed, Julie Livingston suggests that the moral imagination is important to the way we "envision possibilities for a morally better or worse world" and project novel ways in which to frame situations (2005, 19, 63). In this sense, the imagination links people to and frees them from their social and material circumstances, enabling them to safely consider events of which they are a part and reflect on discrepancies, such as the gap between what is experienced and what is desired (Karp 1993, ix, xiv–xv). While it is imaginatively freeing people from their social and material realities, the imagination and its contents are never far or fully detached from these realities.

Material for the moral imagination is shared, but how it is used differs widely across a community (Beidelman 1993, 203). In the case of Nankani spirit discourse, people draw on the circulating cultural models of spirits along with their own circumstances, experiences, and family histories. In contrast to rule-based and objective notions of morality—such as schemas or scripts—the moral imagination permits us to study the dynamic, practiced nature of moral worlds. It helps us to understand how local and global forces influence these worlds and how individuals and communities understand and make moral decisions amid the ambiguity that can pervade social life.

The bush is a space where a range of possibilities of being resides, a space in which the moral imagination is enacted, and a space in which the spirit child, an agent in the Nankani moral imagination, dwells. The use of the bush and its denizen spirits in discourse are a way to make sense of and imagine possibilities for action and ways of living. In conversations, I noticed how people used spirits as characters to imagine outcomes and express fantasies and behaviors that if practiced would be considered socially deviant. Particularly among men, depictions of spirits engaging in wild behaviors or enacting desires occurred frequently.

Stories of male spirits depict them doing things that no mortal man would be able to do. Spirits are able to have indiscriminate intercourse with women without consequence and have the ability to transgress boundaries, act with impunity, and steal another's possessions. Spirits can quickly remove or destroy a person's clothing at will. A man explained how his ancestor would use spirits to steal food. "Sometimes the women may be bringing some local cakes to the market," he recalled. "My ancestor would be sitting at this house and see the women walking by. He would send the *kulkarsi* to get the food. Without a woman knowing, they would take all the cakes from the basin and replace them with cow shit. When the woman reached the market, she would quickly realize that she no longer had any cakes."

Many spirit child stories are sexual. The spirit child can invisibly observe and follow women and approach them while they are bathing at night. A man said that male spirits have heterosexual desires and are able to act outside social norms with impunity. "The spirit is like a wind that is roaming," he noted, "so it sees everything as that you cannot see. It is also like man—it has sexual feelings. If a woman is standing like that, urinating or bending over, the spirit can easily have intercourse with the woman and she can give birth to a spirit child." These narratives direct attention to concerns regarding women who must, for instance, be protected from desirous spirits—much like desirous men—lest misfortune result.[5]

In the following story, which was told in a humorous tone among a group of men, we see an example of a desirous spirit.

There was another time that I heard the *kulkarsi* talking while at the man's house. Those ones that came to him, they even had names. One time as they were dancing, the spirits were talking among themselves. One spirit who arrived late had his clothing open. His penis was out, and it appeared to have sores on it. The other spirits asked what had happened. The *kulkariga* explained, "When I was coming here, I saw something very red and open. I asked, what is that? It was a woman that was exposing herself while urinating in the open. When she saw me, she asked what I had hanging out. I replied that it was a penis. She asked why I hadn't just given it to her. So I started having sex with the woman, but something happened to my penis—it was held in place, and I couldn't get it out!"

There is a certain thrill and amusement involved in sharing many of these narratives. They can end in laughter, like the one above, or shock. In some cases, people begin telling the stories in a joking manner only to become amazed and then serious as the story progresses and the actions become more heinous. I recorded a serious case during a meeting with members of a clan near Kandiga. An elder described a particularly wicked spirit that took pride in the fact that he had had sexual relations with all the virginal women in their section, all of whom remained unaware.

There was a spirit child near our house who was a young man. The family knew that he was a spirit child and called a powerful concoction man to come and treat him. When the concoction man confronted him with the *dongo*, he started confessing many things. He was able to enter all the granaries in the area but one. He announced that he had had intercourse with many women before they were married to their husbands. Their husbands were not the first. You can imagine all the consequences. The spirit child even disclosed that he had killed seven men and eight women in the house. That is why they are afraid here. It means that all women married in those years had intercourse with the spirit. There's much suffering that he has put on us. That is why we are afraid. This spirit child was able to become an adult, and look at everything he was able to do.

The sexual aggressiveness of the spirit is notable, predominantly his power to have sex indiscriminately without being detected, a common characteristic of spirits. He also violated the rules around intergenerational boundaries and privacy by looking into the men's granaries. The narrative demonstrates the power of spirits to kill and disrupt families undetected. Central to this is the fear that one can never truly know the identity of others, even those in one's family.

In addition to the frequent sexual and destructive themes, people describe spirits as longing to access the benefits of the human world by being born into the family. Narratives note that often spirits want to enter a family because they desire the good things a family offers such as food, affection, and protection. In many respects, spirits want to be cared for as if they are infants, to be fed and cleaned without having to reciprocate.

Accounts of tree spirits note that trees can assume human form in order to cause mischief and gain access to the human world. Upon doing so, they can cause confusion and fighting. For example, a tree spirit might be responsible for secretly entering a house to steal food, causing family members to blame each other for its disappearance.

Being approached by a tree spirit in human form begging for water or food is a common way to encounter a spirit. As an example, an individual, who might be vaguely familiar or not, approaches you asking for food or drink. If you give him or her something, he or she will go on his or her way. If you fail to give him or her something, this individual might attack you. "Even if you are in the house eating something," a man remarked, "and the tree wants it and it's very wicked, it can come to you and beg." You must always give to a tree that begs from you; one can never be sure if it is a spirit, a real person, or a family member.

Denying a tree spirit what it desires has consequences. The most common malevolent outcome is mental illness, usually forms of psychosis, and a range of mental disabilities and epilepsy. Afflicted persons are locally described as *gongo*, someone without sense who roams or walks about aimlessly or is considered "mad." A woman remarked, "If you see someone laughing and talking who doesn't know anything or is wandering around like they have no sense, it's the trees that have done that."

Asorigiya recalled a story about a woman who was going to the borehole to fetch water. As she walked along the path leading to the borehole, she was eating groundnuts, a common taboo that attracts spirits. When she passed an evil tree, it decided to follow her and beg for groundnuts. She never noticed the tree begging, as it remained behind her as she collected her water. Angered that she did not share, the tree went on its way. The woman became "mentally disturbed" on returning home. Asorigiya described her as crying for no reason and acting very strange. The woman's family members discovered through a diviner that the tree was the cause of her mental state. During the divination session, the family ancestors talked with the tree spirit and asked why it had made the woman ill. The tree responded, "She was not doing the right thing. I begged for groundnuts, and the woman did not give." The ancestor told the tree that the woman did not see him or have an opportunity to share her food. Therefore, it was not justified to make her ill. The tree soon agreed with the ancestor's perspective, and the family was able to make the necessary sacrifices to placate the tree. The woman's condition improved.

Local understandings surrounding notions of "madness" and "roaming" are also behaviors associated with the bush. In many cases, the very things that can make one bush often come from the bush. Trees live both within the bush and near, or sometimes within, domestic spaces. Partly due to their close proximity, the Nankani incorporate understandings and experiences of trees and the spirits embodied within them into their local social worlds and relationships. Fortes and Mayer commented that the way Tallensi community members described trees as begging is a parody of the way kinsmen or ancestors ask for sacrifices (1966, 14). Indeed, not providing a sacrifice when a relative or ancestor requires one has serious consequences, as does failing to give a tree something when asked. A "correct person" provides sacrifices to his or her ancestors when asked and gives to those in need even when such persons are not known to them, since the individual asking may be an unrecognized relative. Denying that unfamiliar person—or tree—is an outright rejection of one's social relationship with and moral responsibility toward others.

There are connections between the spirit discourse enacted within the moral imagination and what can be characterized as the emergence of unconscious desires and conflicts within the narratives. As noted in several narratives above, spirit children can express a set of central conflicts around sexuality, gender, power dynamics, intergenerational relations and succession, and pleasure. Devereux describes how myths can serve as an "impersonal cold storage" for fantasies, and that the fantasies expressed in stories can be interpreted as projections supported by culture (1969, 123). While I do not intend to offer a full psychodynamic explanation, I wish to draw attention to a Nankani-specific framing of the unconscious, to connect my use of the moral imagination to this understanding of the unconscious, and to link discourse and practices around spirit children to unconscious dynamics that constitute the moral imagination.

Rene Devisch distinguishes between an "everyday consciousness" associated with Congolese village and domestic life and an "imaginative unconscious," which finds expression not within an individual psyche or repressed neurosis but in the hunter or sorcerer roaming in the bush "in search of unknown and untamed forms of being and forces belonging to an extraordinary realm far beyond the domestic order" (1999, 60). Jackson emphasizes that an African-specific framing of the unconscious accounts for the circumstances, social and bodily fields, and perspectives that envision the unconscious as either existing beyond the individual or external to the person (1989, 45). Like Devisch, Jackson suggests that the unconscious exists in a place that is "not so much a region of the mind as it is a region in space, the inscrutable realm of night and of the wilderness, filled with bush spirits, witches, sorcerers, enemies" (1989, 45). Perhaps in this sense, the moral imagination overlaps or in some way engages with these external and socially grounded unconscious dynamics.

The moral imagination and its relationship with the unconscious offer a useful bridge for thinking about the relationship between intrapsychic worlds and the imaginative spaces that enact untamed and undomesticated forms and forces of being. With the bush as the space and the spirits as the agents, people can imaginatively explore and articulate conscious and unconscious concerns, imagine possibilities for action and ways of living, wrestle with disorder and ambivalence, and imaginatively express and enact desires or moral transgressions without consequence (Beidelman 1993; Jackson 1998). The Nankani moral imagination and the discourse circulating around spirit children offer a dynamic cultural model for interpreting abnormality, ambiguity, and misfortune. In other words, the mythical spirits, their wild behaviors, and the intrapsychic dynamics of the humans telling these stories play one of many important roles that influence the way families come to interpret a child's embodied status.

4

Spirit Child
Behavior and
Causation

I accompanied Joe from AfriKids and a community health nurse on a visit to a sick three-year-old girl named Azuma, her mother Abiiro, and their extended family. Joe had concerns not only about Azuma's poor health but also that the family suspected her of being a spirit child. From Joe's perspective, Azuma was at risk due to her medical condition and the chance that family members would administer to her a deadly poisonous concoction. From the family's perspective, Azuma represented a risk to her mother, the family's livelihood, and its continued existence in this and in the ancestral world.

On arriving at the family's compound, we sat in the shade of a baobab tree to wait for Abiiro, along with eight slight children under the watchful eye of the family elder. She soon emerged from her near-collapsing home, limping due to a filariasis infection and carrying Azuma. She sat on a bench across from us with Azuma on her lap. Azuma, arms around her mother, regarded us with concern from an askew right eye as she breathed uneasily, mouth open. After we exchanged customary greetings with the family, the nurse examined Azuma and we talked with Abiiro.

As we spoke about her condition, Azuma made repeated attempts to breast-feed. Abiiro pushed Azuma away, mentioning that she had stopped producing milk several months earlier. "The breast milk alone is not enough for a child at this age," Abiiro remarked, "but she doesn't eat anyway. We assume that's the behavior of a spirit child."

Azuma's medical card, issued by the Ministry of Health at its free postnatal care clinic, indicated that she was consistently underweight, never exceeding

5 kilograms (11 pounds). The nurse tried, to no avail, to get Azuma to stand unaided. Her lean legs bowed outward with each unsuccessful attempt. "She can't walk a step," Abiiro said. "My friends have given birth, and already their children are walking. They are normal human beings. This child, it cannot do anything. It has even given me sickness."

Abiiro's sister-in-law added, "Ever since Abiiro became pregnant, she has always been sick. She has never known good health, right from conception to delivery, and even after delivery she was always sick."

Abiiro estimated that she was around thirty-four years old, although she appeared older. She had given birth four times and had three surviving children, including Azuma, the youngest. Abiiro's most significant complaints were that Azuma cried day and night, rarely slept, and insisted on being carried in her arms, which interfered with her work. During subsequent visits with the family, it became apparent that she was greatly concerned about the disruption and impact of Azuma's condition on the larger family. The family described an increase in conflict that coincided with Azuma's birth. I later learned of significant tensions between Azuma's parents.

Other than her frailty, Azuma's most noticeable feature was a strabismus in her right eye. This "look" troubled family members. Wandering eyes are perceived as evidence that a child or adult is "up to something" spiritual and cannot be trusted.

People were quite suspicious of Azuma's condition. I learned that others in the community had recently begun to shun and avoid Azuma, telling Abiiro, "She can't mix with us." Abiiro, at one point, commented that people were accusing her of giving birth to a spirit child and "just sitting here unconcerned while the child is trying to kill me and destroy my family."

In a discussion several years after we first met, Abiiro recalled that she was the first to claim that Azuma was a spirit child. "I could not sleep at night," she said, and "neither could the child. I had bodily pains and all sorts of things that prompted me to make the statement that the child was a spirit. I thought we had better take a second look at the situation or else the child could kill me." Abiiro recalled that she did not have the strength to prepare food "or the appetite to eat even if there was food." She remembered that Azuma had also stopped eating, cried constantly, and was never well, finally saying, "That is why I concluded she was a spirit child; otherwise she would not behave that way."

As we continued to discuss Abiiro's condition under the baobab, her mother-in-law spoke up: "When these things are happening to your wife, what would you say other than that it is the child that is responsible?"

"Yes, from what people are saying I agree that the child is a spirit child," Abiiro replied. "The child is hiding some features from you to make it appear as if it is not a spirit child." Family members express concern and focus their attention on the interplay between what the spirit child chooses to reveal to people and what it is able to hide. For example, a family might remark that, although a spirit child has chosen to reveal its physical abnormality, it could be hiding other destructive tendencies and simply waiting for the right time to expose itself as a spirit and destroy the family. Others fear that the longer a child is able to hide, the more opportunities it will have to cause misfortune. Consequently, families observe the child's behaviors closely to determine if it is revealing or concealing any other clues to its identity.

The nurse examined Azuma as the discussion unfolded. I was surprised when after a brief examination, the nurse announced that Azuma was fine and Abiiro simply needed to provide her with "proper nutrition" and vitamins to stimulate her appetite. She prescribed vitamins, antibiotics for a respiratory infection, and medication for suspected malaria. "That wandering eye is caused by the child failing to get the proper eye drops during birth," the nurse explained. "The mother must have had gonorrhea when she gave birth. If she had gone to the hospital to deliver, none of this would have happened." The nurse questioned Abiiro about Azuma's birth, stressing that all women should give birth in a hospital. "Why didn't you call the midwife or go to the hospital to give birth?" the nurse asked. "You even had complications and still did not go!" Abiiro said she was unable to send for the local midwife because she went into labor at night and that she lived a five-hour journey away from the nearest hospital.

While hospital and clinic births represent the Ministry of Health's official position, aimed at reducing maternal risk, my subsequent visits with Abiiro and other community members revealed a more complex set of "unofficial" risks that overshadowed sanctioned safe motherhood messages (Allen 2004). First, Abiiro had gone into labor after sunset. Although Ministry of Health midwives encourage families to contact them at all hours, Abiiro later revealed that she did not want to bother the midwife at night. Community members, particularly expectant mothers, rarely travel along paths at night due to the increased presence of dangers such as witchcraft, sorcery, and the presence of various spiritual beings. Giving birth in the family compound is often preferred since those born along a road or path might never become fully integrated into the social and earthly world.[1] Moreover, local interventions for difficult deliveries require the woman to be in the family compound connected to her uterine or agnatic kin rather than in a depersonalized clinic (Cassiman 2006, 234). Several women also equated home birth with a valued ethic of endurance and strength.

While both biomedical practitioners and families wanted similar healthy outcomes, the explanatory models surrounding the notions of causation and responsibility, for example, differed significantly. The nurse redirected and focused on Abiiro's individual responsibilities as a mother disconnected from the social and economic realities of the kin system. This biomedical risk discourse emphasized the importance of regular antenatal clinic attendance, family planning and birth spacing, and improved nutrition. In this and other encounters I observed, it was apparent that biomedical health providers regarded mothers as individual agents responsible for making the choices, as communicated by health professionals and educators, that are in their best interest (Pinto 2008). Nankani mothers and families often have different understandings of causation, risk, and what is ultimately at stake when misfortune, illness, and disability occur. In this case, Abiiro's notion of the cause of and responsibility for Azuma's condition was understood within an epistemology that emphasized the local social and spiritually based perceptions of risk.

Several days before our first visit with Azuma, the family head had consulted a diviner. "The revelations were established there and then," he explained. "She is a spirit child." Despite the evidence confirming her status, family members remained unsure and did not agree about whether they should use the concoction now or wait. Joe convinced the family to wait. AfriKids provided the family with food supplementation, since they were subsisting on one meal a day, and promised to return periodically throughout the next month to check on Azuma and sit with the family to reassess the situation.

Identifying a Spirit Child: Appearance and Behavior

Community members identify spirit children based on their physical appearance, their behaviors, and the misfortunes they cause. Like anywhere else in the world, families are acutely aware of children that fall outside local understandings of normal development. A failure to reach a specific milestone such as walking is a significant indicator, and most spirit children have some sort of physical or behavioral abnormality that figures prominently in explanations. A mother noted that many spirit children "have something wrong with them" and are "stunted, lie on the ground, and can't walk, crawl, or eat." Mothers compare their children to others of the same age and note that the parents of a spirit child see other children "doing all sorts of things, helping their parents, while their child is still crawling or maybe lying on the ground."

Common physical characteristics indicative of a spirit child include an enlarged head due to hydrocephalus, being born with teeth or facial hair, or having various physical disabilities such as misshapen or missing limbs. One elder, when describing a spirit child, noted, "They [the parents] could give birth to a child without a mouth. The legs could be short with so many abnormalities. If you give birth to a child without all fingers, without the toes, what would you describe that child as? What would you say? You have to conclude it is a spirit child."

Since some sort of physical abnormality or disability is central to defining and describing spirit children, one might characterize the phenomenon as simply a cultural model for understanding disability. This explanation is incomplete and fits only one part of people's experiences of spirit children. One way to begin to complicate this association and avoid reducing the spirit child to disability alone is to consider that, while disability is indeed a feature of many spirit children, the vast majority of disabled or seriously ill children and adults are not thought to be spirits. Something beyond disability is at stake and playing a role in families' interpretations.

Forms of disability and other culturally defined states of abnormality can point toward deeper meanings (Douglas 1966, 52–53). To start with, it is important to recognize that abnormality and disability are culture bound, being defined differently within and across communities (Reynolds-Whyte and Ingstad 2007). The interpretation and meanings of disability are also variable. For example, in one society a condition that does not result in functional impairment might be viewed with indifference, whereas in another it calls into question one's origin, status, or ability to enter into expected social relationships. Certain bodily states, according to Julie Livingston, can pose problems or trouble, intensify social relations, and trigger the imagination (2005, 3). Forms of debility and impairment trigger moral and metaphysical complications that evoke questions about meaning, personhood, and responsibility (Reynolds-Whyte and Ingstad 1995, 4).

For Mary Douglas (1973), societies concerned with external boundaries, such as the Nankani peoples' attention to the spaces between the house and the bush, are also vigilant of bodily boundaries and their disruptions. Similarly, Nancy Scheper-Hughes and Margaret Lock noted a relationship between concerns around the violation of bodily openings and boundaries and the breaching of social norms in small peasant communities (1987, 19). With the bodies of Nankani children, who already have a tenuous connection to their families, abnormalities can call into question the moral status of their parents or index disruptions within the household.

There is significant concern regarding the eyes (*nifi*). A spirit child may have a strabismus, fail to make eye contact, or simply look at others differently. For instance, concerns emerged around Azuma's and N'ma's eyes and, in particular, N'ma's refusal to visually engage the concoction man, as recounted in the introduction. Families interpret a child's failure to make eye contact as stemming from a fear of being discovered and evidence that the child is hiding something, possibly its identity. Chronic eye infections are also concerning. In one case, when describing her suspected child, a mother focused on her child's on-going eye infection more than its inability to walk. The eye condition, which she described as "sometimes getting better and sometimes worse," despite being a lesser functional impairment, condensed the family's suspicions and shifting concerns about the child's spiritual status. The focus on eyes is culturally salient. Adults with "eyes" are said to be witches or have the power to see into the spiritual realm. These powers can ultimately be used against others. Eyes and eye contact are also essential in establishing and engaging in social relations. To fail to engage in appropriate eye contact is to deny a fundamental basis of relationality.

Most spirit children are ill. Throughout northern Ghana, serious illness in childhood is a frequent occurrence. Diseases of poverty such as respiratory infections, diarrheal diseases, and malaria are pervasive. Despite the prevalence of childhood disease, there are some patterns associated with the way these conditions are understood in spirit children. Short-term, acute illnesses rarely raise an alarm unless the family already has suspicions and there are other circumstances at hand. In these cases, the illness becomes a focal point for the family's anxieties, an embodied manifestation of the misfortune or conflict. Ongoing illnesses that linger despite treatment can cause concern. For example, a man described to me how a child with a lingering sore on its leg became sus-pect: "The family tried treating the child for many years, but the sore remained. Later they realized that the child was going to destroy the family, so they had to bring in the concoction man to kill it." He said the sore was not the only way they identified the child as a spirit. Tensions and other concerns were present within the family. In cases in which chronic illness is the presenting issue, families will often wait and observe changes in the child's condition or assess whether other misfortunes or strange circumstances are present. If misfortune arises or the situation changes, families will reassess the child's condition and attribute a new meaning to it.

Babies born with teeth or secondary sex characteristics are alarming. A man described spirit children as being "grown but not grown"—referring to children that uncannily possesses adult characteristics or to older children or adolescents that are developmentally delayed. Spirit children can also be gifted, displaying wisdom or knowledge beyond their years. In these cases, families wonder how such children are able to do and know adult things without being a spirit. Being grown but not grown concerns families, since such children repre-sent a breach in boundaries, signify inappropriate maturity or immaturity, and are thus associated with antisocial, maleficent powers.

Descriptions of spirit children standing and walking before this is develop-mentally appropriate are the most common. Recall the example from chapter 3 when a spirit child that could not walk was caught standing on top of a building. Also consider the following account.

> At my uncle's house, there was a child there that could not walk, it could only crawl. In the night while everyone was sleeping, the child was able go across the compound to a different room. The child stood up next to a covered pot with bambara beans, opened the lid, and ate the beans in there. An old man walked by and saw the child. The child cannot walk, how is it able to get there? Because of that, they knew immediately, the child was a spirit child.

Accounts of spirit children occupy a blurry space between the imagination and reality. Narratives incorporate the exploits of mythical adult spirits who resemble children (see chapter 3) into interpretations of abnormal children in this world. Explanations commonly depict family members discovering the child's spiritual identity by accidently catching it engaging in unusual or adult-oriented activities. The following account from a mother invokes the common motif of consuming adult foods.

> A mother placed her child in a room and left the house to do something. As she was leaving the house she realized that she had forgotten something in the room and went back. When she entered the room, she found the child standing and opening a large pot of millet to eat. When the child saw her, it said, "You have uncovered my secret." Then the child fell down, started crying, and died immediately.

While families focus on bodily integrity, they are also concerned about what enters and exits bodily boundaries. Families attend to a child's food intake and feces to interpret and organize their understanding of its status. References to the behavior of spirit children commonly focus on themes of excessive or inappropriate consumption of food or passing abnormal feces. "At night a spirit child is able to eat the leftover food," explained one woman. "The following morning the child's feces will look just like adult feces. What kind of child is that? A child who can only suck the breast has gone out to take solid food?"

Families are concerned that suspected spirit children will steal their stored food and share it with others. A young man described one such incident, which happened within his own family.

> There was a child in our house who couldn't walk. When it was time to harvest groundnuts, the family put all the nuts inside a large pot. The child

who could not walk saw the pot and went over to attempt to open its lid. It fell from the pot and started crying. The mother called everyone to come and see what this child who could not walk was doing. How did it get there? It wanted the groundnuts. That child was actually a spirit child. It doesn't want the groundnuts for itself alone; it wanted to take them to the other spirit children in the bush.

The spirit child's consumptive urges extend to consuming raw animal products and the family's livestock. Families report that, like the mythical spirits, their spirit children suckle the milk of cows and feed other spirits living in the bush surrounding the house. A family might attribute lost fowls or cattle to a spirit child eating or sharing the family's resources. When spirit children refuse to eat, as we saw in Azuma's case, family members suspect the child is secretly obtaining food from other spirits or sources in the house.

Some families see a child's refusal to eat staple foods or valued dishes as evidence of its spiritual status. I observed a family expressing concern over a child who refused chili peppers. In another family, a man claimed that a child's refusal to eat a spicy light soup was evidence that it was not of this world. In another case, a man remarked that whenever a neighboring family would prepare t.z. (*tuo zaafi*, also called *sagebo*, a thickened porridge made with millet flour that is a staple food) their child refused to eat it. "He would only eat the vegetable soup," he explained. "The family said that such a child was a spirit child."

A child's refusal to eat symbolically important foods is indicative of a disruption in its tie to family membership. Refusing food is a refusal of a fundamental act of exchange that ties family members together, as eating together is the basis for sociality and kinship. "Unity in a family means that you eat together," remarked a man. Consuming too much or too little food marks a disruption in the social and relational field. For adults, excessive and uncontrolled consumption and eating alone are tied to witchcraft and are emblematic of social concerns around the breakdown of consanguinity. As a family member, one must eat at appropriate times, exercise restraint, and consume foods as part of a visible and social practice. This is particularly important for new additions to the family.

There is widespread concern that the spirit child will vanish when no one is watching or will disappear at night while everyone sleeps. In the darkness of a room at night, mothers will reach out to feel for their infants and find they are missing when in fact they simply rolled out of reach. The common account of an infant vanishing can result: an infant, sleeping on a mat next to its mother, wakes up and leaves the room to roam about the bush eating, visiting other spirits, or causing misfortune. A mother remarked that before leaving the room a spirit child will tickle the mother's leg: "If it does this for some time, it will know that you are sleeping. Then it will get up and roam about." In the early morning hours, the spirit signals its return by crying, waking the mother and others in the house. The father, on hearing the child cry, will become suspicious. "He might ask the mother where she has gone and why she is not with the child," a woman said. "The wife will say that she's still sleeping and didn't go anywhere. Through that the man will know that the child is doing something or that the child has gone out. They start to think about those things and go to a soothsayer to find out."

A crying child could be ill, hungry, or uncomfortable. Among the Nankani, excessive crying can also be associated with spiritual disturbances or can be an aggressive act disrupting the peace and rhythm of the house. This concern is also found in other cultures. The Machiguenga people living in the Amazon basin consider excessive crying without apparent reason to be an expression of anger associated strongly with antisociality. In these cases, an incessantly crying child that cannot be comforted is more likely to be rejected than a quiet child (Johnson 1981, 64). When looking at crying and temperament across cultures, it appears that infants have to strike a delicate balance. While too much crying is associated with antisociality, a child's lack of crying or passivity also can be perceived as unhealthy (Lerer 1998, 238) or a reflection of a weak will to live (Scheper-Hughes 1992).

The health and postpartum condition of a mother is closely linked to spirit child accusations. One man described his wife's circumstances as follows.

> The day my wife gave birth to it she didn't sleep and was always sick. She told me that the child was a spirit child, but I didn't agree. She said, "Look, the child even has teeth!" I was able to follow the traditions and realized the child was a spirit child. The moment we did the ceremony and the child died, my wife got better. We didn't even have to send her to the hospital.

A grandmother, when talking about spirit children and maternal health, remarked, "They have killed a lot of women." In situations in which the mother is ill or suffering from postpartum complications, greater urgency can surround a spirit child case. "The child wants to kill the mother," a man explained, "so it's better they kill the child first so the mother can live and give birth again." The life of the mother often takes priority over that of the child due to her long-term reproductive potential. People explained that a spirit child interferes with the mother's reproductive abilities by causing illness or demanding excessive or prolonged care (due to developmental delays) because it is selfish and wants to prevent the birth of a sibling so that it can continue to monopolize the family's care and resources.

If the father or other family members are ill, concerns arise that the child might be trying to kill them. When chatting about my research with Patience, a cook who lived in a nearby town, she casually mentioned that her younger brother had been accused of being a spirit child.

"It was when he was born," she said. "My mother had a difficult labor and my father was sick at the time. He had sores on his arm that were getting worse and were not going away. After he was born, my father wanted to bring the concoction man, but my mother refused to believe that my brother was a spirit child. My father wasn't even traditional." Patience and her family were Catholics, although her father did not attend church.

"Why do you think he thought your brother was a spirit?" I asked.

"He may have been worried about things. My mother and brother had to stay in the hospital for a few days. While they were there, my father told me to take my brother from the hospital and bring him to where he was waiting with the concoction man."

"What? He wanted you to take your brother to him? What did you do?"

"My mother refused to let me take the child. She knew what he was trying to do."

Fortunately, the outcome was positive. Within a few days, Patience's mother and brother came home and everyone's condition improved. Her father ended up abandoning his attempts to administer the concoction.

Finally, people made a distinction between a bad spirit child and a good spirit child (*sisigo ditigo*, "spirit child eating"). A good spirit child can help the family prosper; it will not cause harm. A family may determine that it has a good spirit child when a child presents with appearances or behaviors associated with a spirit child, but it is determined, through divination, observation, or other means, that the goal of the child is to bring the family good luck and fortune rather than destroying the house. Community members also commented that little people, such as those with dwarfism, born into families might be identified as good spirit children, particularly if there is no misfortune surrounding their arrival.

A family might fail to recognize that the spirit child in their presence is actually good. A man described one family that misidentified its spirit child. "Whenever the concoction men came," he said, "I would always go to the house and watch. Each would prepare the concoction and give it to the child, but the child refused to die. By the time they found a fifth concoction man, one of the White Fathers [Catholic priests] came and took the child away. The family didn't want the child and freely gave it to the priest. The child is now grown up and even moved to Kumasi and got married. There are good spirit children, and there are bad ones. He was a good one. When he was living at that house, they had so many animals and fowls. Now when you go to the house, you won't see a single one."

Family Misfortune and Illness:
The Case of Victor

The spirit child is associated with a range of family misfortunes; births coinciding with crop failure or the death of livestock are ominous signs. A man explained, "Mishaps in the family will be present, maybe the harvest was poor. They go to the soothsayer and find out that the child who was born two months before is the cause of all the woes in the family. He is a spirit child and will destroy the house, so they will destroy the child."

When other misfortunes strike, particularly when a family already suspects the presence of a spirit child, the misfortune is interpreted as the child "revealing itself." Families say that some spirit children remain hidden for years because additional signs, such as a physical abnormality or a series of misfortunes, are not present. Such hidden children are the most dangerous. A man noted that the sign is not always the physical appearance of the child: "It can be handsome or beautiful. It's about the behavior or the attitude, what it does in the family" that betrays its identity. A normal-looking child can be the cause of its mother's illness.

When I met Victor, he was living with his maternal aunt, Mavis. Mavis was eager to talk about Victor and his circumstances. "I decided I'd better do something about Victor the evening before the concoction man was going to arrive," she said. "His family said that he was a spirit child, but I said, 'No, the child is not a spirit child. He is a normal child! Whatever you intend to do to him, I object. I will take him.'" Mavis was able to convince her sister's family to permit her to take Victor and care for him on a trial basis in order to, in Mavis' words, "determine whether he is really a spirit child or not."

Mavis had been caring for Victor for more than a year. He was healthy, well fed, and energetic. "To me the child is normal," Mavis remarked as we watched Victor, now around two years old, play in the courtyard. "There is no need to kill this child or claim he's a spirit."

Before Victor's birth, Apengo, his mother, was living in the southern city of Kumasi with her husband. They thought it would be best for her to give birth at home, so Apengo returned. The suspicions around Victor arose soon after he was born. Apengo was unable to walk after giving birth and, for a period, was unable to sit up unaided or hold Victor and care for him. Family members took Apengo to the hospital and visited healers. Meanwhile, community members began speculating that Victor was responsible.

"There are people like that," Apengo remarked when I spoke with her later, people "that stand around and say he is a spirit child." Even a traditional healer proposed that Victor was likely a spirit and was attempting to kill her. "At the time, I was helpless," Apengo said. "I didn't know if I was alive or dead. I was in so much pain. If they had given the concoction to my son, I wouldn't have known how to stop them. I only realized what was happening after I recovered."

Apengo's father, Asugya, said they tried everything possible to help Apengo, but her condition did not change. Because of her immobility, she frequently developed sores, many of which became badly infected, adding to suspicions. Asugya was hesitant to attribute her condition to spiritual causes. He described the sores as likely the result of "abject poverty."

Asugya noted that it was primarily her husband's family alleging that Victor was a spirit child. "We went around [talked about it] but couldn't solve it," he said. The in-laws involved Asugya in the decision-making process as a matter of respect and because Apengo and Victor resided at his house. But since Victor was a member of his father's house, Asugya would have little say if the family was committed to giving Victor the concoction.

The in-laws continued to claim that Victor was a spirit child and that trips to a diviner had confirmed their suspicions. However, Asugya did not agree. They even took Asugya to a sorcerer, who gave him treated water to rub into his body and bathe in so he could see Victor's spiritual status with his own eyes. He remarked, "I didn't see any change."

Seven months after Victor's birth, Apengo still could not walk and required assistance for most daily activities. Apengo's in-laws decided to give Victor a concoction and instructed her family to send Victor to their house the following day. Mavis stepped in. "The tradition is that they have to follow the necessary steps to establish the truth about whether or not the child is a spirit child," she said. "Normally, they administer the concoction. If it is a spirit child it will certainly die. If it is not a spirit child, it will continue to live." Mavis, however, did not want to risk testing Victor with a concoction. "Whatever the situation may be, they should not jump to conclusions and have it end badly," she said. "That would not be good at all. I intervened by telling them that this is what I heard [about the child and the concoction], but I have a different view. Just give me a chance and let me take the child away and try to establish the facts about the allegation."

Apengo's condition has improved somewhat. She sits unaided and can walk very short distances while leaning on a walking stick. Her husband still lives and works in Kumasi, and she remains at her father's house. Since Mavis lives only a short walk away, she sees Victor frequently. "I am full of joy when I see him," she remarked. Victor will likely continue to live with Mavis.

"People no longer think that he is a spirit child," Mavis said. "As of now, his mother is still suffering. She might not recover to do anything, but looking at this child, he has a future."

Breaching Boundaries:
Spirit Child Causation

How does a family acquire and give birth to a destructive spirit and where does responsibility for permitting the entry of a spirit lie? Ultimately, explained a mother, while "the spirit child was created by God, there are things in human nature that cause it." That is, the responsibility for the entrance of a spirit into the family centers on human behaviors.

While preparing for fieldwork, I made an assumption, derived from my understanding of spirit possession, that spirit children are "real" human beings inhabited by an external spiritual presence. I presumed that a core of humanness remained in each child and wondered if it was possible, from the Nankani perspective, to drive away the spirit inhabiting a human. During one of my first meetings with a group of concoction men, I asked them if it is possible to remove or "exorcise" the spirit from the child. Everyone laughed. They quickly dismissed the idea, noting that it would be impossible. The only way to remove a spirit, they emphasized, is through death. Several men explained that a spirit child is not a human possessed by a spirit. It is a simulacrum of a human, a spirit that only appears to be a human. For the Nankani, a normal fetus or infant cannot transform itself into, or catch as if by contagion, a spirit. Its status is fixed.

In some respects, the immutable status of the spirit child is similar to that of European changelings. Victorian-era and Celtic folklore describe dwarves or other forest entities kidnapping a child and replacing it with a changeling (Briggs 1976, 21; Silver 1999). In these cases, the child is perceived as nonhuman despite its appearance. Like spirit children, changelings often had physical abnormalities and developmental delays and were frequently tested to determine their non-human origin and then abandoned or killed. Changelings were noted for their lack of a soul, malicious nature, and gluttony and peevishness manifested in an insatiable thirst for milk and frequent crying (Hrdy 1999, 466–68; Silver 1999, 61). Changeling folklore and practice exemplified people's anxieties. Change-lings were understood to be a result of incestuous or unnatural unions (Silver 1999, 6) or, in seventeenth-century France, a product of insemination by the devil (Hrdy 1999, 466–68). Changelings also provided an explanation for illness, death, or bizarre behaviors and often embodied anxieties about disability, difference, and class (Silver 1999, 60).

The cause and arrival of a spirit child embody similar concerns. Most forms of causation involve taboo and boundary violations that intersect with circulating narratives and moral imperatives. One of the most frequently described ways in which a woman can attract a spirit child is if she eats while walking through the bush or along paths and roads. Taboos stipulate that a woman must sit down to eat and not remove food from the home. Spirits crave human food, particularly nuts and seeds, and are always looking for opportunities to eat. If a fertile woman should walk anywhere outside the home while eating, pieces of food may fall to the ground. If spirits are nearby, they will be attracted to the food, will follow the woman, and will take advantage of any opportunity to have intercourse with her and enter her womb. A woman described the dangers.

> If you are fond of eating while walking, those spirit children will follow you and pick up the food as you drop it. They will say, "This woman is good, she likes me. That's why she's dropping all this food." The spirit will follow the woman all the way to her house. If the ancestors are not strong, the spirit will be able to enter the house and find a way to enter the woman. Before you realize it, you give birth to a spirit child.

Gottlieb (1992, 2000a) identifies a similar taboo among the Beng people, although it applies to women who are already pregnant. She notes that a pregnant woman who eats while walking along a path in the forest could drop crumbs that will attract a snake. After eating the crumbs, the snake will develop a longing for human food. In its desire for more human food, it will enter the woman and switch places with the fetus.

While food attracts the spirit, the spirit remains vigilant, watching for any other indication that the woman is interested in it and for opportunities to attack. A grandfather described how spirits stalk a house.

> The spirit will trace you, get to know the house, and watch you. Then they begin lamenting. "This is really a woman! This is really a woman!" When you go to fetch water, they follow you as well. Sometimes they may follow you into your house and have sex with you, and you end up giving birth to a spirit child.

Similarly, a grandmother informed me that a spirit "will loiter around at night. When they [the family members] go to bed, the spirit will follow and have sex with the woman alongside her own husband, resulting in the pregnancy. It will be very hard for the man to think that he is not the one who impregnated the woman." Whistling at night can also attract a spirit.

Spirits are known to inhabit the millet fields, hiding among the stalks or lurking on the periphery. One woman remarked that during the rainy season, just before people are about to sow, the spirit will hang around closer to the houses, knowing that family members will soon be working outside the home in the fields.

Women are advised to avoid places where there are forbidden trees, locations of spirit child burials, and other bush locations where spirit children live, such as rocky outcrops and heavily treed areas. A concoction man assured me that most women who have given birth to a spirit child had visited such a taboo place. Women are also warned about trespassing on a farm or garden plot guarded by a spirit. A woman who has given birth to a spirit child is entitled to use a special medicine, often hung in the corner of her vegetable patch, that will protect her crops. If another woman takes food without permission, she risks giving birth to a spirit child.

Paths play a crucial role in understanding how spirits gain access to women. Paths are obviously crucial for linking dwellings, relatives, friends, and markets, but they also link faraway lands, the bush, and what dwells therein. This link with the bush offers a medium for spirits and other undesirable entities to encounter humans and access the domestic. Witches, sorcerers, spirits, and other entities will travel along, lie in wait, or conduct their business on or near paths. For humans, paths are liminal spaces, and expectant mothers hesitate to use them at night due to the increased presence of spiritual dangers (see Gottlieb 1992, 38).

Since paths terminate at the entrance to family compounds, the entrance is a vulnerable boundary. Recall from chapter 2 that family members are required to use the main gateway so the ancestors can protect them and the family patriarch can watch over their movements. Using unapproved exits for clandestine activities can place one at risk and disrupt the boundaries of the house, rendering it vulnerable to unwanted entities that might take advantage of the breach to follow the person back into the home undetected.

Food (*dia*) and eating (*di*) emerge as central practical and symbolic themes in the prevention or acquisition of spirit children, in detecting spirit children, and in the rituals for sending spirit children back to the bush. Concerns about food reflect themes involving the surveillance, movement, and control of resources in the family. Moreover, food is intimately coupled with and foundational to systems of exchange, forming relationships, and sexuality. Concerns about spirit children are entangled within these fundamental practices of reciprocity and markers of family membership and stability.

When I asked people why they thought the taboo around walking with food exists, they pointed out that if a woman is eating outside the house, she is not eating with the family and is sneaking or stealing food. This taboo points to both resource and symbolic associations.

First, because each harvest must last through the dry season, food management is essential. A husband provides his wife or wives with regular food allotments from his granary. From this she prepares the food for her children, her husband, and occasionally other family members. In general, husbands do not permit anyone to take food from the granary without permission, although in some cases he can give the senior wife this responsibility if he is away.

Second, beyond the apparent need to monitor and conserve, food is foundational to intimate relationships and is closely associated with intimacy. The verb *di* (to eat) has meanings that extend beyond its English meaning. *Di* can mean "to obtain or use something," "to destroy," "to experience something fully," and, importantly, "to marry." In broader terms, it means "to condense," "to take into one's being," or "to transform." Indeed, references to forms of consumption, Paul Stoller notes, are a way to talk about transformation and social relationships (1997, 6–7).

The association of food with relationships, sexuality, and marriage is common in many cultures. Sexual appetite is compared to hunger. Processing, preparing, and sharing food are linked to controlling sexuality, or access to sex, and can be associated with sexual favors (Ingham 1996, 31–32). Smelling and tasting can be associated with intimacy and shared substances (Donnan and Magowan 2010, 52). For example, Beidelman aptly observes that among the Kaguru people of Tanzania, the imagery of preparing food, eating, and the activities of hearth and bed "weld together the social and natural realms where sexual and alimentary appetites are regulated and enhanced through the home by way of the regulations of marriage and kinship, cuisine and etiquette" (1993, 30).

Discussions with Nankani community members about what characterizes the ideal wife often linked sexual and gustatory desires. To not cook or sexually satisfy the husband can be grounds for divorce. Food can also be used to express affection. A wife will be concerned if another woman prepares food for her husband. Eating food specially prepared for you by another woman evokes associations tantamount to sex or marital relations. While discussing the movement of food within a family, a man remarked that if a wife is moving food or eating outside the house, it means she is not cooking for the husband and is likely cooking for someone else.

Sharing food and eating together are the basis of family relations. Engaging in the gendered roles associated with food—generally, men are responsible for bringing food into the house and women are responsible for its preparation—enact the basis of the wife-husband dyad and exchange. Food and eating are particularly symbolic of family relations where family members, for example, ideally not only share one voice in all matters but eat from the same bowl. Eating establishes the ties that link a new wife or child to the family, the ancestors, and the land. An elder commented that when a new wife moves into a compound, she must first learn that food must be eaten together with her new family. To refuse food, as some spirit children do, is to reject family membership. Family members are particularly attuned to how the preparation and circulation of food can be disrupted through poverty, hoarding, or theft and that such disruptions indicate the quality of the relations that these exchanges symbolize.

Ultimately, women are instructed to not eat along paths to avoid attracting a spirit child because of the associative links between the danger and liminality of paths; food, sex, and family relationships; and the presence of desirous and disruptive spirits looking for valued elements that are constitutive of family membership. Even the accidental provision of food to a spirit establishes the hint or basis of a relationship, which opens an opportunity for a spirit—or in other cases a lover—to exploit the circumstances and disrupt the family and patriarchal control. While thinking of the spirits in terms of imaginative and conceptual metaphors, it is hard not to associate spirits and their antics as men and the spirit child prohibitions as ways to limit opportunities for the movement of women and food and the potential relationships it establishes. This becomes clearer below.

For women, the location and method used to urinate are a concern, and they are discouraged from relieving themselves in various prohibited places. The most important are the *tingane* shrines, places spirit children frequent, and other spiritually dangerous or liminal locations. A woman described this concern: "The place where they abandon the spirit children—there are so many spirit children there—if a woman goes there to urinate, the spirit can easily have intercourse with her." As previously established, male spirits are particularly desirous of women and can follow and have intercourse with a woman without her knowledge. "So, at the time the woman is urinating like that," a man told me, "the spirit is also having feelings like a normal human being. It can easily have intercourse with her."

Women are also advised to urinate properly by squatting, not standing. Failing to squat or properly conceal oneself while urinating risks attracting a spirit. One man explained, "Some women don't want to squat; sometimes they want to stand as men do. So, when they do that, the spirit, because they are always roaming about, can easily enter the woman." Other forms of exposure were less often cited as attracting a spirit child. These included bathing late at night when spirits are more likely to be roaming and lurking around the house.

Since the goal of the spirit is to find a way to pass from the bush into the domestic space, the easiest way for a spirit to accomplish this is to enter a woman through illicit sexual activity or exposure. This can occur through the violation of a taboo or, as one youth described it, "illegal sex." Taboo sex is intercourse outside the house or in the bush. Such sexual activity will attract spirits, and the spirits will use this as an opportunity to enter the woman. A man explained, "If a spirit is passing by while you are having sex, [it can enter you] immediately when you finish or just before you start. It can move so fast! That is why it's advisable for men not to have intercourse with a woman outside the house."

Why is sex outside the home so taboo? For some, sex in a public place or the bush defiles the land. Gottlieb describes sex in the forest or fields as polluting and typical of taboos that circumscribe elements of human activity to areas of the forest and village space (1992, 32). Sex in the bush is also antisocial, potentially threatening the health of the family and society. Proper sexual relations, remarks Beidelman (1993), should occur within the safe confines and order of the house. Such human activity, Cassiman notes, is "unoriented and unarticulated and therefore belongs to the liminal, asocial realm of the bush" (2006, 257). People flout this taboo, however.

It seems that everyone has sex in the bush. Friends frequently remarked that they had come upon yet another couple having sex only meters away from a path, and one afternoon a rumor quickly swept through the market that a truck driver from Kumasi was seen having sex with a local women just within some trees nearby. Elders lament that more people than ever are having sex in "evil places." One man noted, "Nowadays you see young men and even old men having sex in the bush or places that are not part of the house. It is assumed that evil spirits are in the bush, so when a woman and the man have sex over there, the spirit will jump into a woman." However, one listener questioned this taken-for-granted logic. "These days, girls are having sex everywhere," he said. "They have dances at schools and other places; wherever they go, this is where they have intercourse. If this were true, then we would have more spirit children on this earth." But today, he continued, there are fewer spirit children than in the past.

Despite the historical, as well as contemporary, taboos on extramarital sexual relations, having one or more lovers outside of marriage was and still is relatively common. Some men remarked that they had their wives and their "friends." It seems it was historically common for men to find other lovers during the multiyear postpartum sex taboo practiced to ensure proper birth spacing. Women might also have earlier lovers that they occasionally visit. The increasing availability of family-planning services are likely affecting postpartum sex practices. Some local reproductive health messages encourage men to continue having intercourse with their wives after they become pregnant, noting that it is not dangerous and that it is important to continue to "nourish" the child. When I asked a health worker about this, she remarked that such messages are intended to keep husbands with their wives during the pregnancy and to discourage roaming.

As it is hard to find privacy in a busy family compound, sex in the bush might indeed be easier, particularly for unmarried couples and those engaging in extramarital relations. It turns out, however, that the directive to not have sex outside the home is less about preventing sex in the bush than it is about regulating who is having that sex and limiting its consequences.

Sex, Belonging, and the Movement of Women

The sentiments, taboos, and practices around sex and marriage have been transformed over the past century due to social and moral changes resulting from contact with various religions and the effects of colonialism and imposed political and legal structures. Hence, it is helpful to interpret the spirit child practice, taboos, and moral concerns in relation to the historical and contemporary context and practices that shaped the phenomena, in particular, the relationship between these understandings of risk and the practices surrounding conjugal unions, extramarital relations, and illegitimate children.

When considering the movement and sex taboos related to spirit child causation, particularly from the explanatory frameworks privileging evolutionary models, one might interpret the taboos as attempts to prevent illegitimate children from entering the patriline by limiting women's opportunities to engage in extramarital sex. That is, one might posit that fathers are not interested in supporting children that are not a part of the patriline and that those they suspect are not genetically theirs are subject to spirit child accusations and infanticide. Concerns about adulterous relations and their impact, however, are more complex than this.

Historical and some contemporary ethnographic evidence indicates that family members are not particularly concerned about illegitimate children. Traditionally, the woman's current husband, not the biological father, determines a child's family membership. Since the woman belongs to the man's family, his patriline can claim all offspring. A child born to an unmarried woman still residing in her father's house can belong to her father's lineage—although in some families the child might not have full religious or political rights.

Family membership is not necessarily determined by the purity of one's blood but rather on the ties established by the exchanges needed to found a conjugal union. Families are quite willing to invest in children that are not biologically theirs. In some cases, when a man has many wives, such as a chief or other powerful person, people recognize and accept that some of the children might not be biologically his, but all are treated as such.[2] People also state that a wife might be encouraged to sleep with another man if she suspects her husband is infertile. Without question, the resulting children belong to her husband.

The circumstances differ when a woman comes to join a new house and is far along in a pregnancy or has already given birth to a child. Her new family might consider this child to be the responsibility of his father's house. I encountered cases in which the mother's children—from either a previous marriage or a pregnancy outside marriage—were rejected. Despite the identity of one's father, being born into the house is often a requirement of establishing one's membership within it.

The birth of an illegitimate child within the family is not threatening enough to warrant a spirit child accusation. If spirit child taboos are not related to preventing illegitimate children, perhaps families are more concerned with the specific types of extramarital acts themselves and the threats around these relations.

The desire to control the movement of women stands out within these taboos. As described in chapter 2, marriages were more fluid, at least historically, and women had greater autonomy, particularly those without children. Before the arrival of Europeans, women in the northern regions had more choice, flexibility, and power to enter into and leave unions (Cardinall 1920, 76; Fortes 1937, 1; Hawkins 2002, 228) and were more independent and able to control their productive and reproductive labor (Hawkins 2002, 286). A contributing factor to the extent of women's flexibility in marriage is that new wives are outsiders and not fully part of their husbands' patriline. It takes decades and the birth of children and grandchildren to establish and then solidify a close link to his family.

Historically, the competition for wives was also significant. Affording a wife required considerable financial resources, many of which were tied up in the wealth of one's father. Younger men had difficulty transforming monetary wealth earned during work migration to southern Ghana into the traditional forms of wealth, such as cowries and cattle, needed to marry. Older men monopolized the control of these resources and hence had more opportunities to marry (Hawkins 2002). With the increased competition, some men forcibly captured, seduced, or eloped with a new lover, even if she was already married. Conflicts with rivals were common, leading to murder, raids, and war between groups. Colonial controls attempted to reduce violent conflicts and transform the formation of unions (Cardinall 1920, 77).

Due to marriage flexibility and challenges from rival men, the movements of new wives were subject to scrutiny and surveillance. For example, an elder explained to me that when a newly married woman arrives at her home, she is "told not to hide or run away. But if you do, you should not pass through the back door; you should pass in front. If you pass through the back door, there is likelihood that you may encounter a spirit, and it could take advantage of you."

New wives, at least traditionally, were also discouraged from returning to their father's house for any length of time. The concern was that she would not return to her husband or, while at her father's house, she would be subject to seduction and courtship by other men (Hawkins 2002, 271). A less frequently noted cause of spirit children mentioned only by elders described the danger of allowing a new wife to visit her father's house too soon or to spend too much time there. If one's new wife has been at her father's house, according to the head of one clan, "You [the husband] have to wait several days before sleeping with the woman. Nowadays, a man will sleep with her right away. That will result in a spirit child." Several women explained that it is dangerous to visit one's mother and father when pregnant. If one does, remarked a woman, "The pregnancy may be terminated or she will give birth to the child and the child will not be able to reason."

A woman can return to her father's house to dissolve her marriage ties. If a wife returns to her father's house permanently, her father will be required to return the gifts exchanged to legitimize the union. Most fathers encourage their daughters to resolve disputes and return to their husbands. An easier way to leave a relationship is to elope with another man.

While men were concerned about competition from others, the most significant fear came from within the clan. Intimate relations between one's wife and a fellow family member are considered incest. For the Nankani and other groups in the region, incest is a grave form of adultery that, at its most serious, involves one's wife having intercourse with her husband's brother (her brother-in-law) or even his father. Sleeping with the spouse of another man or woman in your clan is also quite serious and has grave consequences.[3] This fear surfaces when a woman has complications or a prolonged and difficult labor. Family members may ask the woman, in order to speed delivery, to confess the names of all her lovers, with members of her husband's clan being the most concerning and spiritually damaging.

The consequences of incest are primarily spiritual rather than jurally punitive and can affect the entire family. The ancestors, particularly enraged by this behavior, will lash out against the family by sending sickness to the husband, wife, and other family members. The ancestors might also remove their protection, exposing the family to other misfortunes. Concerns about attracting spirits and giving birth to a spirit child are also likely associated. Notably, the sanctions against adultery and incest are not as much about protecting the legal status of conjugal unions as they are about warding off the spiritual afflictions that might endanger the family (Hawkins 2002, 259).

The spirit child taboos and narratives, particularly those concerning food and the movement and exposure of women, intersect with concerns around women's autonomy, the fluidity of marriage, and the competition for wives. To venture into and linger within obscure areas of the bush, to expose oneself to a potential observer or admirer, or to have illicit or even incestuous sex in the bush, for example, are all linked to and condensed within the spirit child taboos and consequences.

The Role of Men

While chatting one afternoon, I asked an elder to explain what men can do to cause the birth of a spirit child. "Normally," he replied, "a man has very little to do with this, because we have nothing to offer." The role and the responsibility of men in causing spirit children are conspicuously lacking. The few circumstances in which men are implicated in bringing a spirit into a family ultimately involve actions that render women more vulnerable to spirits.

The most common way a man can attract a spirit is failing to take precautions when engaging in extramarital liaisons. After having sex with someone other than his wife, it is important that a man not rush home immediately. One woman remarked, "Coming home from the outside [after sex] may mean that you are bringing the evil spirits into the house." Spirit children are attracted to sexual activity and use the man's "unclean" condition to follow him into his home and to his wife. A man who has had sex with someone other than his wife is advised to bathe before entering his room or to wait to ensure that the ancestors are able to remove the spirits before having sex with his wife.

A man's activities in the bush can also play a role. Some women insisted that men actually have more responsibility for spirit children since when they are in the bush they can unknowingly gather foods from places where spirit children live. "A man will pick those things," a woman noted, "and come to sleep with a woman and give birth to a spirit child." Those entering the bush must exercise care in bringing food, objects, or new practices into the house, since new acquisitions from the bush are associated with its ambiguity and can open a pathway for spirits to follow and cross the boundary into the house.

Finally, when a man is concerned that a woman he is sleeping with will have a child that looks like him, he can urinate on an anthill after intercourse, a place of symbolic importance. Black ant abodes are often the places where concoction men abandon spirit children and where they dig for some spirit child treatments.

A woman described urinating on an anthill after sex as a terrible thing for a man to do. "You don't even love the woman and you just go and sleep with her? Then after that, you go and urinate on an anthill and cause the woman to give birth to a spirit child." It may be that such an act effectively shifts paternity of the potential child to a spirit.

Drawing on contemporary health campaigns, several men and women identified poor-quality sperm as a risk. A young man explained, "Men who are up to sixty or seventy years are still having children! At that time, their sperm are weak. They still have intercourse with women, but they give birth to children who are not properly formed." This is the only medically related risk attributed solely to men.

Integrative Perspectives

It is incorrect to assume that people living in areas where biomedical treatment options are limited lack health knowledge, await biomedical enlightenment, or will readily replace local ethnomedical beliefs. In northern Ghana, government and internationally funded community health clinics and maternal health education programs have expanded families' knowledge of maternal and infant risk factors, and these programs have had a tremendous impact on community health. Despite these programs, such models have not necessarily supplanted local notions of risk. Rather, families frequently transform and incorporate public health messages into their understanding of reproductive vulnerabilities and spirit child causation.

Women who attend maternal health clinics and men and women with some formal public education are increasingly moving between and integrating biomedical notions of causation of illness and disability into spirit child frameworks. Mothers of spirit children frequently move between spiritual and biomedically related causes of their children's condition. For example, they may attribute to spirit children a lack of nutrients or use of harmful prescription medications along with frequenting areas where spirit children are buried.

Many families have food taboos stipulating that eating a specific bush animal, often a family totem, or eating food taken from a spiritually dangerous location can cause one to give birth to a spirit child. Traditional stipulations regarding taboo foods now include contemporary taboos such as the use of alcohol and drugs and the misuse of pharmaceuticals. Other risk factors identified as causing spirit children include failing to get prenatal checkups, premature births, home births, severe malaria, prolonged labor, and a heavy workload during pregnancy. One woman explained the role of prenatal nutrition, noting, "In the old days there were not as many nutrients; they were not eating the way we do today. That's why in the old days there were more spirit children. Today we learn what to eat. If you don't get the proper nutrients, your baby will not develop well and you can easily give birth to a spirit child."

While access to biomedical services are increasingly recognized for their ability to reduce risk, families explicitly identified poverty and the cost of many biomedical services as a cause of spirit children and a barrier to accessing prenatal and antenatal care. "If you are poor and give birth to a child, you can't go to the hospital," a mother said. "If the child is sick, you can't care for the child, you can't buy drugs, you can't do anything. It's because of all these things that it's a spirit child." Another woman added, "You have to buy this thing, that thing, get eggs, and eat more so the child will form well. But, when you come home and tell your husband, he will tell you he has nothing, that he has no money. If you have some money it helps, but if not, you will not be able to help the child, so it will be abnormal, a spirit child."

Education is increasingly playing a role in shaping the understandings of spirit children and disability. A group of educated men described the spirit child as "just a way of thinking." They agreed when another man said, "People don't understand the circumstances of nature. That's why they say that a child is a spirit child." I expect as access to education and health services increases, the understandings and practices around the phenomena will continue to transform.

5

Detection and
Decision-Making

The presence of abnormalities and misfortune alone is insufficient to confirm the existence of a spirit child because humans cannot, in the words of one man, "see beyond the focal point" and into the spiritual side of reality. Families explore anomalies known to be indicative of a spirit child and attempt to glimpse what cannot be seen though additional tests or trials, divination sessions, and discussions with others.

The most common test involves detecting a spirit child's covert movements around the compound. One technique involves covering the soles of the child's feet with oil to see if it gets up to walk while everyone is sleeping. "In the morning," a man described, "if they find dirt on the feet, it means the child has gone out walking. The child cannot walk. Where did he go?" Families will also place ash or sand at the entrance to the room where the child is sleeping so it will leave footprints if it rises to visit the bush at night. Ash is also placed near steps leading to a rooftop, near walls, or near other exits not under the ancestors' gaze.

In some of these cases, spirits outwit family members. A local health researcher recalled that a neighbor's spirit child, too young to walk, would get up at night to eat any leftover food and drink any remaining water. "He was making more work for the women in the house," the researcher said. Family members proceeded to spread ash around the food so they could see the child's footprints the following morning. However, the spirit child put food tins on its feet to disguise its tracks. The next day they awoke to find the food had been eaten. "But they didn't see any footprints!" the man continued. The following night they smeared oil on the child's feet, but when it got up it attached the tins to its hands and walked on them to reach the food.

Small seeds are also scattered around the entrance to the room of a suspected child. Community members described the seeds as being so small that only a spirit child could pick them up. Their love for the seeds is so strong that spirit children are compelled to drop everything to consume them. "If by the following morning the seeds are not there, you know it's a spirit child," one woman said.

A small number of families use the *dongo*, the symbolic object used to treat spirit children, to test all infants soon after they are born.[1] They may hang the *dongo* where the infant sleeps or use it to gently touch the newborn. In these cases, the *dongo* alone is powerful enough to kill a child before it has an opportunity to cause problems. I encountered a family that pours water over the surface of the *dongo*, spiritually imbuing the water with the power to catch a spirit. In this case, a family member holds a calabash below the *dongo*, collecting the runoff to feed to each child soon after its birth. If the child is a spirit, it will die. These methods ensure that no spirit children remain in the family.

Rarely, families use a concoction composed of herbs or medicines to test each newborn. Alukoom, an elder concoction man, explained that his family gives all its children the concoction. "The father comes to take the medicine [from me], and it goes to the mother of the child," he said. "The mother grinds it and places it in water for the child to drink. If it is a spirit child, it has to go back. Even myself, I have done it. All people in my family have had this to drink."

"Have many died?"

"Many died," he replied. "They have all been tested, and many have passed away."

People are frequently concerned with the hidden qualities, powers, and intentions of others, particularly children who have yet to be firmly established within the family. Testing with the *dongo* reveals the unseen identity of the child. Families find that spirit children that do not display any visible evidence of their identity and remain hidden in the house are the most concerning. A grandmother described these children.

> There is another type of spirit child; it is dangerous if you're holding it and care is not taken. Such spirit children are not stunted, they don't fall sick, they are normal children, normal growth, but they are mischief, very destructive to families. They can kill a whole lot of family members then will later take over the family. In such families, you can't tell what is actually responsible for their woes. By the time you realize it, almost every important

individual in that family is gone and it is the spirit child alone that will now take over the family.

To hide its identity, a spirit child can also distract the family. A diviner explained that a spirit child might feign a mild or treatable illness or other problems. "Those diseases are ways of pretending," he said. "The sickness will not kill the child, yet the child can be sick for a long time. They are only pretending while they try to find a way to kill the parents. It is not actually sickness." Spirit children also feign illness to attract additional attention and care.

While families look for objective evidence indicating the presence of a spirit child, no one form of evidence unequivocally proves the presence of a spirit. Even if a child is born with teeth or facial hair, Alukoom said, one still must consult a diviner since "you can't use your naked eye to see if the child is a spirit child." Consultation with a diviner provides the most objective form of evidence and insight needed in spirit child cases.

Divination

In many African cultures, divination systems play a pivotal role within society (Peek 1991, 2). In northern Ghana, divination plays a central role in decision-making, identifying deviance, maintaining social cohesiveness, and upholding the jural authority of elders. Despite the fact that many people's lives are affected by divinatory decision-making, community members, researchers, and development workers in the region who do not divine have several misconceptions about the process. Speculation and misunderstandings commonly identify the diviner as controlling the interpretations. A common belief is that one pays the diviner to answer questions and, in spirit child cases, to tell the family if it has a spirit child. Additionally, the role of diviners is sometimes confused or conflated with that of concoction men.

Divination probes the inchoate, concealed, or mysterious in an effort to acquire knowledge, validate understandings, or imbue decisions with authority. Fortes (1987) characterized divination as a ritual means of making a choice. Among the Nankani, men communicate with ancestors through an interpretive form of divination in order to make decisions, uncover the hidden, and seek explanations for misfortune. Divination also can clarify emotions and interpersonal circumstances and performs an important political function by imbuing decisions with authority and explaining social conflicts. Among the Nankani, divination (*bogero*)—locally referred to in English as "soothsaying"—is a mediative practice involving the clients' active engagement with their deceased ancestors in a ritualized dialogue involving symbolic objects and objective trials. During this dialogue, the clients' experiences, uncertainties, and questions are formulated, articulated, and made meaningful in reference to their perceptions, the opportunities and constraints dictated by their social fields, and individual psychodynamics. A diviner (*bagadanna*), explains why people divine.

> The reason people soothsay is because they are having problems or troubles in the house. Maybe you raise fowls and you find that at the end of the day they all have died. Or you or your children are sick, or there are people dying. So, you are going to soothsay in order to know the reason why those things are happening and address them. Soothsaying connects you to your ancestors so you know about that problem.

Through divination, a client can obtain solutions to problems and ascertain the sacrifices necessary to gain ancestral favor and protection from spirits or malicious persons and their hidden intentions. There is considerable variation between individuals and their reasons for divining. Divination determines the cause of a sickness, or *ba'a* (usually ancestral), offers an explanation (the ancestor is demanding a sacrifice), and fixes other actions necessary to affect a cure (*tibiga*). A person might divine to determine an infant's name and destiny (*paala*); determine the proper sacrifices required to make amends with the ancestors or to offer thanks (*kaabegɔ*); identify sorcerers, witches, and sources of enmity or envy; implicate family members engaging in antisocial acts; make hidden forces and intentions known; and assist in daily or long-term decision-making. Of these, the most important use of divination is in the detection, management, prevention, and redress of misfortune, individual and collective. Ultimately, through divination, individuals and families are provided with a ritual and symbolic system that offers a set of culturally prescribed choices, facilitates the generation of answers, and negotiates solutions to problems (Mendonsa 1982).

Divination serves an important sociopolitical function as well. It is one of the more important ritual institutions within the immediate household and patriline, playing a central role in family decision-making. Only men have the authority to divine, although there are occasional exceptions to this norm. This exclusivity in divination reflects the traditional power and authority structures within Nankani families.

A man with a question or concern usually goes to a diviner's compound early in the morning, the time when the veil between human and spiritual worlds is the thinnest, and enters the divination room. He briefly greets the diviner and declares his intentions to divine by placing his offering of grain or money in a basket for the ancestors to accept. The session begins when the diviner calls on his ancestors directly. For example, after shaking a gourd rattle (*sinyaka*) and playing a few notes on the local guitar (*kɔlegɔ*) to entice the ancestors with pleasant sounds, the diviner asks his ancestors at the beginning of a session to "listen to what he [the client] is saying" and to facilitate the connection between the client and his own ancestors.

After summoning the ancestors, the diviner opens a goatskin bag containing the various symbolic divining objects (*yale*), which consist of an array of common everyday items, each with symbolic and moral significance, and empties the items onto the floor. Familiar objects include animal bones or hides, a cow horn, seedpods, stones, pot fragments, shells, cloth, a section of rope, a lock, and old coins. The meanings of the objects, which can range from thirty to seventy items depending on the diviner, are relatively consistent across diviners in the area and, when considered within the cultural and ecological context, are a matter of common sense. For example, a mango seed indicates something sweet. A small calabash or gourd represents a woman or issues involving a woman. An elephant tooth indicates something powerful or strong. A snail shell means that someone has done something harmful to one and one should retreat and not retaliate or one will be harmed again. Clients also bring outside items to check the divination process or assist in resolving questions. Gestures are also used; for example, pointing to the floor or earth indicates the Gods of the land or a shrine.

When the diviner's and client's ancestors are present, attentive, and willing to participate, the client and diviner, usually sitting directly across from each other, take hold of the *bakoldoore*, the divination stick. The *bakoldoore*, a two-foot-long root with a forked top and metal affixed to its base, is the primary means by which the ancestors identify the objects and direct the client's interpretation. The *bakoldoore* "is like a magnet," said one diviner. "It is the thing that will see what the problem is, and it will be attracted to the *yale*." Another diviner described the stick as a "shadow that goes out; you will not see it, but it goes around in the spirit world and gathers the information and comes back."

The diviner lightly grasps the top of the stick, and the client lightly holds the base with his fingers rather than clenched in his fist. All diviners and clients denied controlling where it landed. To prove his point, one diviner mentioned that there are blind diviners. "How are they going to direct you?" he asked. "The stick itself directs. I have no hand in it." Other diviners often looked away or closed their eyes during sessions. All diviners described their role and the stick as a conduit for ancestral communications to be interpreted by the client and emphasized that as mechanical facilitators they have no role in controlling or influencing the messages.

Most clients divine verbally, voicing their questions *and* speaking the ancestor's responses in a dialoguelike manner. The words the client utters for the ancestor are seen as coming directly from the ancestor. In the ritual's most basic form, the client asks binary questions of the ancestors and the ancestors

A client and a diviner (*sitting on stool*) during a divination session (Stephen Fisher)

respond by directing the stick to strike one of two or more metal objects, usually flat pieces of scrap metal, representing choices. The ancestor also works through the stick to identify the symbolic objects, guide the divination session at critical points, provide answers, identify problems, or offer a solution. As the stick responds to the questions, the client interprets and narrates the ancestor's reply in his own voice and then offers another question.

The divination process surrounding a suspected spirit child can be complex and involved. I was told that at a minimum the family head would consult the diviner at least twice, but more often he would visit multiple diviners on several occasions to find the truth. A man explained that the first diviner he consulted confirmed the presence of a spirit child in his house. Days later, he consulted another diviner and discovered that the child was not a spirit. A third consultation confirmed the second, and he no longer had any suspicions. In another example, a concoction man described a lengthy process: "The man will visit a soothsayer and come home and sacrifice a fowl to the ancestors. Then he will be rushing here and there seeking a solution to the problem. Then he will get up again and go to another soothsayer. He may go to a soothsayer three, four, or even six times in a month to make sure it is the child who is causing the problem."

Other families emphasized that it was important to have multiple men from the family go to separate diviners simultaneously to ensure that they get an accurate result. When finished, the men return to the house to discuss their findings. Multiple consultations are necessary not only to confirm suspicions but also to ensure that the spirit child is not distorting the answers. A spirit can

interfere with or "cover" the divination in an attempt to remain undetected. If
the divination is inconsistent or the client receives mixed messages, he may find
a distant relative, someone the spirit child might be unaware of, to divine for
him. A man explained:

> A spirit child can prevent you from finding it. You can go and divine the
> first time, and it will say it is a spirit child. You go a second time, and it will
> say that it is not. So, we normally get a relative, someone close to us, and
> give him two sticks. One [stick] is good, and one is bad. We don't tell him
> which is which. He will go soothsay, and [the ancestors] will choose one.
> He will bring the sticks back and say which one was chosen, either the stick
> indicating it is a spirit child or the one indicating it is not. The next day,
> you do it again and give the sticks to three other people. If they all come
> back with the stick saying it is a spirit child, then you know. If you follow this
> [procedure], the spirit child will not be able to prevent that disclosure.

Despite these objective measures and precautions, divination is still not
foolproof. Powerful spirit children can interfere with divinatory communications
by bribing the ancestors. "They will sacrifice as men sacrifice to the Gods of the
land," an elder woman said, "so no one will disclose their secret so they can grow
old." Accordingly, a man might travel to another section to consult through a
different set of ancestors as a countermeasure.

There is no one divinatory object that signifies a spirit child is present. Rather,
the clients will identify several items that together lead them to interpret the
presence of a spirit. In the following example, I show how a client might identify
and interpret a selection of symbolic objects as a spirit child. Since divination
sessions are complex and can be obscure, this illustration is simplified and condensed for clarity.

In this session, the head of the house suspects the infant born to his son is a
spirit child. Since its birth seven months ago, the infant has been sick, frequently
cries throughout the night, and has been behaving strangely. The infant's
mother has also been sick, and others in the family are starting to claim that
the child is responsible. He is hoping the divination session will clarify what is
happening. In this session, we arrive after all the preliminaries have taken place
and the client has connected with the ancestors. The diviner is shaking his rattle
loudly, closing his eyes while holding the top of the stick and humming along
with the rhythm. The client grasps the base of the stick and begins (C = Client,
A = Client speaking for his ancestor):

> c: Is there a problem? The problem, is it in the house [*touching first a metal object
> representing a choice*] or from the bush [*touching a second choice*]?

A: It is in the house, the house, the house [*the stick impacts three times on the first choice*]. It is hiding, hiding in the house [*the stick touches an enclosed seedpod among the objects*].

C: Ancestor, what is hiding [*the stick digs through the objects*]?

A: It is with the woman [*the stick identifies a small calabash*]. It wants to die [*the stick knocks aside the* loko, *a quiver for arrows*].

C: The *loko* . . . is this thing that is wearing the *loko*, is it for the bush [*touching choice 1*] or for the house [*choice 2*]?"

A: The bush.

C: Will it kill? Ancestor, tell me, will it kill or remain peaceful in the house [*the stick hovers over the objects*]?

A: It is not known. We don't know. It is shifting [*the stick touches a multicolored dark stone*].

C: Why? What is it?

A: It is hiding. It is shifting. It is hot and wants to kill [*the stick rapidly identifies a seedpod, a multicolored stone, a piece of red cloth, and a round black stone*].

I offer a summary. During the consultation, the *bakoldoore* pointed to an impenetrable seedpod from the *kairga* tree. The pod is sealed and difficult to open, suggesting that something is hiding and growing inside the house. Next the *bakoldoore* indicated a small calabash. This means that it is hiding inside a woman or is with a woman. Then it pointed to an item that symbolizes the *loko*, or quiver, which is significant in the Nankani funeral ceremony. The *loko* indicates that whatever is hiding wants to die or is already dead (it can also mean that it wants to fight). The man then determined that the thing wearing the *loko* belonged in the bush. He then asked if it is going to kill or be peaceful, and the ancestor indicated a multicolored stone. This means that whatever is hiding is attempting to fool him or is hiding its identity or intentions. The stick pointed to a red cloth, indicating that it is hot, dangerous, and wants to kill people in the house. If the stick indicates other colors, it means the spirit child has not yet decided to kill. The back stone means death. In this case, the spirit child is ready to kill. The red cloth and the black stone together indicated that the situation was urgent.

Divination is a constructive, provoking, and reflective activity that is encompassed within a ritual and symbolic system of culturally prescribed choices and meanings. On the surface, it might seem that divination is simply a matter of talking to oneself, since the client narrates both his own questions and the ancestral responses, and that any insights gained are self-serving and manipulated for self-interest. Indeed, divination can simply be a way for men to back existing decisions or preconceived notions with ancestral authority. However, a more complex process often occurs. Divination works by examining questions, uncertainties, and sentiments that remain diffuse or unclear. It organizes and directs the client's attention, formulates experiences (Stern 2003), and enables the client to act on newly acquired or formulated insights. The resolution of uncertainty through divination involves, in part, probing the spaces within and disjunctures between what is known, what is assumed, and what is unformulated, with the goal of transforming the ambiguous or "not known" into full awareness.[2]

This divination process results in a narrative that the client takes home to share with others. When the divination concerns a spirit child, this narrative might include a confirmation or denial of its presence, explanations for misfortune or the child's behavior, insights into how or why the spirit entered the family, or possibilities for action. Divination offers a space where the available evidence is considered, integrated, and made meaningful through divination's ritual and symbolic form.

The interpretive process does not end when the divination session is finished. When the client brings the divination results or narrative back to the family, it can generate additional questions or scenarios, necessitating another trip to the diviner. The need for multiple consulters, diverse diviners, and multiple divination sessions demonstrates the way some decision-making processes can extend beyond the sole authority of the head of the house yet remain located within the patriarchal system of authority. Involving multiple people in the detection and verification process is a check that can limit one individual's decision-making power and open an interpretive space around the child and its circumstances.

Families observe spirit children and the events surrounding them closely. Tests are used to confirm the presence of the spirit, and divination provides the most objective method through which to evaluate evidence, consult the ancestors, and uncover a spirit. Despite the power of divination, families remain unsure. As they continue to search for evidence, families hope their child is not a spirit and that their circumstances will change. People understand that administering the concoction to the suspected spirit child is ultimately the only way to confirm its presence and know for sure. Before families administer the concoction, however, they continue to observe the child, look for additional signs, and discuss the evidence.

Detection, Conflict, and Decision-Making: Azuma Continued

In the weeks following our first visit with Azuma, AfriKids provided her family with supplementary food. They also gave Azuma vitamins and various medicines—antibiotics and antimalarial drugs—and Abiiro medication for her leg. When Elijah and I returned to the compound after Abiiro had completed her course, Apaanzo, the family head, greeted us, still looking bedraggled. Azuma, however, appeared better. She was not as cranky, her eyes seemed brighter, and she was more active. She could stand without assistance and take a few steps forward before falling. However, when I asked Abiiro how she thought Azuma was doing, she emphasized in an irritated tone that Azuma was still a spirit child.

"Your health," I asked. "Has it changed?"

"When I took the medicine, I was getting better. Now that I do not have the drugs, I am not as good. The child, it does not sleep, it is always awake. It will never sleep at night." She still looked exhausted, and there was desperation in her voice. "Anytime I want to do anything the child will be crying. Night and day, it's the same. Anytime I want to do work, it cries."

She told us that she frequently attempted to leave Azuma in the care of other children, but Azuma would cry incessantly until she returned and held her. Azuma never left her side, refusing to be left with anyone else. Abiiro reported that Azuma had been eating well and that the other family members were healthy, but she interpreted these changes as small. She suggested that it would be best if AfriKids took Azuma away since nothing was working for the child.

Apaanzo, who until this point had been quietly listening, spoke up. "As the day breaks, the mother has to go and do work," he told Elijah. "But she can't because she is with the child. Should I follow the procedure for a spirit child?"

Elijah did not respond directly and instead asked if Apaanzo had visited a diviner recently to inquire again if Azuma was a spirit. He had not. Apaanzo paused for a moment and then turned to question Abiiro about the ongoing crying and disturbances as if he was unaware of them. He admonished her for not telling him that the child was keeping her awake. He said he did not know the extent of her suspicions, partly because his younger brother Azaare, Azuma's father, was rarely home to talk or even sleep with the family.

Abiiro became angry and cut Apaanzo off before he could speak again. "Why are you bringing this up?" she demanded. "We should focus on how AfriKids can help rather than bringing up these things in the family."

"What is your husband saying about the child?" Elijah pressed.

"He has no time for me and the child," Abiiro replied. "He wakes up drunk every morning. He doesn't even know his own mind. He just gets up and goes wherever he wants. If the child is crying, he pays no attention. That's been going on for three years now! Even a few nights ago, I had a disagreement with him, I told him it's been three years and there is no solution to this. I don't even know what he thinks about the child. He's never with the child, so he doesn't care!" She then continued to describe their frequent disagreements. Elijah suggested that Azuma's father should stay with Abiiro to learn more about what was happening before any decisions were made.

Later, Abiiro's sister-in-law, in a separate discussion, said that Azaare was a part of the problem. "He's a drunkard. He doesn't even know his left from his right! It's because of the father's actions, and Abiiro not being healthy, that they claim Azuma is a spirit child."

Azaare was rarely present when I visited the family. He spent most of this time working and sleeping at his bush farm some distance away. When I asked about him, Apaanzo would explain that Azaare could not be bothered because he was an "important man" with important things to do.

It was becoming clear that Abiiro wanted to be free of Azuma. AfriKids and the concoction man were, to her, the only option remaining. As the conversation progressed, Apaanzo, now frustrated that Abiiro was openly criticizing his younger brother, inflamed the discussion. "The way that women behave these days!" he exclaimed. "A woman can just go out and do anything. Abiiro should just take the child to the concoction man herself to see if it's a spirit child. It should drink the medicine."

Everyone started talking at once. Abiiro's two older sisters-in-law argued that it was inappropriate for Apaanzo to leave everything up to her. They claimed he really knew more than he implied and that he was trying to dodge his responsibilities. One of the women stated, "Apaanzo is at a point where he believes that we should just bring the concoction man to see if she is really a spirit child. Since AfriKids is here, however, we should try to solve the problem with them."

"No!" Apaanzo stubbornly declared. "We should just bring the concoction man. There's no need to hide what is happening here." From his perspective, the concoction man would be able to end the family's discontent. "What you are saying," he continued, "is that AfriKids should just take the child away. I don't agree with that. She's not been telling us what is really happening. She has to tell us everything she sees in the child and then let the tradition take its course." If Azuma was a spirit, as the evidence indicated, Apaanzo felt the concoction was the safest bet. If a suspected spirit child went to another home or the hospital, it could still fly to the house at night and attack the family. In these cases, the only viable solution is to administer the concoction.

Elijah suggested that because family members greatly disagreed, Apaanzo should call a meeting with his brothers to determine a solution. Apaanzo agreed, adding that "these women frequently cause confusion for the family. So, we [the men] have to make sure to take proper care of it."

A few days later, the brothers met and decided they should see if any treatment could help Azuma before using the concoction. Soon after, Elijah and I returned to take Azuma and her mother to the hospital for a checkup and to a feeding center for malnourished children and their mothers in the city.

One of the goals of spirit children is to break the family apart by instigating conflict and disagreements or causing confusion in the house. "The child can even let the father beat the mother," one woman explained. These are all signs of an unresolved problem within the family and signal the breakdown of order and authority.

Nankani family members live in close proximity to each other, and the maintenance of domestic harmony is paramount. An elder offered a clear analysis of disruptive conflict within the home and described the relationship between fighting and spirits.

> We should not quarrel as a family. We were always told this. If you are often quarrelling as a family, it could enable forces outside to come and take advantage of the situation in the house. The spirits or forces could take advantage of the family's quarrelsome nature and probably cause deaths without you knowing. So, if you live in a family, for the sake of unity and peace, it is better to share ideas and counsel and live together. Excessive quarrelling will bring many issues and untold hardships to your family.

In other societies, a child's illness is often understood to be a result of family conflict (Lancy 2008, 53). Among the Nankani, disagreements and conflict can weaken a family, rendering it vulnerable to attacks by spirits, which can cause further division, disruption, and a perpetual cycle aimed at destroying the family. In these cases, vulnerable children identified as spirits come to embody the conflict within the house and can function as a scapegoat. In this sense, as David Lancy notes, the child's condition can provide a ready "pretext" for addressing the disharmony and root issues in the family (2008, 54). I return to the theme of scapegoating and Azuma's circumstances in subsequent chapters.

Decision-Making

Azuma's case demonstrates the complex family dynamics and decision-making processes that can surround a spirit child case. When confronted with a possible spirit child, a range of variables shapes a family's considerations. Decision-making is not limited to the specific moment when a family chooses to give a child the concoction but is part of a larger continuum from initial suspicion to resolution. In this section, I consider the trajectory of decision-making within the context of related gender, power, and other structural processes. I discuss these dynamics apart from the rationales and sentiments surrounding spirit children. This bracketing is artificial, yet it has proved to be descriptively and analytically helpful. In chapter 8, I build on the themes discussed in this section by introducing the complexity of family sentiments and rationales.

The assessment of a suspected child is an ongoing process of gathering evidence, seeking help, and evaluating options as new information becomes available or changes occur. Throughout this process, families question the status of the child and look for evidence that will either disprove or support their suspicions. Detection and decision-making are fraught with ambiguity and uncertainty; many family members feel they can never know for sure.

Ethnographic accounts frequently depict the way mothers control decisions around infanticide. In particular, the mother generally maintains greater control over the life of the neonate in circumstances where decisions are made immediately after the birth. Often only the midwife or birth attendant assists in evaluating the child and informing the mother of its viability. !Kung women are described as having control over the decision for or against infanticide because the decision is made while they are giving birth alone in the bush (Shostak 1981, 238). Sargent observed among the Bariba that, although other members of the family expressed suspicion, the mother was central when it came to identifying a witch-baby (1988, 84). In Brazil, Scheper-Hughes (1992) noted that mothers, in a context of scarcity, decide the fate of the child. In her general description of infanticide practices, Laila Williamson observed that mothers, with occasional support from the father, made most decisions to keep an infant (1978, 66).

Among the Nankani, multiple people are involved in the spirit child decision-making process. While certain people within the family have the greatest power to push an agenda, it is rare to see one family member of his or her own volition decide that a child is a spirit and send it to the bush. Important decisions affecting the family are rarely made in isolation. While the discourse indicates that unilateral decisions are occasionally made, particularly with neonates (Allotey and Reidpath 2001), I did not assess such a case directly and rarely encountered credible accounts of this occurring. This may have been due to improved neonatal services in the region.

In each spirit child case, we have seen family members and others offering their thoughts on the fate of the child. For example, in Azuma's case, the mother raised suspicions, the head of the house considered the circumstances and went to the diviner, people outside the family provided gossip and comments, and an NGO and the Ministry of Health intervened. Additionally, the family continued to discuss Azuma's status as new perspectives emerged and her circumstances changed.

If a formal decision-making body can be recognized within any family, it is found when the head of the house, the father, and other senior men sit together to discuss important issues. "Sitting" with adults in the family is a common practice and the time when a problem is presented, perspectives are shared and discussed, and, ideally, the group achieves consensus. It distributes the decision-making responsibility among all concerned. Despite this process, not all family members will agree in the end. Women's voices are often excluded, and decisions to give a child the concoction can be made against the wishes of the mother and father.

While the father can sit with the other men of the house to discuss the case, his wife, depending on her age and status within the family, is usually unable to sit with her mother-in-law, who has significant authority, to discuss her child's future. Younger married women, who as outsiders have a tenuous link to the patriline, have limited decision-making power. The child is ultimately "for the house," not for the mother, and decisions prioritize the best interests of the extended family.

A mother described this process. "They will talk to the father," she said, "[but] they have the right to make the decision that the child is a spirit child before they inform the woman or the man. Whatever position they have taken, they [the parents] will also have to take."

Others echoed this position but added that these decisions are the responsibility of the men of the house. Furthermore, some women wanted nothing to do with the decision. "The decision will be from husband and the *teŋdanna*," said one mother, "because they have got the upper hand [knowledge and power] and know what to do to save my life or save the child's life." Abiiro also said that divination and discussions concerning Azuma's status were ultimately the men's responsibility.

While women are less likely to engage in the visible or formal decision-making process, they still play a significant role in adding or withholding evidence, actively resisting decisions, and attempting to influence decisions or manipulate family members.

Perspectives on the detection and decision-making contributions of each gender are diverse and largely depend on the family, its experiences and power dynamics, and its degree of exposure to religious and social change, education, women's groups, and outside agencies. There is no doubt that my presence and that of AfriKids shifted the power balance in family conversations. In Abiiro's case, at least initially, it seemed that our presence actually placed her in a decision-making position outside her expected gender role and comfort zone.

In other cases, the presence of outsiders in family discussions seemed to give women more voice and agency, possibly circumventing processes that are more traditional.

The diversity of decision-making across families was demonstrated during a women's group meeting when I asked attendees whether men or women initiate spirit child suspicions.

"It's always the men that have the problem," a middle-aged woman said as she stood to address the room. "Even before a woman is pregnant, some men start going to the soothsayer's house to determine the fate of the child. Many times they will go. Then they finally tell us that it's a spirit child. So, it's the men."

Others responded that women also play a role. Another woman noted, "It is not always the men; the women also bring it out. It is women that are sleeping with the child. Sometimes they say the child will be crying in the night, or you will be sleeping and turn and put your hand there and you don't feel the child. So, it is that woman who is going to tell the man that the child is behaving [strangely] or that she is sick. So, you are informing the man. It is through that that the man will start looking for other actions. So, sometimes it comes from the woman."

Taking a different tack, another said that, despite who decides, it is possible to disagree and resist a decision. "Women who are very determined won't agree," she said. She noted that a woman can run away and use her network to find an alternative place for her child.[3]

As noted above, family disagreements can be dangerous. Most concoction men recalled situations in which family members disagreed. A concoction man described a case in which a relative's refusal to accept that his child was a spirit resulted in the child killing the mother. If everyone had agreed it was a spirit child earlier, he said, they could have prevented the death. Most concoction men indicated that they would not treat a child when a family is unsure or not in agreement.

Gossip, rumor, and unsolicited advice from people outside the family also play an important role in shaping suspicions and decision-making. However, "you cannot step outside your family," a grandmother emphasized, "and decide to solve someone else's family problem." A proverb among the neighboring Kasena holds that "a man cannot enter another's compound to dispatch its spirit child" (Awedoba 2000, 190). Still, people talk about each other's children, and mothers with abnormal children are subject to gossip and unsolicited recommendations, and might experience shame, ostracization, and pressure to see the child as a spirit. Having to care for a child with special needs can also exclude mothers from communal work and social activities.

Even when overwhelming evidence is gathered, many families noted that they can never know for sure until the concoction is administered. When evidence is lacking or inconclusive, they might wait and see whether the child will eventually return to the bush on its own. While hesitation brings disaster to some families, others wait for months, looking for changes in the child's condition and pursuing potential remedies. For example, a concoction man kept me informed of one of his spirit child cases. His relatives living in southern Ghana had a four-year-old daughter that was unable to walk and talk. Her family suspected that she might be a spirit child and waited to see if further indications emerged. As no other problems in the family developed to definitively indicate that she was a spirit, these suspicions were abandoned after three months. "She was just crippled," the concoction man said.

Discourse describes the spirit child detection and decision-making process as urgent and rapidly progressing. That is, families suspect, detect, and give the concoction within a period of hours or days. Possibly observers only encounter spirit child cases when they learn that the family is calling for a concoction, thus missing the trajectory of events that led up to the decision. The process can take weeks or months, and a situation might only become urgent and visible to others when a family reaches a crisis point. Hence, decision-making should be framed as a trajectory rather than distilled into a specific moment or event, such as a consultation with a diviner or a family meeting.

Neonatal cases wherein family members reject an abnormal infant within days or weeks of its birth could be an exception. While a portion of these neonates is possibly subject to infanticide, my sense is that some actually die of other causes, such as complications related to the birth or the child's condition. These neonates are identified as spirit children around the time of their deaths as a post hoc diagnosis wherein infanticide has not occurred (Denham et al. 2010).

For older children, when family members have reached the point of calling for the concoction man, they are often at their limit, things are not improving, and they have run out of options. Fear and a lack of choice compound worries that the child has gained the upper hand and will kill others. We saw this in N'ma's case when the family head was concerned that the spirit was aware of their plans and therefore would target him first.

As such, it is felt that families should conceal their investigations from the child. As a young mother explained, "It knows that you are trying to follow it, and [it] will cause harm to the family." Another woman said that only after the decision has been made and a diviner has confirmed it do you "go to the concoction man to tell him. But you will also have to hurry because the spirit can kill you. Sometimes it can invite other spirits from the outside into the family to kill you."

Finally, it is important to put family decision-making into a broader regional and global perspective. The presence of the Ministry of Health, NGOs, researchers, religious organizations, and the police and legal systems directly and indirectly influences decisions through forms of surveillance, education, and services. Each organization brings with it differing conceptions of the human body, alternative notions of risk and responsibility, diverse disciplinary structures, and unfamiliar notions of human rights. Some of these parties play an important role in the improvement of health outcomes in the region. They may also transform families' decision-making process by providing assistance and alternative options or by helping people better understand a child's condition. The consideration of these additional options and variables, when compared to the past (before the 1990s), provide alternative models for understanding the child's condition and the reasons for misfortune and ultimately lengthen the decision-making process.

These changes are positive; however, they are also insufficient. For example, basic health services may address a child's immediate medical needs, and the threat of police intervention might deter an intentional death. However, the lack of long-term care and education services for chronically ill or disabled children, coupled with families' misunderstandings of the capabilities of biomedicine and hopes for Christian-derived miracles, for instance, engenders new needs and pressures. From this perspective, the very transformations that can protect the health and rights of children may also prolong their suffering and generate new moral and ethical questions for health providers, NGOs, and Nankani families.

6

Concoctions and Concoction Men | TREATING SPIRIT CHILDREN

The concoction man, or *dongodaana*, is the ritual specialist with the power and authority to use the *dongo* to send spirit children back to the bush. It was late in the afternoon when Asaana and I met in the Sirigu marketplace to chat about his experiences as a concoction man. On market days, Asaana would have been sitting with a small group of men selling bundles of handmade rope or softball-sized balls of tobacco at the base of the large tree at the market's bustling center.

Asaana was initially hesitant to tell his story, instead describing the *dongo* and its powers. "As I mentioned, the concoction man is someone who represents our ancestor," he explained. "He represents our ancestor using what is bequeathed to us, the *dongo*. It is the *dongo* that has the power to help us send away the spirit child as our ancestors did."

He paused to smoke his pipe. "It's like a wild animal discovered in the bush," he said. "At some time, an ancestor, our distant grandfather, as he was traveling home killed a powerful animal and removed all its skin and with this," he said, gesturing to a cow horn, "this is what became the *dongo* and its power. So, I am a representative of that." He paused for a moment. "But you cannot send a spirit child away if you have never given birth to one or had one in your family."

"Did you have a spirit child?" I asked.

"My wife once gave birth to one," he replied. "You cannot become a concoction man if you never had a spirit child. When my wife gave birth to the spirit child, the child was bearded all around. As a result, the child killed my wife."

121

"What did you do?"

"My father was still alive, so he went and consulted a soothsayer. The soothsayer confirmed that it was a spirit child and that I needed to dispose of it. At that point, my father wasn't using the *dongo*. However, he was supposed to be using it, according to tradition. But when he stopped using it, the *dongo* got angry and inflicted pain on the family. That is why the spirit child was conceived and born into the family. Because of this calamity, my sister was killed, followed by my wife."

Soon after the deaths, his father began sacrificing to the *dongo* again, and people once more brought him their spirit children. But the *dongo*, he said, no longer responded to his father. When it was clear that his father could no longer continue using the *dongo*, it became Asaana's responsibility.

I asked him if he would say more about his spirit child.

"Well, we were a bit disturbed about the whole situation," he said. "It had killed another human being, my wife, so we were a bit peeved. Certainly, you wouldn't be happy if there was death in your family. I was angry about the death of my wife but not the death of the spirit child," he added, laughing deeply.

As our conversation continued, he reflected on the changing role of concoction men now that there was greater awareness of spirit children and improved access to health care. "So, these days the spirit children live with us," he said. "In the past, there were situations where I would go with the concoction to give to the child. I would hang the *dongo* on the child. We no longer do that. Well, the end result? If it's a human being, then, well, it's good for society. Why not? It's good. So, the work of the *dongo* is finished. We don't kill them. We don't do it anymore."

The *Dongo* and *Dongodaana*

The *dongo*, or "horn," is the spiritual and medicinal object used by concoction men to send spirit children back to the bush. *Dongo* refers to a medicinal substance given to a spirit child, the spiritual power present within the concoction, and the object itself. The *dongo* consists of a six- to eight-inch-long cow horn encased in sacrificed chicken feathers affixed to it with dried blood. An older and well-used *dongo* can grow to the size of a soccer ball. A small rope attached to the *dongo* allows it to hang within a house or around the neck of the concoction man or spirit child. The term *dongo* is quite general; it also describes horns that act as medicines and containers for different substances. People hang these around their necks, near their farms, or in their homes for protective or medicinal purposes.

Asaana told me that the *dongo* originated from the killing of a powerful animal in the bush. Other stories describe hunters or others who went into the bush to search for and acquire the powers necessary to send spirit children away. One concoction man said his ancestors had sent a cow, a significant resource, to a distant location to acquire the *dongo* and its powers in order to, in his words, "save humankind."

The concoction men and traditional community members describe the *dongo* and concoction men as essential to saving, protecting, or working for the good of humanity. They exist "for the health of children, for the benefit of all people," remarked one man. Another man explained the importance of concoction men.

> The spirit child is full of destructiveness and destroys lives and property. So, the concoction man saves many lives. I think his work, his activities, help a lot. Many spirit children kill human beings, I have been witness to that, and if the spirit child is out to destroy, the concoction man has to kill it. He has the medicine to give it so it will die, and there will be peace in the family.

Concoction men have become increasingly stigmatized. Although they rarely encounter them, younger and educated community members describe concoction men as remnants of the past and, in some cases, murderers only interested in food or money. Others do not approve of what they do but maintain a romantic or nostalgic perception of their spiritual powers.

Being a concoction man is not a primary identity or occupation. Like other community members, concoction men farm and engage in small trade. Some also practice local forms of healing. Concoction men downplay the significance of their role and are humble about their power. They emphasize that the power to send spirit children back to the bush resides within the *dongo*, not within men. "A concoction man is a human being like anyone else," one remarked. "It's just that he is the one that holds the *dongo*."

The *dongo* is a discrete spiritual entity with agency and a persona. The relationship between a *dongo* and a concoction man rests on exchange obligations and a ritualized system of reciprocity. Without the *dongo*, a concoction man is powerless against spirit children. The *dongo*, on the other hand, depends on a concoction man for its sustenance and comfort.

The *dongo* has a "mouth" located at the opening to the inside of the horn, which stores the medicine used to treat the spirit child. The mouth also eats and drinks the food sacrifices that the *dongo* requires for encouragement and reward. The *dongo* prefers fowls but also eats goats and local food staples and drinks *pito*. The concoction man feeds the *dongo* each time it "catches" a spirit child and occasionally throughout periods of inactivity to ensure that it remains

A *dongo* receiving a *pito* libation before a spirit child ceremony (Stephen Fisher)

satiated and loyal. "It needs meat," the concoction men would say. "It's becoming restless!" These maintenance feedings are necessary to prevent the
dongo from maliciously striking out in anger or leaving its owner. The consequences of not attending to the *dongo* were apparent with Asaana's father. A
breakdown in reciprocity permanently damaged their relationship.

The *dongo* is temperamental, insatiable, and vindictive. Concoction men
described a range of misfortunes and illnesses resulting from the failure to care
for it or meet its demands. If you neglect, abuse, or improperly handle the
dongo, it can even kill you. "The *dongo* can let people give birth to a spirit child,"
said a concoction man. "Then it will kill that one and make you give birth to
another spirit child. Kill it, and cause it again. It does these things to get something to eat." In another example, a concoction man recalled how a hungry
dongo had also caused his wife's death.

> Years ago, my wife gave birth and would not stop bleeding. The child died
> soon after it was born. I went to get herbs to treat my wife, but she, too,
> died. After that, I went to the soothsayer and found that my wife had given
> birth to a spirit child. The reason was because my family had hung the
> *dongo* for a long time and never fed it. The *dongo* was angry and caused the
> birth of the spirit child.

It often seemed that the concoction men projected on and communicated
their desires and expectations through the *dongo*. When interacting with AfriKids,

which hosts a concoction men's association involved in transitioning them to roles that help spirit children, the concoction men would forcefully communicate their *dongos'* demands. During the association's first year, the *dongos*, according to the concoction men, became increasingly difficult and demanding. For example, one man said that his *dongo* demanded compensation, exclaiming, "The *dongo* is going to cause harm. It will not harm AfriKids. It will harm us!" The concoction men rarely demanded anything directly from AfriKids; they expressed gratitude for any support. However, the *dongo* occupied a space that permitted the concoction men to aggressively express desires and frustrations that they might not otherwise communicate. AfriKids often met these needs by satisfying the *dongo*.

The concoction men communicate with the *dongo* through divination. Ayisoba remarked, "When things become critical, the spirit child talks through the *dongo*. So, when I go to a soothsayer, I hear what the spirit child wants." In these cases, the *dongo* works as an intermediary and asks what sacrifices the spirit child desires. To avoid having to administer a concoction, the concoction man or the family may conduct sacrifices for the spirit child in an effort to encourage it to leave the family.

The use of the *dongo* for purposes other than treating spirit children is limited, and the concoction men generally balk at using it for other purposes. Its owner cannot summon the *dongo*'s power to send a spirit child to another family or harm someone. The only example of its use to cause a woman to give birth to a spirit child is when a woman defensively uses a *dongo* to protect her crops from theft.

The *dongo* protects the concoction man when he is engaged in actions directed against a spirit child. He might hang the *dongo* around his neck when traveling to conduct a ceremony or when visiting a suspected child. Even if the *dongo* remains at home or is not in the concoction man's possession, it can still warn him of and protect him from spiritual threats. Its protection, however, is not guaranteed. An elder concoction man told me that once, as he was returning from burying a spirit child, he fell into a ditch and injured his leg. He attributed the fall to spirits. Three months later, while returning home from conducting another spirit child ritual, he again fell and reinjured his leg. Laughing, he explained that spirit children were either becoming too powerful or the *dongo* was no longer protecting him from spiritual attack. He reckoned it was time to retire.

The *dongo* is passed between generations, usually from father to son. It can skip a generation, passing from grandfather to grandson, or it might go to a man's nephew within his patriline if there are no eligible sons. The inheritance of the *dongo* follows the rules for inheritance and succession. After the death of its caretaker, the inheritance will temporarily go to the youngest son until the family performs the final funeral rites, releasing the deceased's spirit to the ancestral world. This often occurs two or more years after his death. After the final rites, the *dongo* is given to its successor. If no successor is identified, the *dongo* will hang in the home of the eldest son—who is responsible for the family's shrines—until someone is identified, often through the birth of a spirit child.

As noted above, one does not choose to become a concoction man. A concoction man explained that after the death of his wife and child, the *dongo* "chose me to use it. If it doesn't choose you and you try to learn it, you can die." It is significant that each concoction man must experience the loss of a child and other family members before he is able to involve himself in another family's misfortunes. Similarly, in other social roles, such as becoming a diviner, misfortune and suffering are calls to become a ritual specialist. It is common across other cultures for healers and related practitioners to emerge from a community of similarly afflicted sufferers (Finkler 1994). Nankani people prioritize and grant authority to direct experience over vicariously passed knowledge. To become ill, experience a loss, or suffer is part of what Ayisoba considered necessary to become hardened and be able to withstand the physical and spiritual assaults inherent to being a healer, sorcerer, or concoction man. Suffering is a call, a test, and a rite of passage to determine if one is strong enough to assume responsibility over a power and endure the challenges and risks associated with it.

One learns to use the *dongo* by observing and assisting. The instruction is direct, and the concoction man will explain what he is doing as it occurs. The future caretaker usually performs menial tasks such as cleaning sacrifices during rituals or digging the child's grave. The knowledge is specialized and potentially harmful; concoction men do not share knowledge of how to use the *dongo* with those who do not need to know.

The *Dongo* as a Dog

The concoction men experience the *dongo* as a self and a relational being that simultaneously exist within the spiritual world and among the living. The concoction men perceive and interact with the *dongo* in a manner similar to a dog (*ba'a*). Like the hunter and his hunting dog, the *dongo* is tasked to hunt for and catch spirit children for its caretaker, and it searches for a spirit child much like a hunting dog searches for and pursues game. The ritual invocation used to wake the *dongo* petitions its doglike nature to "not sleep or sit down, but go out as a dog . . . and get the spirit child so I can feed you." During thanksgiving sacrifices to the *dongo*, the concoction man voices a similar plea, urging it to continue to hunt for spirit children. The *dongo* can direct the concoction man to a spirit or, when someone calls on him to treat a spirit child, he will understand that the *dongo* led the individual to him.

There are good reasons why doglike characteristics are useful for catching spirit children. Traditionally, when wild game was plentiful, hunters used trained dogs to hunt it in the bush. Not only were the hunting dogs effective at detecting game and dangerous animals, but they were also able to detect spiritual threats. When his dog's ears prick up and it begins to pursue something unseen ahead, a hunter might conclude, particularly if no game is present, that the dog is chasing a spiritual presence. Dogs are well suited for protecting humans from unseen dangers in the bush because spirits dislike dogs and dogs are invulnerable to spirits. In her work with the Beng people, Gottlieb similarly noted that spirits fear dogs and hunting dogs scare away spirits (1992, 103).

Nankani dogs, which resemble the Basenji breed, are largely independent, nearly feral, and always hungry. They frequently roam alone or in small packs within liminal spaces, such as the periphery of the bush and house, usually in the evening and early morning hours when the veil obscuring the spirit world is thinnest. People own dogs as pets, but close affectionate relationships are less common. Dogs typically have a great deal more freedom, and they are associated less with the domestic sphere than Euro-American pets. People also eat dogs for sacrificial reasons and on special occasions.

Like the *dongo*, dogs occupy the boundaries between important realms. People often view dogs with ambivalence due to their wild and unpredictable nature and their ability to cross spatial boundaries such as between the house and the bush. While at times dogs behave like wild animals, people also observe that they have their own social networks, hierarchies, and other humanlike characteristics. In mythical accounts, dogs have also been helpful to humans. The narrative in chapter 2, for example, describes dogs that became substitute humans and played an intermediary role in helping humans understand and manage spirits' demands.

Concoction men explain that they can direct the *dongo*, like a hunting dog, to do their bidding. However, the *dongo*, and dogs in general, can act autonomously and stubbornly refuse requests. The relationship is uncertain. A Nankani dog may quickly turn on a family member and growl or bite. The *dongo*, too, can act aggressively and attack if aggrieved.

In her analysis of the Beng people's relationship with dogs, Gottlieb aptly explained that dogs resonate strongly because they "act both as Self and as Other to humans," journeying between mythic and social time and between animal and human (1992, 107). In many respects, the *dongo*, too, occupies a middle ground between spirits and humans, self and other. As a mediator, the *dongo* helps to reestablish order, return entities to their respective domains, and suture the boundaries in between.

Treating Spirit Children

Families hope the time will never come when a child of theirs requires a concoction. After a period of help seeking and decision-making, families might seek out a concoction man after visiting a diviner. A mother summarized this process:

"When we give birth to such children, we will always try to find treatments for them. We will go to many herbalists. When we fail, we will go to the soothsayer's house and find out if such a child is a spirit child. Then the concoction man is summoned." Even if a soothsayer confirms the presence of the spirit child, families may remain unsure. "It's only the *dongo* that has the power to determine if a spirit child is a spirit child or not," a woman said.

Families hope that the suspected spirit child will depart on its own. Indeed, some spirit children die before a concoction is given. An analysis of verbal autopsy and demographic data collected by the NHRC demonstrated that 36 percent of the spirit child cases recorded did not involve active death-inducing behaviors (Denham et al. 2010). For example, one man said that after visiting a diviner and confirming the presence of a spirit child, "We normally pour a libation. When we pour it, the spirit will run away at that point [without the need for a concoction]." Families also described spirit children that had died on their own because they were satiated, wanted to return to the other spirits, were given the correct sacrifices, and were banished by the ancestors.

It is not difficult to find a concoction man. If a clan has a history of spirit children, it is possible that someone in the clan keeps a *dongo*. People can locate a concoction man through word of mouth in a short time. I was aware of at least sixteen concoction men in the eastern sectors of the Kassena-Nankana districts.

The sections below describe the spirit child rituals as they were demonstrated and explained to me by concoction men and Nankani community members. I focus on the diversity of concoctions, the procedures used, the experiences and roles of the concoction men, and the context wherein spirit child rituals and deaths occur. The diversity of methods used to "treat" spirit children raises important questions around how spirit children die and whether all such deaths are infanticidal.

I begin with a description of the content of concoctions. I group the preparation and contents into three categories: the symbolic use of the *dongo* only, the use of the *dongo* and black medicine mixed with water, and the use of the *dongo* and black medicine mixed with herbs and water.

THE *DONGO* ONLY

Three of the concoction men I worked with did not use herbs to treat spirit children. Two simply poured water over the exterior of the *dongo*, collected the runoff in a calabash shell, and administered the water to the child. "It is not about the medicine; it is about the power of the *dongo*," one explained. "When the water flows around the *dongo*, its power makes the child pass away. The power goes inside the water. If it is a spirit child, then it has to die." Apiah, another concoction man, explained that he ritually places the *dongo* in the room with the suspected spirit child, as the presence of the *dongo* itself causes the child's death.

"We don't give any medicine to the child [to consume]," Apiah said. "But any woman that gives birth in our family, they will take the medicine, the *dongo*, and go to the house. They will put the black medicine from inside the *dongo* on the ground and put the child on the medicine and it will lie there when it sleeps. On the third day, if the child is still alive, it is not a spirit child." During this time, the family still feeds and cares for the child.

"Do you also hang the *dongo* in the house?" I asked.

"We hang the *dongo*. When the child is sleeping, we hang the *dongo* on the wall above the child. Anyone in the family that gives birth, they take the *dongo* there [to the house], hang the *dongo* above the child—three days, it can sometimes take that long—then take the *dongo* back." People from outside his family also request the *dongo* when they suspect a spirit child. Apiah estimated that ten to fifteen women give birth in a given year in his clan and that at least one or two spirits are detected and die each year from the *dongo*. I asked him if the children were cared for differently while the *dongo* hung in their house. He emphasized that nothing changes and life goes on normally.

"How old was the oldest spirit child your *dongo* has treated?" I asked.

"About fifteen years old," Apiah replied.

"How will an older child accept this, lying down on the medicine?" I asked.

"The child will agree because of the power of the *dongo*. They will hang it above his head where he is lying."

"So, the *dongo* can really work on its own?"

"Yes, the spirit or the power of the *dongo* can work and fight with it."

Similarly, a mother I spoke with in another village noted that her family members did not use a concoction. "They go to the concoction man, and he will bring the *dongo* to place in the room where the child is sleeping. If it is a spirit child, it will die."

Stories about the power of the *dongo* alone were common, and no one denied the effectiveness of using the *dongo* without substances. While I was sitting one afternoon with a group of elder men, one described a neighbor that had a spirit child. Laughing, he said, "When the concoction man came to the house, the child just took off running down the path. The concoction man took aim and threw the *dongo* at the child. The *dongo* hit the child, and he fell down and immediately died!"

On a separate occasion, a man offered a story about a woman believed to be a spirit. "She was a very old woman," the man explained. "The family had to call a concoction man to come and give her the concoction to drink. While the concoction man was approaching, the old woman was inside grinding millet flour. When she knew that a powerful person was coming, she cried out, 'There is something coming to get me.' There was another woman inside with her watching this. She quickly ran out of the room. As she exited, the concoction man was waiting outside for her by the door. He said, 'I've seen you, I've uncovered your secret, I've seen your wicked nature.' When he said that, she just fell down and died. He didn't even have to use the concoction."

What is important about this particular use of the *dongo* is that it demonstrates a set of practices in which the spirit child does not ingest any substance and no obvious, active death-hastening process occurs. While a minority of concoction men did not use substances, I believe that the symbolic means of managing the intrusion of a spirit into the family—including families' sacrifices and appeals to their ancestors—is more common than is usually acknowledged. Notably, these cases demonstrate that when families describe the death of a spirit child, it does not necessarily imply poisoning or other death-hastening or infanticidal actions.

THE BLACK MEDICINE WITH WATER

The second treatment method involves orally administrating the black medicine to the child. Black medicine (*tiim sabelega*) refers to a general category of medicines commonly associated with significant but hidden power, nefarious activities, and harming others. Black medicine can be contrasted with white medicine (*tiim peelega*), which is associated with curing.[1] These medicines are also called black because the roots, branches, or bark in them are calcinated or burned in their preparation and can be consumed as small pieces of charcoal. The black medicine in the *dongo* consists of one or more roots that have been calcinated, crushed, and mixed with shea butter to form a paste, which is stored inside the horn.

All the concoction men I spoke with used the black medicine in some manner, either placing it on or near the child (as described above) or forcing the child to consume it. Three of the concoction men prepared the black medicine without other substances for the child to consume, including Ayisoba, who people regard as one of the most powerful concoction men.

The concoction men have two perspectives on the origin of the black medicine. Some claimed that the ancestors or unknown forces consistently replenish the black medicine inside the *dongo*. "It has always been there," a man said, "and it will never finish. If we have been using it, if it gets halfway, the next day we see it full. We don't know who refilled it." Others say it is necessary to collect the bark and roots of herbs and trees to prepare it.

Ayisoba prepares the black medicine using a range of trees and herbs. Significant are the roots of trees where black ants (*gurne*) commonly live. Ants and ant abodes are often associated with spirit children, either playing a role in causing a spirit child (chapter 4) or, in other societies, and in some cases among the Nankani, serving as a place where spirit children can be buried.[2] During the day, Ayisoba takes the stone that he uses to grind the herbs for the black medicine and places it on top of the ant nest "to drive the ants away." He then ties a black or white fowl near the nest. Late at night, he returns to the nest to see that the fowl has died and begins to dig into the nest, "taking the roots from the ants." When he finishes near daybreak, Ayisoba collects the remaining four herbs and parts of trees nearby. The most important and abundant of these are the stems and bark of the *kalga* tree (*Piliostigma reticulatum*), which is spiritually dangerous. On returning home, he boils the dead fowl, grinds the material collected, and smolders and chars the mixture in a small fire. He then crushes and mixes the calcinated material with shea butter, forming a black paste that hardens over time.

"The *kalga*, it's a bad tree," Elijah said while we were discussing the black medicine.

"When the tree wakes up it is very dangerous," Ayisoba added.

"What does it do?" I asked.

"It can turn into a normal human being and scare people," Ayisoba replied.

Elijah added, "Men or women don't pick the roots. In the stories our fathers give, the tree can turn into a donkey. Or when you pass it, it will throw stones at you. If you are in the bush you won't find it unless you know how."

Ayisoba added, "If you're not strong, you can look but will not find the tree. Only those that are powerful can do that. It can turn into anything." Ayisoba explained that, despite the danger, its roots can be used to treat illness, protect the ancestors, and drive spirit children away. It is important to exercise care around these trees, as they can cause confusion. "Sometimes in the bush," Ayisoba said, "it can turn into a human and will be sitting there. If a fellow walks by and it greets it and it responds, it means you will die." People also identified the *kalga* as responsible for causing madness.

According to the concoction men, the black medicine is the most powerful substance used to treat spirit children, particularly compared to other herbs and preparations mentioned below. Without the black medicine, either added to a concoction or used externally with the *dongo*, the treatment will be ineffective. People indicated that just a small amount of black medicine is often enough to send a spirit away. The concoction men perceive those that only use the black medicine as having significant power because they do not need additional substances.

In the ritual involving the black medicine alone, the concoction man brings the *dongo* to the spirit child's house and mixes the black medicine with water.

A concoction man preparing the black medicine in a calabash while sitting next to the *dongo* (which has recently received a sacrifice); the mouth of the *dongo*, filled with black medicine, is facing forward (Aaron Denham)

When Ayisoba prepares it, he removes half a teaspoon of black medicine from the mouth of the *dongo* and adds it to water in a small calabash. While he told me that he adds the black medicine to hot water, in practice I never observed him heating the water. The medicine does not mix with cold water very well, clumping on the water's surface. An older woman who can no longer become pregnant will administer the concoction, usually after laying the infant on her lap. The volume the infant consumes is small, likely less than one hundred milliliters. It is questionable whether the infant ingests much of the black medicine in the calabash. I asked Ayisoba about this. "It doesn't matter how much it consumes," he said. After the concoction is administered, a family member hangs the *dongo* on or near the infant. The family continues to care for the infant until it passes away, usually two to three days later.

People acknowledge that the black medicine cannot harm a normal human being; however, few were willing to sample it voluntarily. While learning Ayisoba's spirit child rituals, Ayisoba and I sampled the black medicine several times, both the medicine mixed with shea butter and the calcinated roots alone. I experienced no discomfort or ill effects. It is hard for me to imagine that the black medicine in small quantities is very toxic.

BLACK MEDICINE WITH HERBS

The most common treatment involves mixing the black medicine with an herbal infusion. Ten concoction men described this preparation. They use a plant referred to as *bunbunlia*. They dig the root of this semiwoody shrub, found in low, moist ground, when it is roughly "knee high" or still young.

Preparations of *bunbunlia* vary. Some men crush or grind the root and soak it in unheated water for roughly fifteen minutes. Others boil the uncrushed root for approximately five minutes. Before giving it to an older woman to administer to the child, they add the black medicine to the preparation.

Development workers and researchers commonly ask about the scientific identity of *bunbunlia*. Based on samples and the ethnobotanical literature, I posit that *bunbunlia* is likely *Sapium grahamii* (Stapf) Prain (family Euphorbiaceae). It is important to note that my identification process does not satisfy scientific ethnobotanical standards. Although I attempted it multiple times, I was also unable to obtain a chemical or toxicological analysis of the concoction. Despite this, the effects of *Sapium grahamii* are relatively well known.

Sapium grahamii is found throughout West Africa, primarily in the savanna and some forest areas. Various societies have used it for arrow poisons, as a poison in food, to bait and kill animal pests, to treat guinea worm during extraction, to treat skin afflictions, as a vermifuge, as a purgative, to induce abortion, and for scarification. The Nankani use it to clean sores and treat parasites in addition to spirit children. In neighboring Dagbani communities, it is referred to as *kpárípìhìgà* (Blench 2006) or *pampiga* (Burkill 1985). In his notes, Robert Blench (2006) described *kpárípìhìgà* as a small shrub with toxic milky latex sap that is fed to children said to be afflicted with evil spirits. The root latex is powerfully caustic and when applied to the skin causes swelling, resulting in a permanent scar or colored tattoo (Blench 2006; Burkill 1985; Neuwinger 1996). Indeed, people always advised that I carefully wash my hands after handling the root and never touch my eyes. H. M. Burkill reported that it is immediately fatal when given to pigs (1985).[3] Severe diarrhea with bleeding in the intestinal tract is a primary symptom of ingestion (Traore et al. 2014).

Nankani accounts state that intestinal or stomach distress is associated with its use. A concoction man explained, "You know this thing is poisonous! If you are able to eat it, depending on your intestines, if your intestines are strong, maybe you can fight it." A woman said, "Sometimes they boil the water with the herbs and they give it to the child, it is a lot of water. Sometimes when the child takes the water, it will cause harm, it will kill the intestines or something like that. That is why the child will die."

The concoction men and the families of spirit children indicated that the consistency of the child's feces is the primary indicator that the child is a spirit or that the *dongo* has caught it. "It will not look like the feces of a normal human," a woman said. "The child will keep releasing animallike feces. That is how you know it is not a normal child. It keeps doing that until it becomes tired and dies." Some people remarked that if the child does not urinate or defecate after receiving the concoction, this means that it is not a spirit child.

A Spirit Child Ceremony

Each concoction man follows his family's tradition when treating spirit children. While elements of each practice differ, several structures and practices are shared. I describe the elements involved in treating a spirit child by recounting Akaare's ritual, which I found to be similar to other practices. My description of Akaare's ceremony is derived from interviews and a hypothetical spirit child case we enacted together.

When families summon Akaare to treat a spirit child, he first visits a diviner to determine whether the child in question is indeed a spirit and if there are any unforeseen issues of which he should be aware. He also determines through divination whether there are any particular sacrifices he and the child's family should perform to encourage it to leave. At the agreed-upon time, Akaare gathers the *dongo* and the herbs and walks to the family's house.

When Akaare and the other concoction men travel to confront a spirit child, they adopt a disposition different from their everyday way of being. They are vulnerable while in transit from the safety of their ancestrally protected home to the disordered house of the spirit child. There is a chance that the spirit knows the concoction man is en route and can attack or call on other spirits to stop him. It is essential for concoction men to harden themselves, walk directly to the house without stopping, and focus their attention solely on the task ahead. Some concoction men will also arm themselves with medicinal objects and consume medicine to fortify themselves against danger. Their faces become somber, their gaze focused. One concoction man said, "My eyes turn, and everything looks different." Treating a spirit child is like going to war.

Akaare speaks to no one when he is holding the *dongo*. On reaching the house, he remains attentive to the family's sentiments, particularly if anyone disagrees. If there is a disagreement, he will not treat the child. While preparing to boil the *bunbunlia* and the stems of a plant he refers to as *yegipia*, he sends all the women of the house away except for the spirit child's mother. Other concoction men send away only the women that are still able to give birth, including the mother. The concern is that the departing spirit will enter one of the women present and be reborn into the family.

After boiling the whole, uncrushed roots in a small pot for ten minutes just outside the compound's entrance near the ancestral shrines, Akaare pours a small amount of the nearly clear liquid into a small calabash. He adds one teaspoon of relatively dry, chunky black medicine from inside the *dongo*. Although the water is hot, the black medicine does not mix well.

Akaare, one of the few concoction men that administers the concoction, asks the parents if he should proceed. Just a small amount is needed to kill the child, Akaare says, showing me an amount of less than 150 milliliters. He notes that even older children and strong spirits cannot resist the administration. "Because of the power of the medicine," Akaare said, "they will not have the power to struggle with me. So, when I give the medicine, they will drink."

After giving the concoction, he gently touches the child twice with the *dongo* and places the child in a room before returning home. The family continues to care for the child, feeding it normally. Death usually occurs within four hours, he said, but it can take up to several days. Akaare believes, as do the others, that if the child does not die, it is not a spirit child.

When the child dies, the family calls Akaare back to the house to perform the burial. He rolls the deceased child in an old sleeping mat and ties it closed with scraps of cloth. At this time, the danger has not yet passed and the spirit still lingers around the house. It can attack others, enter another woman, or cause problems. As Akaare prepares to depart for the bush with the child, the mother remains behind wearing the *dongo* around her neck for protection in case the spirit attempts to enter her again. If the mother is not at the house or if Akaare is concerned that the spirit is powerful and his well-being is at stake, he will hang the *dongo* around his own neck.

Burial locations are a map of social relations. Families bury children who are not spirits within or at the edge of a farm or a similar periphery between the domestic sphere and the bush. The regenerative symbolism of being buried at a farm or on the periphery of a house is strong. Since a child is not fully integrated into the social order, it is not buried in the ancestral graves located below the remains of an old, collapsed compound. Not having any link to the social world, spirit children are disposed of in the bush, often where other spirits are known to dwell.

On this occasion and with all ceremonies, when leaving the house, Akaare asks the family for a calabash full of sorghum and millet seed, which he takes with him into the bush along with a hoe to dig the grave. The father often accompanies Akaare to the burial. The only others allowed to assist are those that have had a spirit child. When ready, Akaare places the bundled body of the child under his arm, hangs the hoe over his shoulder, and, wearing a stern expression, sets off, walking in a direct line toward a nearby hill located within his clan's territory.

The spirit is compelled to follow and attend the burial. When entering the bush, Akaare prefers that those accompanying him walk in front, since spirits prefer to stalk and attack from behind. Again, no one is to speak to him, and he remains silent, walking swiftly during the five- to ten-minute journey. He climbs the small hill and enters the trees. Near its crest, Akaare stops walking and immediately identifies a relatively fresh mound of dirt covered with a pile of stones — a recent spirit child grave not of his creation. "This is my place," Akaare says. "No one else is allowed to bury here."

His son, who was accompanying us, notes with concern, "The one burying here might not have done the necessary things [rituals]."

"No," Akaare replies. "It was likely another concoction man." Akaare continues for a few additional meters and stops between two trees. "Here," he says, placing the body and the calabash on the ground.

Akaare digs a shallow grave. He places the child in the grave and, with the father's help, covers it with dirt. Akaare works quickly lest the spirit child rise up and attack him or return to the house before he performs the ritual to permanently send it away. He and the father then gather stones and place them on top of the grave to prevent the spirit from rising. Some concoction men do not dig a grave, choosing only to cover the body with stones, tree branches, and other debris. Many people describe returning to a grave a few days after a burial to see if the child remains. All find that the body has disappeared into the bush with the other spirit children.

After placing the last of the stones, Akaare scatters seeds around the grave to distract the spirit if it rises. Spirits will stop everything to eat the seeds. "Maybe the spirit child wakes up," he says, "and before he is able to pick up all the seeds I will have made it back to the house and performed all the rituals. The seeds prevent the child from coming back to cause harm to the father or mother." While quickly walking home, he also tosses the seeds over his shoulder every few strides to delay the spirit if it follows.

On returning to the house, Akaare begins the ceremony that will send the spirit away. He boils a selection of "healing roots" mixed with some of the *bunbunlia* and the *yegipia* used in the concoction. He covers the earthen pot, symbolic of womanhood, containing the roots and herbs with half of a broken pot. Akaare places the head of a hoe directly on the cover and sets the *dongo* on the hoe. A hoe, symbolic of fertility, is exchanged as part of bride price and brought to the funeral of one's wife or mother. Constructing a shrine with these items establishes a link, which, through sacrifice, works to repair and reestablish reproductive normality and continuity.

Two sacrifices are made. First, Akaare sacrifices a chicken, traditionally identified as men's food, immediately followed by a guinea fowl, traditionally women's food. This sacrifice urges the *dongo* to send the spirit away. If the spirit child has made a specific request through divination, such as for a goat or a fowl of a particular color, it is sacrificed at this time. On a separate occasion, an

A concoction man preparing to sacrifice a fowl to the *dongo* (Aaron Denham)

elder described these sacrifices as the spirit child's share of the family property. He said that the spirit must "take the items and leave the family in peace." If the spirit child had any claim to family membership, accepting this sacrifice solidifies its permanent separation from the family.

Similar to the way ancestral sacrifices are made, the concoction man cuts the fowls' necks while holding them directly above the *dongo*. As the blood falls on the *dongo*, Akaare affixes to the outside of it the feathers plucked from the fowl and offers the following invocation.

> Now, *dongo*, go and hunt for the spirit child. After collecting these things, you should not sleep or sit down but go out as a dog, go out with the ancestors, and get the spirit child so I can feed you. As the day comes to an end, you should go out and hunt for more. Collect, collect, collect this fowl and be awake. Today it isn't free, today it isn't free, you have to go out and work. Collect these things. We are here to help each other. I give this fowl here, and the guinea fowl, but three fowls and a goat still remain.

On a later day, the concoction man sacrifices a goat along with three chickens if the spirit child was a girl and four if a boy. These numbers are

A concoction man offering the *dongo* its share of the food (Aaron Denham)

commonly associated with each gender and used in a variety of settings. This second sacrifice is the final payment to the *dongo* for its services. Although the concoction men eat the meat, they emphasize that the animal sacrifices are not a payment to them directly; they are strictly for the *dongo*.

After the first sacrifice to the *dongo*, the mother and father take a small sip of the specially prepared water contained in the pot beneath the shrine and wash themselves in the mixture for purification so that, according to Akaare, "The spiritual sickness will be cleansed." Other traditions also require the mother and father to shave their heads and remove their clothing for disposal. In these cases, the mother and father place their hair and clothing in a large basket along with the child's clothing and the cloth used for carrying the child. The concoction man removes the basket from the house and scatters the items, which are polluted and can draw the spirit back to the family, in the bush. The roots used to prepare the water, now imbued with the spiritual disorder, are buried outside the house.

The two sacrificed fowls are boiled, and only the *dongo*, the concoction man, and those who have had a spirit child eat. The family prepares additional food and *pito*. When the food is ready, Akaare asks everyone's permission for the next offering to begin. Squatting, he takes the *dongo* and says, "*Dongo*, get up, wash your hands. That is your t.z., meat, and *pito*. Get up, wash your hands, and collect these things. As day breaks, don't sleep; you should get up and hunt, as people have spirit children. Come and collect these things."

Akaare stands, holding a calabash filled with *pito*. He dips his hand in the *pito* and flings his hand in the air, sprinkling *pito* toward each of the four directions while declaring to his ancestors that they should also take part in the meal wherever they are living. He then tells the *dongo* to come and collect its share. It is at this point that the spirit is committed to the bush and can no longer return to the family.

Concoction men will perform a similar ceremony for children that have died for other reasons or if a family determines that a previously buried child is a spirit and responsible for any disturbances. Occasionally, in these cases, the concoction man exhumes the body and reburies it in the bush in a similar manner.

While there are variations between the spirit child rituals performed by other concoction men—ranging from different types of sacrifices to alternative concoction types and administration methods, as discussed above—the general structure of many ceremonies is quite similar to that of Akaare.

7

Causing Death and Prolonging Lives

In the introduction to this volume, I ended my discussion of N'ma's case with Ayisoba telling me that her family was asking him to administer the concoction. Although Joe urged the family members to let her die on her own, they were convinced that N'ma was a spirit and wanted to take action. Roughly a week later, Elijah and I visited Ayisoba at his house to learn more about the outcome.

"Ayisoba!" Elijah called out from outside the compound. "We went by your house the other day, and you were not there. We heard that you had gone to the spirit child's house. We were afraid that the child was very powerful and had killed you there." Everyone laughed.

Ayisoba replied with a serious face, as he exited his house to join us, "The child was not able."

"Were you not able?" Elijah asked.

"How would I not be able?" He laughed. "Because my ancestors are here, there is nothing that I fear. Sit down. Let's talk about what happened."

In the early morning, before leaving for N'ma's house to treat her, Ayisoba had consulted his ancestors and the *dongo* via divination to determine whether he should proceed and what sacrifice the spirit demanded. After divining, Ayisoba sacrificed a black fowl to the ancestral shrines in front of his elder brother's house. During this sacrifice, he explained to the ancestors what was occurring and sought their guidance and protection. Next, moving inside the compound, he sacrificed a guinea fowl to a female ancestor at a shrine embedded within the external wall of the traditional woman's room. Ayisoba declared,

"Grandmother, you should collect this fowl through the Gods of the land, so that they are able to communicate with the ancestors and make sure that what I'm using is used well and will catch more spirit children."

Wearing the *dongo* and carrying his goatskin medicine bag, Ayisoba walked directly to N'ma's home. Most of her family members had already left, and only the head of the house and his wife remained. In a calabash, Ayisoba mixed a concoction consisting solely of black medicine. The elder woman administered the concoction to N'ma. Ayisoba was uncertain as to how much water and black medicine N'ma actually swallowed, but he noted that it did not matter; even if she spit it out, she would still die if she were a spirit child. After receiving the concoction, Ayisoba placed the *dongo* around N'ma's neck, and she was set alone in a room.

Ayisoba noted that death usually occurs quickly; if the family gives the concoction in the morning, the child dies by midday. However, in N'ma's case it took much longer than expected. Ayisoba said that when the woman gave the concoction to N'ma, "nothing happened. The child was still lying there. It didn't die."

Through divination, Ayisoba determined that the concoction had failed, as had those of the concoction men before him, because the sacrifices offered to N'ma did not contain exactly what the spirit child desired. To ensure success, Ayisoba and the family head made another sacrifice, being careful to include exactly what she wanted. On the second day, he described N'ma's behavior as "picking up." Ayisoba observed that the people present "really knew for sure she was a spirit child." The grandmother administered the second dose. This second concoction also failed.

"I did it a third time," Ayisoba continued. "I gave a third concoction to the child! Shortly afterward I went back into the room and found that the child was dead. I went out, but by then there was no one at the house. I found the family head and told him that the medicine had caught the child. He came back to the house, entered the room, and saw that the child was dead. As the other family members were returning, I prepared to take the child to the burial site, but then I saw it move and open its eyes. It was awake!"

He explained to the family that N'ma must want something else and he would divine in the morning to determine what it was. Ayisoba returned to his home. The next morning, he arose early to divine and so determined that the spirit wanted a special fruit located far away in the bush. He went out, found the fruit, sacrificed it to the spirit, and told a child to run and tell the family that he had completed the sacrifice. Later in the day, the child came back and notified Ayisoba that N'ma had died. Ayisoba, who claimed he was skeptical at this point, particularly since the spirit had followed him back to his house on the second day and made his family sick, walked back to N'ma's house to confirm the death. She had indeed died, so Ayisoba took the body to the bush for burial and completed the necessary ritual. He sacrificed a white fowl, a red fowl, and a goat for the *dongo* and then made several *pito* and flour water (*zoom ko'om*) libations to the *dongo* and ancestors. The family head sent a message to N'ma's mother and father in Kumasi, telling them to come home, drink the medicine, and perform the ritual so the spirit would leave them.

Ayisoba emphasized to me, "You can't owe the spirit child a single thing. You always have to provide whatever it has asked for so it will go away. Maybe you have a spirit child and you are poor and do not have the necessary things to give the spirit. Unless you are able to perform the ceremony to send the spirit away, if you are unable to do that, it will always come back to the family. Within a year, the spirit can come back to the house."

Ayisoba points to an important feature of the spirit child ceremony. It is expensive. The ceremony requires a significant number of sacrifices. On average, his ceremony costs a family several gallons of *pito*, a hoe, six chickens, one guinea fowl, a goat, a small amount of sorghum, other prepared foods, and other sacrifices specifically demanded by the spirit child. If the animals are purchased and the rituals conducted during the dry season when prices are high, the total cost can easily exceed seventy US dollars. Many families cannot bear this expense or the loss of their own animals. While parts of the payment can sometimes be delayed for several months, at significant risk to the family, the cost of identifying a child as a spirit and proceeding with the ritual emphasizes the significant commitment involved in providing or purchasing the animals when the family is already stressed. Sending the spirit to the bush is not an easy way out.

After Ayisoba finished his account, we continued to chat about N'ma. "She was not the most dangerous or powerful spirit child I've encountered," Ayisoba remarked, "but she was close." I asked him how the family felt about her death. "The mother is happy that the child is dead," he replied. "Even the in-laws are happy the child is dead. Their daughter is now safe."

Catching the Spirit

Concoction men and families know when the *dongo* has "caught" the spirit child by evaluating the consistency of the child's feces. "It will not look like the feces of a normal human," a woman said. "The child will keep releasing animallike feces. That is how you know it is not a normal child. It keeps doing that until it becomes tired and dies." Alternatively, some community members and concoction men said that if the child does not urinate or defecate after receiving the concoction, it means that it is not a spirit child. While the *bunbunlia* likely causes the diarrhea, the concoction men that do not use the shrub also describe changes in the child's feces as being indicative of the treatment's effectiveness.

After N'ma died, I talked with Ayisoba about the physiological events he had observed surrounding her death and the deaths of other spirit children. I was curious, partly because he does not use *bunbunlia*. Ayisoba said that after the first dose, N'ma "was passing feces but still eating. But when the medicine and the *dongo* started working, when she passed feces they were not like those of a normal human being."

I tried to get this clear. "So, when the *dongo* started working the feces looked different?"

"They were different," he replied.

"How? Was she running diarrhea?"

"Not when she took the first one [concoction]. . . . The first one she was passing feces like a normal human, and on the second day it was the same. The third day was different. She was passing feces like mucus."

N'ma's account is also notable because the family and the concoction men made multiple attempts to treat her, calling into question the common discourse among nearly all those involved with spirit children with whom I spoke that if the child survives the concoction, it is not a spirit. In practice, however, I documented several cases like that of N'ma in which families firmly believed that a child was a spirit child and repeatedly administered the concoction when it did not die because the child was "wise" or powerful. In N'ma's case and others, family members justified repeated concoction administrations by concluding that they had failed to perform the correct sacrifices to encourage the spirit to leave. When asked about the need for multiple concoctions, concoction men suggested that unresolved matters with the ancestors, problems with the divination, or other issues in the house could have been interfering. In these cases, a concoction man noted, once the family addresses the matter or satisfies the ancestor or spirit, the spirit child will die when given the medicine again. If a family is convinced of the child's status, surviving attempts with the *dongo* or concoction does not result in a reprieve; rather, it requires additional efforts.

Perceptions of Efficacy

N'ma's case raises important questions around treating spirit children, particularly concerning the efficacy of the concoctions used. Notably, Ayisoba had to administer the concoction three times. The family had also previously consulted two others, who had given N'ma a concoction that differed from Ayisoba's each time. Recall that the amount of the concoction the child consumes varies and is dependent on the concoction man's tradition and the person administering the concoction. Thus, in some cases the child will receive a particularly strong dose due to the preparation or quantity given, or it will ingest a relatively small amount.

One might expect that the concoction men using only water or the black medicine alone would report high failure rates; however, those using the poisonous *bunbunlia* described a similar lack of success. Based on my interviews and discussions, roughly half the children given the poisonous *bunbunlia* did not die or required multiple concoctions over a period of days. Why was there such a high failure rate? What might the questionable potency or lethality of the varied concoctions tell us about the spirit children and the circumstances around their deaths?

For community members, the variations in concoction preparation and the need for multiple administrations are of little concern. The efficacy of the concoction rests not with its chemical or poisonous composition but with its symbolic power. From the perspective of the Nankani, and the concoction men in particular, the power of the *dongo* is the primary force that causes the spirit to depart. The black medicine, whether remaining within the *dongo* or administered to the child, is also essential and closely identified with the power of the *dongo*. The narratives of the mere presence of the *dongo* causing death support this perspective. The addition of *bunbunlia*, an essential component of many concoctions, was recognized by concoction men and others as lethal but less important spiritually. The *bunbunlia* is needed to kill, yet its importance is secondary when it is used against spirit children.

Attention to whose subjectivity is privileged brings up important differences in perceptions around concoction efficacy and the cause of death. Outsiders seek efficacy in the chemical composition of the concoction, often assume that all concoctions are poisonous, and categorically reduce all spirit child deaths to infanticide.[1] Members of the community believe that efficacy primarily rests within the power of the *dongo* and black medicine. When evaluating the spirit child practice, assuming that all concoctions are poisonous and assigning sole responsibility for death to the concoction men misses the complexity of the practice, alternative perceptions of what is occurring, and noninfanticidal causes of death. In practice, a variety of factors shapes the period surrounding the death of a spirit child—in particular, the type of concoction, the child's health status, and the level of care it receives after it is identified as a spirit.

Causes of Death

I group spirit child deaths into four categories. The first includes cases in which the family uses the spirit child framework as an explanatory model for misfortune or understanding why the child died. These include postmortem determinations wherein a family concludes that an already deceased child who was not diagnosed as a spirit or given a concoction was actually a spirit and returned to the bush on its own. For example, I met a family whose members suspected a child that had died two years before was a spirit and responsible for the misfortunes they were currently experiencing. After consulting a diviner, they asked a concoction man to exhume the body, rebury the remains in the bush, and conduct the ceremony. This category also includes cases in which a spirit child died of other causes before the family called for a concoction man to treat the child.

The second category encompasses children that families and concoction men describe as dying from the use of the *dongo* employed as a ritual or symbolic object. These children are touched with or given the *dongo* to wear in order to kill them. The power of the *dongo* alone catches the spirit, causing death. From a biological perspective, the family did not administer a concoction or other substance in these cases; use of the *dongo* alone is perceived as having caused the child's death.

Third are the cases in which the family uses the *dongo* as a symbolic object and gives a nontoxic or mildly toxic substance to the child, either water poured over the exterior of the *dongo* or black medicine. The black medicine has uncertain but likely limited toxicity.

The fourth category includes cases in which death involves the consumption of the *bunbunlia* or other toxic substances. I estimate that these comprise roughly half the spirit child cases. In each instance, the strength of the concoction varies and the concoction men have mixed results. In some cases, it works quickly, while in others it requires multiple attempts. It is important to keep in mind that when children are malnourished, weak, or ill—as most spirit children are—a small dose of even a mildly toxic substance can have an adverse effect and possibly result in further dehydration. In other words, a concoction of any toxicity is likely more harmful to a sick or malnourished child.

Rarely did discourse arise indicating that people abandoned living children, placed a child in a dangerous situation, or used physical violence, such as beatings or suffocation, to kill spirit children. Most accounts of violence came from people outside the Nankani community. I did not encounter credible contemporary cases of violence, and the concoction men denied that this occurred, although several claimed that it might happen in neighboring ethnic groups. There remains a chance that such deaths occurred in the past. It is also possible that these were not technically spirit child cases but forms of infanticide practiced outside the cultural model for spirit children. Ultimately, using "the *dongo* is the only way," people said, to ensure that the spirit returns to and remains in the bush.

In circumstances in which a toxic substance is not used, what is the cause of death and can such deaths be described as infanticidal? In these cases, the most significant contributor would be the child's underlying condition, be that illness, malnutrition, or related complications. Additionally, I want to leave open the possibility that in these cases, passive means such as a reduction in feedings or human contact in an identified spirit child might contribute to a decline in the child's condition and its death.

While there is a tendency to focus on the biological death of a spirit child, it is important to understand that spirit children can experience a social death before a physical death (Cannon 1942). The child's embodied status, its link to misfortune, and its inability to engage in fundamental forms of reciprocity such as eye contact and forms of consumption essential to establishing subjunctive personhood and family membership situate it in a zone of social exclusion associated with the bush. Within this space, people's negative responses to the suspected child may be perpetually reified. As families become more certain of the child's status, feelings of fear and aggression can emerge, particularly when they hold the child responsible for misfortune or death and wonder who it will target next. These sentiments can ultimately influence caregiving.

Unlike Scheper-Hughes's (1992) extensive accounts of maternal neglect in Brazil, I have less overwhelming evidence of parental distancing and neglect in practice. The degree to which a family distances itself from a child depends on several factors. First, families and concoction men are adamant that once families suspect a child, they continue to feed and treat it as a normal child. Even after giving a child a concoction, families and concoction men indicated that care continues. I did not encounter strong evidence of families completely neglecting a spirit child under their care, by, for example, letting it starve. It seems that most families attempt to meet the child's basic needs relative to their own nutritional and economic positions.

I believe that maintaining a basic level of care occurs because many families with spirit children are never entirely sure their child is a spirit and maintain hope for resolution of whatever issue or condition is at hand. The circumstances can differ for families that are positive their child is a spirit or that refuse to entertain alternative explanations. In these cases, my sense is that subtle distancing and changes in the intensity and quality of care occur and that for children that are ill, malnourished, or otherwise fragile, even small changes in attention and caregiving can influence their health. While families report no changes in caregiving, I suggest that as circumstances deteriorate, particularly if the mother is ill or the family is in chaos, caregiving patterns shift from the ideal described.

Some families with spirit children did appear to be less attentive and responsive to their children's needs and engaged in less close contact and face-to-face engagement, particularly compared to the attention given to normal children (this was not so for all families). This could be due to a range of factors, such as fear of the child and its spiritual aggression or simply feeling overwhelmed, sick, and exhausted. For example, Azuma progressively became more burdensome as her family became increasingly suspicious and stressed. Caregiving was minimal and done with reluctance, and she was rarely passed around or played with. The family did not meet her demands quickly or with enthusiasm, feedings were infrequent and short, and family members frequently complained about her. Neighboring families noted that they were not surprised that Azuma was not receiving the food supplementation provided by AfriKids, and that the adults and other children were consuming it. This resulted in a cycle in which Azuma's disengagement and failure to thrive reinforced the family's detachment and suspicions.

As I detail in the concluding chapter, however, Azuma's family's attitude toward her was transformed after she was sent to a feeding center, gained weight, and began to walk. After the crisis period passed, the family went from minimally interacting with her to overwhelming her with attention and affection. In the following years, Azuma remained healthy and well fed. The head of the household, who once rejected and wanted nothing to do with her, cared for her. Family members worked to integrate her into age-appropriate activities and roles despite some remaining additional needs. The change in care and attention was dramatic. Without it, Azuma would not have recovered from her illnesses and begun to thrive. In other words, if Azuma had continued to experience the same level of care she was receiving when I first encountered her, she would have died regardless of any concoction treatments.

Finally, many people are curious about the demographic characteristics of spirit child deaths, particularly the age at which the deaths most often occur. I previously published demographic and verbal autopsy data from a limited time frame and area, and I discussed the challenges of enumerating spirit child deaths (Denham et al. 2010). Although a detailed descriptive analysis of the larger districtwide data set is not available, the more than ten years of data do indicate that more than half the spirit child deaths, whether intentionally caused or the result of illness, occur within the first year of life. Only rarely does a death occur after the age of four. Additionally, there are no gender differences. My ethnographic data support these general observations.

Spirit child deaths cannot be directly attributed to an act of poisoning or infanticide. Spirit children die because of their medical conditions, poverty, and inability to access medical care and ongoing support. Spirit children die because existing health issues and other vulnerabilities are exacerbated by subtle, passive, and possibly unconscious means, such as changes in familial engagement and caregiving, which can speed their decline. In these cases, families might attribute children's deaths to the *dongo*, if one was used, or simply to the child's own desire to return to the bush. Spirit children who are fragile or ill die, in some cases, because families administer a concoction of mild toxicity and questionable potency. Finally, some spirit children die because families give them a strong, toxic concoction.

Prolonging Death:
The Case of Samuel

Samuel is a child with cerebral palsy supported by AfriKids. After exhausting his treatment options and under pressure to do something about Samuel, his father, Apoore, sought out a concoction man. The concoction man he found happened to be working with AfriKids to identify and help suspected spirit children.

After a lengthy drive into a section near the Burkina Faso border, I followed Joe along a path that snaked its way through the tall millet until it ended in a small clearing in front of Samuel's family compound. A small child ran into the fields to find Samuel's father, and the mother was called from inside the compound. There were several goats and fowls milling around the compound, most of the rooms had sheet-metal roofing, and the senior brother, who worked as a public servant in a nearby city, was finishing the construction of a modern-style cinderblock house next door. I later learned that, despite the general appearance of wealth and the extended family's status, there were significant economic differences between family members.

The older brother supported much of the extended family and paid for Samuel's treatments. However, in the previous year, the brother had withdrawn his support, saying that he could no longer afford or justify Samuel's expensive biomedical and traditional treatments. He encouraged Apoore to consider whether Samuel was a spirit child, a sentiment that was already circulating throughout the extended family and community. Apoore and Awoko, Samuel's mother, increasingly recognized that he might be a spirit child. His condition was not improving, and it was becoming increasingly difficult for them to meet not only Samuel's needs but also their own.

Awoko emerged from the compound with Samuel hoisted on her hip. Apoore soon came in from his work in the fields. Samuel was wearing only a shirt. Although this makes toileting easier to manage and is common with an infant, at twenty-seven months of age Samuel should have been wearing shorts and been under the supervision of the other children, who had now gathered around to see what was happening. Joe took Samuel into his arms and sat next to me. It was apparent that Samuel had poor motor control and muscle tone: he could not hold his head upright, his body was stiff, and he could not coordinate his movements.

I asked Awoko when she had noticed that something was different about her son. While handing me his Ministry of Health record containing his birth, developmental, and medical history, she explained that right after his birth, he started to exhibit "stiffness" in his body, which spread among all his limbs. His medical record indicated that he was consistently below the World Health Organization's weight recommendations; six months before my visit, he had weighed 7.3 kilograms (16 pounds), and judging from his current appearance he had gained little in the interim.

I learned from the medical record that in his first six months of life, Samuel had made five trips to the community health clinic. On October 27 Samuel was diagnosed with malaria. Two weeks later, the card indicated that his mother brought him to the clinic because he cried loudly when urinating and defecating. No diagnosis was recorded. On December 1 Awoko reported a fever and crying again and, on the twelfth, a fever, vomiting, and cough. On the twenty-fifth, he was again diagnosed with malaria. Ten months passed before the next entry in his record, which indicated a diagnosis of cerebral infant paralysis. It was difficult to determine from the record whether the cerebral palsy was attributed to brain damage resulting from the fevers, a difficult birth, or a prenatal issue, although Awoko's later description points to a difficult labor. The last entry on his medical card recommended that he receive a pediatric and neurological consultation at a hospital in Kumasi, six hundred kilometers away. The cost of such a specialist consultation was out of the question for the family.

Awoko, who was likely around thirty-three years old, looked healthy. She has been caring for Samuel, her third child, full time since his birth and was unable to do much work around the home or farm, a serious concern for her and other family members. She also had a twelve-year-old daughter, her second child. Her first child had died soon after she gave birth.

Awoko said that when she was four months pregnant with Samuel, she noticed something was different from her previous pregnancies. She tired easily, frequently having to stop and rest while walking or working.

"Was the birth itself unusual?" I asked.

"The labor started in the night. There were some pains, but it was not time for him to come. I thought it must be a sickness or something. I could not urinate, and it was very painful. So, I waited until the next morning, and we went to the hospital. When I got there, they said it was labor. I had to wait awhile, and they said they had to do an operation. They did the operation [caesarean section], and I had the child. They kept us in the hospital for nine full days."

Four days after returning home, Awoko heard Samuel cry out in the middle of the night. She said he was experiencing *tiisi* (lit. "trees"), which brought on seizures or convulsions (*niiŋa*). Conditions in the general category of mental abnormalities, such as seizures and mental illness, are understood as being caused by malicious tree spirits.

During Samuel's first year, family members visited a range of biomedical providers, traditional healers, and herbalists without success. Desperate, they traveled to Burkina Faso to visit a noted healer at the suggestion of a friend. The healer attempted to determine the true cause of Samuel's problems, Awoko said. He sacrificed a fowl and made a small incision in Samuel's forehead where he applied a mixture of herbs. The treatment was unsuccessful.

At four months, Samuel stopped breast-feeding. Awoko switched him to powered milk when she was able to purchase it, and *koko*, a watery millet porridge with added seasonings and sugar, which provides inadequate nutrition. The possibility that Samuel was a spirit child arose and was confirmed by a diviner. Despite the rumors within the community and their own suspicions, Apoore and Awoko remained uncertain and continued to search for a treatment.

"Do you think he might be a spirit child now?" I asked.

"To be a spirit child," Apoore explained, "there must be other things that determine it, not just sickness. With Samuel, it's only sickness. He doesn't do any other abnormal things in the house. But when we had done all the treatments and there was no improvement, the only thing that we could do was go to the soothsayer to find out."

Apoore hesitated, then continued, "When his mother was pregnant, she would go to the clinic for prenatal care. Once, as she was walking there, she stopped to rest beneath a baobab tree and picked a baobab fruit to eat. She didn't know it, but that place is where they usually bury spirit children. That is what happened; they gave her a spirit child."

Awoko agreed that this was probably the best explanation. She noted that other children Samuel's age were already walking and were able to be left with others while their parents went out to work. "I cannot go anywhere to work," she said, "and this child will not even be able to help us work. It's a hardship."

"She will help with the sowing or the harvest, the millet, groundnuts, rice, all those things," Apoore added. "But now she cannot do that kind of work. The child cannot go anywhere, and it is always crying."

Despite their suspicions, Apoore and Awoko remained hopeful that one day Samuel would be able to sit alone or even walk. They put a great deal of faith in AfriKids and biomedicine and continued to seek treatment. However, over the next year they recognized that a cure was increasingly unlikely. AfriKids attempts to find residential homes for children with special needs, but in Samuel's case the few homes in the country were unaffordable or at capacity and had long waiting lists. In the meantime, he went from one illness and medical crisis to the next. Somehow, he would always pull through.

In an effort to give Awoko the opportunity to earn some income while caring for Samuel, AfriKids gave her a small loan to purchase items for a mixed-goods trading business at the market. When she would arrive at the market, however, Samuel would begin to cry and demand constant attention. People made comments about him as she tended to his needs, speculating that he was a spirit. Meanwhile, Apoore's brother continued to pressure them to send Samuel away rather than relying on the microfinance project.

Despite their difficulties, over the next year Samuel's parents moved away from the possibility that he was a spirit child. This was due in part to their fleeting hope that his condition would improve and because of AfriKids' assistance. AfriKids staff would also frequently emphasize that, despite Samuel's condition, the family should let him die naturally. I wondered if the family would make a different choice if AfriKids were not involved.

Apoore and Awoko were in a difficult position. They wanted to be free of Samuel's and their ongoing suffering, but they lacked the skills and resources needed to care for him while meeting their own needs. AfriKids brought disability specialists to show them how to care for Samuel by, for example, exercising his limbs and using sand and props to help him sit upright. These services were sometimes helpful. However, their lives were seemingly on hold as they waited for a miracle or death. They diligently cared for Samuel while longing for a return to normalcy. They wanted to have another child but recognized the impossibility of this unless a dramatic improvement in Samuel's condition freed Awoko.

I continued to visit Samuel every few weeks over the next year. During most visits, he was sick, crying, and malnourished. Awoko was regularly taking Samuel to or from the nearby health clinic. My field notes from each visit included lengthy descriptions of his poor physical state and accounts of Awoko's struggles. Each visit chronicled some condition that placed him near death, such as malaria and ongoing respiratory infections. Once he had terrible sores in and around his mouth that prevented him from swallowing. Awoko often described him as not sleeping, crying frequently at night, and screaming when having to defecate, possibly a consequence of his chronic dehydration. My notes describe eye infections, stiff and nearly immobile limbs, and severe malnutrition. He could not sit unaided and needed to be constantly held. His physical presence was unnerving, partly because we (his family, AfriKids, and I) recognized that he was suffering terribly.

Physicians visiting the region to whom I described his condition were not optimistic. A pediatrician commented that, although it was admirable that the family was able to do such a good job of caring for him, it was likely that Samuel was one infection away from death. Many people were surprised that he was still living.

In the context of their suffering, it was hard not to reflect on the notion that death would be a welcome release for all. In conversations with fieldworkers and others, both within and outside the community, we wondered whether it would be more humane if the family still viewed him as a spirit and gave him a concoction.

"You know," Apoore said, gesturing toward Awoko, "it's hard, what she is doing. It's very painful to take care of the child. But I say not to kill the child, but wait until a time comes for him to pass away. Still, having something like this is very painful."

"It isn't easy," Awoko agreed. "You know that this child will not be able to do anything on this earth."

Joe and I nodded our heads in agreement and told them we would visit again in a few weeks. As we were walking away in the midday heat, Joe said, "Really, Aaron. The child, he is suffering. The family wants to set him free."

Samuel died early in 2009, likely from malaria or an infection. He was five years old. The same day I learned that he had passed away, I also heard that his mother was pregnant.

Saving Lives or Prolonging Death

From my first visit with Samuel and his family, I wrestled with the ethical perspectives around prolonging the lives of spirit children that were, because of the lack of local resources and services, unlikely to survive. Community members, NGO workers, health professionals, and others familiar with Samuel and similar cases also questioned whether some spirit children would be better off not receiving life-prolonging or "extraordinary" care. Cases like Samuel's and N'ma's raise questions not only about the potential that organizations and interventions have for saving lives but also about their power to prolong death. Do some interventions simply prolong suffering that would not be present if the family received no support or was able to find a concoction man?

Such questions can lead to a slippery slope. Who decides and how do we determine which lives are worth living or how long to prolong a life? Where does one draw the line? I do not tackle these questions directly partly because no single moral or economic framework is suitable for all cases. It is, however, important to consider the points these questions raise in the context of unique cultural, political, and economic circumstances.

I do not raise the issue of prolonging suffering or death to downplay the work of AfriKids and others who have helped spirit children. However, it is important to be aware of the underlying assumptions and models that shape the way interventionists conceive rights and how this influences aid and the moral space of caregiving. AfriKids uses the United Nations Convention on the Rights of the Child (UNCRC) and takes as its foundational position that all lives matter. It does not condone the killing of spirit children. Families are free to make their own choices, but AfriKids encourages them to let the child die on its own regardless of its condition. In practice, a middle ground consisting of discussions and considerations of tradition plays a role, and fieldworkers generally know when to step away (as they did with N'ma).

Nongovernmental and other organizations often tap into globally circulating moral and ethical systems that might not clearly map onto local moral worlds. Other sources critique the UNCRC's universalization of rights, its cost to disempowered groups, and other problems. What is important herein is to recognize the ways in which global discourses and ideologies easily and rapidly circulate without the required technologies, infrastructures, and other resources that the places of origin of these moral systems take for granted. In this sense, the imposition of human rights discourse within the UNCRC is much easier (and, some may argue, cheaper) to extend across social and political-economic divides than providing the concomitant access to resources essential to the enactment and practice of those ideals.

Historically, and to some extent today, families made decisions around the life of a child, and the state or biomedical systems of authority did not impinge. Today, even in rural areas, increasing intervention by systems outside the family, whether it be the state or NGOs, can be framed as a Foucauldian act of "biopower" in which decisions to let someone die, or the power to decide which lives are not worth preserving or prolonging, are removed from family control (Das and Das 2007, 86–87). Scholars have questioned attempts to save the lives of poor children that might not otherwise survive, since such efforts, if successful, can result in increased human misery (Cassidy 1987; Einarsdóttir 2004, 175; Miller 1987). Scheper-Hughes similarly writes that poor children have no say and "cannot protest the international child survival programs and campaigns that can cruelly (although unintentionally) prolong their suffering and death" (1992, 285–86).

Policymakers and NGOs do not have to live with the decisions they influence. Human rights promotion needs to consider the context and long-term perspectives that comprise, for example, the care needs of disabled children throughout their life spans. Local health systems and families, particularly in rural areas, often cannot meet the ongoing needs of infants and children with limited viability or severe disabilities. Surviving with a disability in rural Africa depends on a set of intersecting social and structural factors that, according to Benedicte Ingstad, include the attitude, availability, and resources of the caretaker; the health system; and poverty, unemployment, and the need for rural-urban migration for employment (2007, 239–42).

Universalized ideals and the presence of aid lengthened Samuel's life at a questionable cost. It is easy to target AfriKids in these cases; however, that might be misguided. First, it is important to recognize that AfriKids and other organizations are able to save the lives of many spirit children with treatable conditions. In only some cases are deaths prolonged. Second, from a broader vantage point, I see the protracted deaths as less of an ethical problem concerning intervention and more of a reflection of the global political economy and inequality that reduce life chances and increase the suffering of the poor. The problem of prolonged death and spirit children in general goes deeper into the responsibilities that societies, national and international governments, and multilateral global agencies have to bear to ensure that the necessary infrastructure and services are available to back their conception of rights. In other words, spirit children are not necessarily dying because of a harmful cultural practice, nor is their suffering prolonged due to intervention alone. Samuel and other children would not be spirits if they had been born with access to the resources and support that give families an alternative.

To End a Life:
Mercy Killing and Euthanasia

Not far from people's concerns regarding the ethics of intervention is the question of mercy killing and euthanasia. Are the intentional deaths of spirit children a culturally specific form of euthanasia for children of uncertain viability? The euthanasia question is seductive, as it is easy to reframe the spirit child practice as a culturally sanctioned way to expedite an inevitable and painful death. Perhaps what draws people to compare spirit child deaths to euthanasia is how it seemingly limits the suffering of nonviable children and their families. It can also be an attempt to soften and potentially humanize an infanticide practice that presents to some people a set of uncomfortable realities.

Is the spirit child practice akin to euthanasia? Moreover, what is revealed or concealed by framing it as an act of euthanasia rather than infanticide alone? The Nankani perspective is central to these questions. It is easy to filter spirit child cases through a Euro-American lens shaped by a cultural history of mercy killing, ongoing public debates about the ethics and boundaries of euthanasia, and, in some countries, the availability of euthanasia and related medical services for neonates and others facing extreme suffering and inevitable death.

Euthanasia has an established European history, with evidence of its practice dating to the Greco-Roman world before it was influenced by Christian doctrines that upheld the sanctity of life (Dowbiggin 2007; Van Hooff 2004). While various religious, medical, and philosophical positions are found in European texts dating back hundreds of years, and with additional research and ethics papers

appearing regularly, there is, however, limited evidence and discussion of euthanasia or mercy-killing practices and their associated moral contexts in both
historical and contemporary non-European societies, and of people living in
resource-poor and underdeveloped communities in the Global South.

The absence of euthanasia in these contexts could be explained by the
prevalence of religious or moral prohibitions on killing or suicide or because
there are few identifiable cultural models in other societies that are comparable
to European notions of euthanasia. For infants and children, one might argue
that because infanticide is practiced globally, mercy killing or euthanasia practices are likely common and subsumed under infanticide. However, it is important not to conflate euthanasia and infanticide. A careful distinction needs to be
made between committing infanticide because an infant is nonviable, disabled,
or unwanted and practicing infanticide as an act of mercy to relieve a child's
suffering.

The cross-cultural questions concerning the prevalence of euthanasia are
as much resource and biomedically driven as they are moral, in part because
euthanasia is a medicalized construct and practice and because having access
to medical resources radically redefines the margins, or the beginnings and
endings, of life and one's quality of life. Biomedicine can save or improve the
lives of those otherwise subject to death-causing practices, rendering euthanasia
unnecessary. On the other hand, cases abound in which individuals, particularly
neonates that would have died without sophisticated medical technology, are
unnecessarily kept alive.

I return to the role of biomedicine and resource inequality shortly. I now
define *euthanasia* and examine the representational issues present in euthanasia
and infanticide. I follow this with an analysis answering the question of whether
the spirit child practice is an act of euthanasia.

Euthanasia and related actions intentionally causing an infant's death fit
within infanticide's larger map of induced death (Fletcher 1978, 13). Often people
invoke infanticide within euthanasia discourse in order to promote specific representational strategies and moral agendas. Narratives often draw on the extensive
history of infanticide practiced in Greek city-states, for example, to establish
links among contemporary euthanasia practices, infanticide, and notions of
civilizational and moral progress. Slavoj Hontela and John Reddon caution
that people often deploy infanticide in euthanasia discourse as a "pejorative
term which in ethical and moral terms construes the termination of a neonate's
life as equivalent to murder" (1996, 1275). Einarsdóttir reflects on infanticide's
harsh associations with illegal activities and practices confined to the past or
primitive societies (2006, 197). Indeed, in legal terms, infanticide is associated
with illegality and murder while euthanasia, which is widely practiced and legally

sanctioned in some contexts, often is not considered infanticide (Savulescu 2013, 257) and does not attract primitivistic associations.

Likely noting the diversity of infanticide practices, scholars have attempted to distinguish or qualify forms of infanticide as being "benevolent" (Kohl 1978, 5) or "altruistic" (Resnick 1969). Describing infanticide as benevolent or placing it within the frame of euthanasia notably softens the term by evoking, in part, the notion of a good or gentle death rooted in beneficence rather than brutality or grounded in compassion, not aggression. Notably, the medicalization of euthanasia has also contributed to a sanitization of euthanasia and infanticide by rendering them more palatable. This places them in a frame of controlled and calculated decision-making that evokes clinical associations and the authority of biomedical practice.

The meaning of *euthanasia* differs across individuals, and it is frequently misunderstood and misused in end-of-life debates (Michalsen and Reinhart 2006). A great deal of the confusion results from contextual differences and the fact that many of the fundamental terms and descriptions are used interchangeably. This confusion can have harmful consequences. Terms such as *mercy killing, withdrawing care, terminal care, assisted death, neonaticide, infanticide, benevolent infanticide,* and *postbirth abortion,* for example, overlap or convey different moral and practical meanings, which results in unintentional confusion within and between patients, clinicians, families, and the media (Verhagen 2013, 293). The contemporary discourse around *euthanasia* and the role of the media, among other factors, have broadened the term to the point where *euthanasia* has come to encompass a range of death-inducing practices (Sklansky 2001).

The term *euthanasia,* derived from Greek words meaning "good death," "denotes the practice of ending life in order to bring relief from incurable suffering" (Gesundheit et al. 2006 621). This is possibly the broadest definition. Mark Sklansky (2001) describes euthanasia as a mercy-motivated effort conducted to avoid prolonged and futile suffering by deliberately bringing about the death of an individual in as painless a way as possible. Jeff McMahan's (2002) definition includes the acts of killing and letting die and emphasizes that these actions are motivated by beneficence. In this sense, an act of killing or letting die must satisfy two conditions: "First, that death benefits, or is good for, the individual who dies and, second, that the agent must be motivated to do what is good for that individual and must intend to benefit the individual in bringing about his death" (456).

Euthanasia is distinguished by active and passive inducements of death. Active euthanasia, also commonly referred to as mercy killing, involves deliberately bringing about the gentle death of an individual to avoid unnecessary suffering. Passive euthanasia occurs in the absence of intervention that would have prolonged life (Slansky 2001) and involves withholding further treatment, such as efforts to resuscitate, or the withdrawal of life-prolonging treatment (Gesundheit et al. 2006, 622). Neonatal euthanasia involves the termination of life in situations in which there are serious medical problems with no hope of improvement (Verhagen and Sauer 2005). In these cases, the family and physicians question the viability and quality of life of the neonate or infant due to a number of birth defects. While a range of factors are considered, the goal is often to end the unnecessary suffering of a terminally ill infant, mercifully speed an inevitable death, or end a life that would require extensive resources, long-term dependence on high levels of care, or care that might not be available.

An Act of Mercy?
A Nankani Perspective

For a spirit child case to be considered a form of euthanasia based on the above definitions, Nankani families would need to recognize the suffering of the child; have a motivation rooted in mercy or the alleviation of undue, incurable suffering; act in the best interests or benefit of the child; and cause a gentle or easy death. Before addressing these characteristics, I must clarify the Nankani distinction between killing and murder.

Murder is killing with a moral and often legal judgment attached. Laws in Ghana stipulate that intentionally caused spirit child deaths constitute murder in a legal sense. There is no legal provision for mercy killing. For many Nankani, however, killing a spirit child is not an act of murder. This is not because community members permit indiscriminate killing; killing a human is a reprehensible act. Even during conflict or war, spilling another person's blood on the land is polluting, and sacrifices must take place to purify the land. Decisions around life and death are for God and the ancestors. For many Nankani, killing a spirit child is not murder because the spirit is not human and does not have the traits necessary to attain personhood.

The first characteristic I use to define *euthanasia* is the family's recognition of the child's suffering and its motivation to alleviate undue suffering. When considering and discussing possible spirit children, many Nankani families will split their interpretations into two areas. Depending on the condition of the child, families often simultaneously consider the possibility that the child is a human and the possibility that the child is a spirit. That is, families can speak of the child as a suffering human in need of help while also articulating the distinct possibility that it is a malicious spirit that should be destroyed. Families are often unsure.

If families recognize that the child is suffering, their first priority is to end the suffering by finding a treatment and restoring order within the home.

Families hope that the child's condition will improve, and many will speak of new treatments, miracles, and other transformations that can alter the child and reveal that it is not a spirit. However, families can also move toward perceiving the child as an aggressive object responsible for misfortune. Later, when there is no change in the child's condition or the situation deteriorates, families more seriously consider the child's nonhuman status. When the time comes to cause the death of the spirit, they do not kill to relieve the child's suffering. Killing protects the family by sending the nonhuman spirit back to the bush.

The next characteristic of euthanasia stipulates that the actions are in the best interests of the child. Particularly in the early stages, Nankani families will engage in help seeking in an attempt to heal the child or change their own circumstances. Rather than viewing a death decision as in the child's best interest, families view the decision as in the best interest of the group.[2] In neonatal euthanasia discussions outside Ghana, making decisions that consider the interests of the family can play a role, but it is not as central as in the Nankani case. For example, European families with severely disabled neonates and infants remark that if the child lives, it can dramatically constrain the lives of current and future family members. The financial cost of supporting a severely disabled child, the imposition of lifetime caregiving responsibilities, the differential caregiving burdens placed on mothers, and the degree to which society is able to take some caregiving responsibility are common themes that arise.[3]

The final characteristic concerns a good death. What constitutes a good death will differ across individuals and societies and likely extend beyond Western concerns over maintaining control and peace or, as Frances Norwood (2009) describes, the desire to align the social death with the biological death. In general, for the Nankani, a good death is largely predicated on living a full and good life—living to old age, having children, and sustaining a large cohesive family. Deaths, particularly those that occur early or due to tragedy, are often indicative of some disturbance in the house or other problems, such as spiritual disruption, social disorder, ancestral anger, bad fate, or the malevolence or witchcraft of others. A good death should be swift and without undue suffering. Suicide is unacceptable. While people recognize the suffering of a child and see that death is a preferable outcome, I did not encounter notions of actively speeding a death to reduce pain and suffering. To actively endeavor to kill a family member to ease his or her suffering would be seen as taboo, likely polluting, and an affront to the ancestors and God, in whom the decision to take a life rests. Spirit children are different because of their nonhuman status and the threat to the family they embody.

Finally, I think the Nankani and other observers would say that the manner in which many spirit child deaths occur is far from the good death characterized by euthanasia or done with the intent of easing the experience of the child.

The level of medical technology and support available within a social context and historical period shapes the way the beginnings and endings of life are defined (Einarsdóttir 2008). Euthanasia debates around the active or passive facilitation of death and the unnecessary prolonging of life are largely bound to the financial and biomedical resources that can ensure a good death or contexts that can widen the margins between life and death and ensure a future quality of life that without resources would not be attainable.

Although this is a moral question, it is also important to recognize that the option of euthanasia today is about having the necessary resources to make it a possibility. Conversations about euthanasia in low-income contexts are not simply about how death occurs. They are discussions about having the resources to identify, treat, and manage conditions and then having the opportunity to make the choice for death with compassion and mercy rather than with fear.

8

Why Infanticide? | SENTIMENTS AND THE DYNAMICS OF CHOICE

Esther was four years old when I first met her and her mother, Maria. Esther's family suspected that she was a spirit child when she was a year old and living in the village, after cerebral spinal meningitis left her with brain damage. "It all started with something like a small headache, then a cold," Maria told me. "It was midnight when the whole thing became serious." The local health clinic sent Esther to the district hospital when she started to have seizures. She stayed in the hospital for two months. When she was sent home, she was unable to breast-feed, continued to have petit mal seizures, and was always crying. The family refused to allow her to return to the hospital for a follow-up visit or to purchase her next course of phenobarbital, which was too expensive at fourteen dollars per month. The medication and hospital visit may have stabilized her, but the family was expecting a complete cure.

"When we came back from the hospital they sent her to so many herbalists," Maria recalled. "Some of the herbalists and family started to say she was a spirit child. I knew it was a sickness; some children fall sick and become paralyzed, so I told them it is sickness. But they were saying that if it's sickness, how is it that you stay in the hospital for so long and are not cured?"

I asked Maria what her husband thought.

"At first," she replied, "he didn't believe she was a spirit child, but at last he believed that she's a spirit child."

Within a few months after Esther left the hospital, and as her condition continued to deteriorate, the family indicated that it wanted to give Esther the concoction. Maria refused and fled with Esther to Accra. When they arrived in

Accra, Esther was not eating. Fortunately, Maria had a friend with a child who suffered from a similar disability who showed her how to feed and care for Esther. Esther's mother and father decided that it would be best for them to stay in Accra and see if her condition improved. Over the next three years, with her mother's careful attention, Esther grew but could not walk, talk, respond to sounds, or feed herself. Although she was apparently very well cared for, there were no signs of improvement. Since Esther required full-time care, Maria could not work. According to Maria, Esther's father, who worked as a general laborer, could not support them both on one income. Exasperated, he decided it would be best for Esther and Maria to return to his family in Sirigu and not go back to Accra until the child was, in his words, taken care of. Esther was Maria's first child.

Researchers have speculated that the spirit child phenomenon seemingly disappears when residents migrate to urban areas in southern Ghana. According to Fred Binka, former director of the NHRC, migrants bring divination, social structures, and other cultural familiarities with them when they relocate, save for the spirit child. "How do you leave that behind?" he asked. "Somewhere in that mystery is the answer" (Lothian 1996).

Indeed, people do not necessarily abandon their beliefs and social networks when they migrate, and migrants remain connected to their families at home through visits and remittance payments. Families do, however, carry spirit child beliefs to the south; it is the treatment of the spirit child that physically remains in the north. The ritual power of the *dongo* remains ecologically fixed. Suspected spirit children must therefore return to their ancestral land for treatment and burial, as the local landscapes, both physical and imagined, are essential to positioning the spirit child and returning it to its origins.

Despite a lack of improvement and the grim prospects associated with a return to the north, Esther's mother remained hopeful. We took Esther to the doctor for a checkup, and he explained that little could be done to reverse her condition. Maria, a Christian convert, placed her faith in God: "What the doctors say is very hard for me. For me, I believe that God can do anything at any time. When the doctors say they cannot do anything, I leave everything to the hands of God."

As it did for Samuel, AfriKids attempted to place Esther in a home or residential school for disabled children but was unable to do so. AfriKids also arranged for a disability specialist to visit Esther and her mother several times a month, offering support and education. Her husband's family, with whom Maria continued to live when I was conducting fieldwork, knew that AfriKids was looking for a home for Esther and became suspicious of its failure to find a solution. "My family was saying that the child was so powerful that AfriKids has been through all the schools and they have not found any for us," Maria explained. "When the family talks about Esther, they do not come in the house but stand outside and talk. This last time, I heard them saying that the child has some powers."

Three months after Esther and Maria returned to Sirigu from Accra, the situation became more critical. One afternoon, while Esther was napping, her mother left her in the care of a family member and went to the market. As she was leaving the house, she saw a strange man entering but did not think this was unusual until she returned from the market. Esther was crying, and something was not right about her. She refused to eat or drink, could not swallow properly, and was unsettled. Later Esther developed red sores in her mouth and throat. The mother was sure that one of the elder women of the house, maybe her mother-in-law, had given Esther the concoction. She suspected that the man entering the compound as she left for the market might have been a concoction man delivering the poison.

Family members were strangely silent about what had occurred when she was away at the market despite rumors in the community that a concoction man had come to the house. Over the following two weeks, Esther refused all food and most liquids, then slowly regained her appetite. Maria never left her side again, carrying Esther, with considerable difficulty, everywhere she went.

Several months later, Maria reconnected with her friend in Accra who also had a disabled child and found that she was opening her home to other children with disabilities. AfriKids facilitated a trip to Accra for Esther and her mother, where Esther was given a place in this home. The arrangement soon fell through, however, and they returned to the village. Over time, despite the setbacks, it seems that her family became more accepting of Esther as she continued to live in its compound and life proceeded without incident. Months later, I found that Esther's grandmother had become more accepting of her. Rather than avoiding her, she held, smiled at, and fed her.

Ester died in late 2009 at the age of six from an unrelated illness. Maria, devastated, returned to Accra to live with her husband.

Unlike N'ma's case, Maria refused to accept the spirit child accusations and devoted herself to caring for Esther despite family pressure and the poor prognosis. This case is one of several in which mothers resisted a spirit child diagnosis and, in some cases, the will of family members. Why do some family members protect nonviable and spiritually dangerous children? What roles do love and hope play in their responses?

Parental Sentiments and the Dynamics of Choice

Soon after I met Esther and Maria, I mentioned to Joe at the AfriKids office that Esther looked very well cared for. "You know mothers," he said, "they will never leave their children just like that." I frequently encountered declarations, particularly in the context of well-cared-for spirit children, that mothers would never give up on their children. Many of these explanations also referenced innate characteristics of attachment and maternal love. The presumption of maternal love or devotion was shared mostly by outsiders and educated or Christianized Ghanaians, whereas rural, traditional Nankani people offered a more diverse range of sentiments and positions concerning spirit children and infanticide.

Serious anthropological debates concerning maternal sentiments did not emerge until the 1980s, following feminist-oriented movements that assumed a universal notion of motherhood and reflected a growing public interest in attachment parenting and theory. These perspectives were often based on Euro-American assumptions. Sara Ruddick's (1980) rooting of maternal practices within love and the notion that such love is a human universal is an example of this perspective. Few scholars before the mid-1980s published research directly addressing the social and political-economic contexts that surround maternal sentiments toward child neglect, infanticide, and decision-making—domains that are indispensable to informed theorizing on the notion of a "natural mother." Notably, Maria Piers (1978), a psychologist, viewed infanticide practices as a consequence of the underdevelopment of women and the oppression, emotional starvation, and negative life experiences of victim mothers. It is not that maternal love does not exist, Piers argued; rather, it is that a range of social problems interfere with the motherly drive.

It wasn't until Scheper-Hughes's research on scarcity and maternal thinking in Brazil that rich ethnographic evidence disputing the discourse of universal maternal love was provided. She stated that "maternal thinking and practices are socially produced rather than determined by a psychobiological script of innate or universal emotions"—the very determinants suggested by biomedical literature and feminist scholarship (1985, 292). Her research demonstrated that mothers practice a form of passive infanticide or selective neglect with infants that are perceived as being of low quality, while those with a knack for life are saved (Scheper-Hughes 1992). Scheper-Hughes's research emphasized that maternal indifference is closely shaped by the greater political-economic context and structural violence confronting the mothers. She suggested that in impoverished regions with high fertility and infant mortality, mothers will be more likely to neglect their children, particularly those that are vulnerable. In these deaths, culture and psychological defenses such as denial spare mothers feelings of grief.

Scheper-Hughes's work inspired both support and criticism. Some critics suggested, for example, that the withdrawal of parental nurturance was due to powerlessness, the consequences of poverty, and bureaucratic and geographic barriers rather than death-accepting fatalism and selective neglect as an active survival strategy (Larme 1997, 1720–21; Nations and Rebhun 1988). Others, emphasizing complexity, cautioned against universalization of the neglect thesis across cultures (Einarsdóttir 2004). Nonetheless, her work marked a much-needed critical shift in recognizing, conceptualizing, and representing the historical and sociocultural realities embedded within maternal sentiments and passive infanticide practices.

Based on her ethnographic research among the Papel people of Guinea-Bissau, Einarsdóttir contended that cultural values and ethical considerations related to religion and ideologies of kinship also play an important part in shaping reproductive practices (2004, 7). She took a needed integrative approach that moved away from any one universalizing script or position concerning maternal neglect or love. She cautioned against dismissing or reducing practices around nonviable or "nonhuman" children as superstitions that contribute to natural selection, since these perspectives alone do not help us better understand a child's fate in its local context (162). Einarsdóttir's work offers several useful points of comparison with Nankani spirit children.

Meira Weiss's (1994, 2007) research on disability in Israel questions the naturalness of parent-child bonding and offers an alternative, nonmaterialist explanation. Most compelling are her considerations of how disabled or "appearance-impaired" infants challenge symbolic boundaries between the human and nonhuman and the natural and supernatural, leading to stigmatization and rejection. Additionally, she illustrates the relationship between family perceptions of bodily boundaries and the political borders of Israel and describes a relationship among body image, the soul, and how sin is understood to result in abnormal bodily conditions (2007, 120–21).

Infanticide accounts often focus on the mother because infanticide decisions are often hers alone.[1] Similarly, theories concerning the role of attachment, innate drives, and sentiments in infanticide decision-making are maternally focused (Driscoll 2005; Hrdy 1999) and, I posit, can often overlook the role of the entire family system. The challenge is to strive for nuanced understandings of how larger forces such as maternal investment and love, innate traits or drives, and political-economic circumstances are lived, negotiated, and shaped. Since Nankani mothers rarely make decisions concerning the life or death of a child alone, attention to the diversity of families' religious positions, material circumstances, histories, moral worlds, power relations, and other influences help move the conversation beyond maternal drives to more "practice-oriented" explanations (Ortner 2006).

My position on attachment and sentiments around spirit children is flexible and quite similar to Einarsdóttir's (2004) assertions. I posit that no one model of parental sentiments, rationales, or decision-making can be deployed to encompass the range of spirit child variability within Nankani communities or, more generally, of infanticide cross-culturally. The following sections present a range of family sentiments and responses to spirit children.

As described in chapter 2, families begin to develop a relationship with the child as soon as the mother realizes she is pregnant. The father and the family head will consult diviners throughout the pregnancy in an effort to "get to know" and understand the coming child—particularly its gender, desires, and destiny within the family. The divination functions in a similar way to an ultrasound, being able to detect not only potential abnormalities but also the intentions of the newcomer and the family's current relational dynamics. The coming of a child is fraught with ambiguity, and in the first months after a child is born, the family closely scrutinizes it to confirm its intentions. Despite some ambivalence, families engage infants, attempt to interpret their behaviors, and personify them from an early age. My sense is that families can simultaneously remain cautious of a child, particularly an abnormal child, while also forming a relationship and emotionally investing, even tentatively, in that child. Attachment is not necessarily an all-or-nothing or either-or process.

The delayed bestowal of names or attributions of personhood is often cited as evidence demonstrating that families postpone attachment. One rationale is that parents form tenuous bonds with infants that have a low likelihood of survival, particularly in difficult ecological or economic contexts, and that they wait for an important milestone to occur before naming the child (Hrdy 1999, 468; Scheper-Hughes 1992, 413). Late naming is supposed to make grief following the loss of a child easier to endure (Lancy 2008, 55–56; Scrimshaw 1984, 443). While this may have been the case historically, I did not see a consistent contemporary connection between delayed naming and bonding with Nankani infants. I do not doubt that late naming, such as in N'ma's case, plays a role in shaping some parental sentiments or is a reflection of a family's degree of attachment. Indeed, a generic name could offer some psychological distance from a potential spirit child that would likely soon die or be killed. However, I observed a number of family members name and emotionally and economically invest in a disabled or significantly ill child, such as Leah. Delayed naming can be one of many ways families manage or attenuate their attachment to an ambiguous or suspicious child.

As with naming practices, the sentiments expressed around the loss of a child are often used as evidence to assess parental attachment. For the Nankani, the grief surrounding the loss of a child, normal or otherwise, can be significant and illustrates—as Marjorie Shostak also noted in her observations of the !Kung—that living within an area of high infant mortality does not make the pain resulting from the illness or death of a child any less profound (1981, 182). Following the deaths of children in a range of health statuses, I often witnessed profound parental grief, despite a taboo in some families that forbade crying upon the death of a child under two years of age. Crying might interfere with the child's passage back to God or crying during the burial could result in the child being reborn to its mother. Displays of grief around the death of a child are not the most reliable measure of attachment. Withholding grief in public or even among family members does not indicate that parents are cold and indifferent to infant mortality.[2]

The positions people take surrounding the identification and death of spirit children vary. "When the men go to the soothsayer's house," a grandmother said, "and say that a child is trying to kill you [the mother], some women will never go near the child again. Other women, no matter what you do, no matter how the child behaves, they will never give up and allow them to kill the child." Einarsdóttir observed similar diversity in maternal responses to spirit children among Papel mothers, describing how some mothers fight for the survival of their disabled or deviant children, some hinder the diagnostic process, and others resist, without success (2004, 160).

Family power relations also play an important role. During a women's group meeting, a Nankani opinion leader explained that a mother's response to an ill or abnormal child is dependent on family gatekeeping, such as whether the father is amenable to sending the child to a clinic or wishes to manage the illness traditionally. "It also depends on the woman," she said. "If she is capable of sending the child to the hospital without telling the husband, she can do it to save the child. But there are some women who are submissive to the extent that even when the child is dying, they still respect the husband by not sending the child."

Nankani people generally held at least one of three positions or inclinations toward spirit children, each demonstrating how individual dynamics intersect with family power relations and contextual constraints. In the first group, women and men refused to accept the spirit child diagnosis and actively resisted attempts to pursue a diagnosis and give a concoction despite allegations or pressure. Second, some people said that, while they might not agree or feel comfortable labeling a child as a spirit, they would (or did) consent to the diagnosis and supported using the *dongo* because they felt they ultimately did not have the power to decide otherwise or they feared that their lives or the lives of others would be at risk. Finally, some expressed a strong aversion to a suspected spirit child and would distance themselves from the child and support its death. In each of these categories, tensions often emerged between individual feelings and desires and the needs, constraints, and decisions within the family.

Resisting the Diagnosis:
Empowerment and Its Consequences

When mothers and fathers commented on the strength and innateness of parental bonds as a reason for remaining invested in their children, the affective qualities were not referenced as much as the mothers' physical investment in, and their anticipation of, the child's future. A woman would never give up a child, people said, because mothers "suffered" during pregnancy and childbirth. "This is the way God made us," remarked a woman. "Being pregnant for nine months and carrying the baby. We know how all the suffering is. So, when we give birth to children, no matter their condition, we always have mercy on the child. We won't say it's a spirit child and be forced to throw it away."

This perspective is not unique to the Nankani. Einarsdóttir similarly discussed Papel women who perceived mother love as originating in the suffering and burdens of birth and in caring for the child (2004, 86). This suffering, however, has great rewards. For both the Papel and Nankani people, children bring joy, extend the lineage, and help ease one's workload later in life. Reciprocity is thus central to parent-child relationships. Many parents expect their children to continue to reciprocate as they age.

Notably, a spirit child can disrupt expected exchanges since the child in question may never reciprocate. However, for some families, the future return makes little difference. Family members who resist the spirit child diagnosis, despite the evidence, remain hopeful that the child will be cured or that their circumstances may change. For the Papel people, hope for a cure keeps mothers breast-feeding (Einarsdóttir 2004, 161). For the Nankani, hope presses family members to search for treatments and alternative explanations and can spur resistance to accusations.

Some mothers remarked that no matter what other family members might say, they would not agree with a spirit child diagnosis and their perspective would not change even if they believed their child was responsible for a maternal illness. "I would allow the child to do whatever harm it caused me," one mother said. "I would not agree that they should kill the child." The concoction men also described circumstances in which they went to administer the concoction and mothers would disagree with the decision to kill.

When a mother disagrees, her family may distract or deceive her, as in Esther's case. A family might hide the *dongo* and administer the concoction when she is not looking. Before modern boreholes were installed (when a water source was distant), family members would send resistant mothers to fetch water or run some other errand so they could administer the concoction. Many mothers admitted that they had little power to stop others intent on giving a concoction. In some cases, however, both mothers and fathers said that if they suspected their family was going to trick them, they would run away with the child.

Although it is risky and requires determination, running away with a child is an option. A mother who chooses to run needs to draw on her network of sympathetic friends or family members willing to take her in and hide the child. Mothers who run usually travel to a distant city or urban area. "There's a woman at my house," a middle-aged mother said, "who they told had a spirit child. She ran away with the child and then sent the child away somewhere. The family was not able to collect the child and, as of now, the child is living. So, if the women are courageous and they do not entertain any fear, they can find a way out."

Curious about this process and its consequences, I asked a man what might happen if a woman ran off with a child and was caught. "Is it serious?" I asked.

"No, you can only hide and take the child away," he responded.

"But can she ever return to the family? What would the husband do?"

"If the condition of the child is better, she can return. The husband can't kill [the mother]."

"But he can make her life difficult." I said.

"You see, it will be some time, maybe a month. She and the family will not be on good terms for that time."

People described the child's temporary departure as allowing time for its condition to improve, issues or misfortunes to be resolved, tensions to dissipate, and any urgency to pass. Family members may later accept the child back into the home with the realization that it is not a spirit after all.

The removal of a spirit child from the home, however, does not work in all cases. Several families expressed concern that a spirit child, even one living hundreds of kilometers away, can still spiritually travel or "fly" back to the family to kill and cause misfortune. I heard accounts of families actively seeking out suspected spirit children understood to be continuing to cause misfortune from distant locales.

Some mothers are able to resist and fight the diagnosis and use of the *dongo* while remaining at home. For example, one mother, who had already experienced the intentional death of her child, adamantly refused to allow the concoction man to use the *dongo* on a subsequent child. In a similar situation, a man, recalling his sister-in-law's response, said, "She came out of the room to the front of the house where we were discussing the situation and said that she would not agree that this child was a spirit child, that we should allow the child to do whatever it wanted to do to her. In that case, nothing happened. Now the child is in grade five."

Fathers also actively refuted spirit child diagnoses. I recorded the case of a man who refused to accept that his child was a spirit child despite his wife's insistence. "Everyone gathered to see the child," the man's brother said. "They all described it as a spirit child, but my brother said it was not." Consequently, his wife fled alone. "Our family even tried to kill the child, but my brother sent it to Tamale [to live with relatives]. That was ten years ago. Today the child is very active, even normal."

Despite doing everything they can to stop spirit child proceedings, some parents are unsuccessful. Successful resistance depends a great deal on the family and the strength of its conviction that the child is dangerous. When describing her sister-in-law, a woman remarked that, despite her protests, resistance, and threats to run away, the family administered a concoction and the child died. "The mother wasn't happy at all," she said. "After that happened, she wept and wept and wept for months."

The mothers and fathers that are best able to go against their family's wishes are those that feel empowered to do so and have the necessary network and social capital on which to draw. The more social capital a mother has, the better chance she has to find an alternative option. A woman observed that a mother might not directly approach an NGO or someone for help but might consult a close friend and "whisper into the person's ear: 'They say my child is a spirit child, but I want to save my child. Can you help me?'"

From the perspective of some families, resistance can be deadly. People told of a mother's or father's resistance that resulted in delays and further misfortunes or loss of life. A concoction man described a case in which a mother did not agree and the family delayed giving the concoction. "Later the child killed the mother," he said. "At another house nearby it was also the same thing."

A mother who resists is usually subject to stigma and the added burdens associated with caring for a high-needs child. "It's hard doing what I'm doing," Maria said. "It's very painful to take care of Esther. But I will not say to just kill the child. If it should die, it should see its own end." Despite this, she continued, "It is painful to see other people walking with their children, being free, doing their own things."

Scholars describe mothers that use practical reasoning and behavioral strategies to vary their investment in infants depending on their potential, circumstances, and future reproductive capacity (Driscoll 2005, 273–74; Hrdy 1999, 316). According to this position, the mothers of costly or nonviable spirit children will rationally respond by adjusting their attachment to the child and supporting infanticide. In these terms, such decisions make good practical sense. However, some Nankani mothers and fathers, despite family pressures and evidence, such as in Esther's case, refute this theory and expend time and resources on children that will not survive or will require a disproportionate level of continuous care. A combination of several factors can shape each decision. Maria's circumstances encompassed many of these, including her education (completion of primary school), her age (early twenties), prior residence in urban Accra, marriage into a relatively high status family, relationships with mothers in similar circumstances, and access to biomedical services that can prolong life. Her Protestant faith, which forbids infanticide and emphasizes the possibility of divine miracles, also played an important role in shaping her expectations, hope, and commitment to continue caring for Esther.

Spirit child cases highlight the importance of considering a broader set of factors that shape the patterns and sentiments around caregiving. If there is an innate script for parental attachment or infanticide, the script and its enactment are molded by culture, context, and range of individual and family circumstances.

There Is No Other Choice:
A Double Bind

A woman summarized the bind that some mothers and fathers confront with a spirit child.

> Some women will easily give the child up. Some of the women run away, because of their love for the child. Some of them, the family will tell them that if you don't do this, something bad will happen. Because of that pressure from the family, they are afraid and they will have to give the child up. Even though they love the child, it's the pressure from the family that makes them.

Women often remarked that even if they objected to the spirit child diagnosis, they ultimately were powerless to influence the outcome. This was perceived in two ways: powerlessness vis-à-vis those with more authority in the family and powerlessness in the face of fear and the perceived consequences of allowing the spirit child to live.

"When the man says that a child is a spirit child," a mother noted, "the woman can't dispute that fact. She has to agree. In the house there's nothing I can do because the man has the power. After giving the child up, I will not be happy for a long time." Similarly, a man said that in some families women have little opportunity to agree or disagree. "The women can't do anything about it. The men decide. Once the men have decided that it is a spirit child, sometimes they come and take the child away without telling the mother. Sometimes the mother will be weeping and they will just ignore her and take the child."

References to the "men" do not implicate the father alone but rather the larger patriarchal decision-making system. In many cases, fathers have minimal decision-making power and are subject to the dictates of the senior men. Recall that a child is traditionally not the property of the mother or father specifically but of the larger family. Fathers, too, are often subject to relationships and circumstances that overshadow their preferences. Other family members said they did not wish to kill the child but that it was unavoidable because the child could continue to cause sickness and death in the family.

I occasionally asked mothers if they would agree if they were told that their child was a spirit child. Most answered no with minimal explanation. However, the responses differed when I asked whether their decision would change if they were sick. For example, while working at a maternal health clinic, I asked a woman, after we had finished weighing her infant, "If your family told you that your child was a spirit child, would you agree?"

"No," the mother responded.

"But what if you were sick?" I asked.

"If I'm sick and they say that it's a spirit child, I will agree that it's a spirit child. I would send that child to the hill. It's because of the child that I'm sick."

"Even if it's this child?" I asked, gesturing to her infant.

"Yes, because he is making me sick." She paused and then continued, "You see, it will not be easy for me, but I will have to do it. If I do not do it, I may die. I won't be happy about it, but I have to allow it to happen."

In a separate conversation, another mother offered a similar response: "It's not easy. You have to kill the child, otherwise it will not be something good for the house. You will not be happy." Another woman remarked that if a child is indeed a spirit child, it is out to get her: "If it showed that it wants to kill me by making me sick, I will not have any feelings toward it." A grandmother explained, "It is very painful; that is not what a woman would wish for, to give birth and kill the child as a spirit child, but sometimes circumstances warrant certain actions."

People frequently say that giving birth to a spirit child is painful. Two interrelated characteristics are generally associated with how families articulate the pain and loss of a child confirmed to be a spirit. First, women and men experience the loss and pain in terms of what the child was expected to be or could have been—a loss of potential. As noted above, family members also characterize this pain as a loss of the time and effort invested in the pregnancy and birth.

People described the birth and death of a spirit child in a manner similar to what Levinas (1998) characterized as "useless suffering," suffering that is absurd, evil, or meaningless. In this sense, it is painful to be pregnant for nine months nurturing expectations and suffering through the birth, only to find that your child is a spirit.

Second, families, but particularly men, experienced distress in terms of the existential shock of having a spirit enter the house. A father commented that when one gives birth to a spirit child, "it's very difficult to understand why that has happened to you." He continued, noting that his concern was not over the loss of the child but over which rituals he needed to perform to ensure that it would not happen again. In these cases, there is great unease over the origin of the spirit, or how it entered the family, and the causal boundaries or moral violations. For example, one man described the pain of having lost his wife shortly after she gave birth to a spirit child but said he was particularly upset over the circumstances that permitted the entry of a spirit in the first place. In another account, a man commented that the most painful part was accepting that the child was from the bush: "Even if you have a child that is a normal human being and it returns [dies], it's better than [the experience of] giving birth to a spirit child."

For family members caught in the bind of having no choice but to kill, significant evidence must be present, and few will support baseless rumors or suspicion.[3] People's attitude toward a child can also shift in either direction as circumstances change. As noted above, power relations, changing family circumstances, improving or worsening health, and fear closely shape responses to spirit children.

I spoke with Mavis about the role of suffering and love and how families change their perceptions of a child and decide it is a spirit. She explained:

> The ailments cause so much agony. Every sickness, the mother goes through hell. If the sickness is on the father, he goes through hell. Because of these, one is compelled to think or accept that allegation. The assumption is if the child is killed, those misfortunes, the trouble or the ailments, will become better. If it is about the destruction of the whole family, the belief is that if the child is killed, peace will return to the family. That is often why the mother has to let go of that kind of affection [love] for the child.

Mavis's explanation emphasizes that family circumstances and fears surrounding a child limit choice, supersede sentiments, and dictate responses to a suspected child. As I explain in detail below, families draw on the spirit child in this case as a cultural model for understanding and for neutralizing the suspected source of the misfortune in an attempt to restore normality.

It is difficult to say how the death of a spirit child affects parents decades later. Mothers and fathers from older generations usually offered pragmatic, brief responses supporting the child's death or noting that they had little choice. One day, I visited an elder named Agotiba to chat about her grandson Amos, who had a mild cognitive developmental delay and was blamed for his mother's illness and death. As we sat down to talk, she declared that she, too, had a spirit child in her younger years. I asked her to tell me more. After some hesitation, she said that her child was sick and her family thought he was causing a food shortage. Like others, she did not see any alternative to his death.

Agotiba took pride in Amos, and our visit that day emphasized how well he was doing. While reflecting on her disclosure and its timing, it was hard not to view her motivation to intervene on Amos's behalf as a respected elder as an opportunity to act on and prevent a death when decades ago she had felt she lacked agency and had no options. Moreover, I recognized that for children like Amos and Victor, a sympathetic grandmother or elder aunt with enough power or distance from the family could provide an alternative and make the difference between life and death.

It Is for the Bush

In previous chapters, I described the circumstances that contribute to families' concerns about spirit children. These include the child's nonhuman status, fear that it will bring further misfortune in an effort to disrupt intergenerational continuity, its inability to participate in relations and reciprocity, and, as I detail in the next section, the cultural models that shape how families come to perceive, condense, and project a range of meanings on its embodied status. While some family members resist accusations, envision and access alternatives, or acquiesce due to family power structures and limited options, a number of people unquestionably support using the *dongo*.

The support of a spirit child diagnosis can involve the intentional initiation of suspicions, and/or facilitating the diagnostic process and use of the *dongo*. A mother, while feeding her six-month-old child, noted, "If the man goes soothsaying and comes back saying it's a spirit child, I won't even touch it. They should just go and kill it." Supporters referred to the immediate dangers posed by a spirit child and/or the threat to their future reproductive potential. "If I die," one mother said, "I'll be unable to have children. If I live, I can have more." One mother's account drew on the common metaphor of a deadly snake, using it as an aggressive object to which to the child's identity can be transferred. "The child is a snake," she said. "When a snake gets you, what can you do? It will bite you, and you will die."

In their fear of the child, families adopt an antagonistic position as a defense against it. The presence of fear can also speed the decision-making process, distancing and further hastening the social death of the child. "It is a wild thing in the family," said a man commenting on a spirit child in his family. "It's a wild thing mixing with humans [and] trying to find the means to quickly kill and destroy the family. If I don't hurry up, it will destroy me first."

The Spirit Child as a Cultural Model

People's experiences and interpretations of spirit children are derived from a range of spirit-related discourses that act as a "source model" used to construct and organize perspectives, experiences, and practices related to misfortune, conflict, and childhood abnormality (Moore 2007, 32). Interpretations of spirit children are at once shared and idiosyncratic. The larger cultural model of the spirit child intersects with the unique moral worlds of families, their relational dynamics, and their histories with abnormal children.

Cultural models play a role in shaping people's interpretations of the world and their behavior in it (Quinn and Holland 1987, 4). They are often taken for granted, convey essential information and ideas, and help to determine meanings. Health-specific cultural models convey ideas about symptom reporting, treatment processes, and possible outcomes and are, importantly, resources that closely shape illness experiences (Kirmayer and Sartorius 2007).

The spirit child is a cultural model that mediates family experiences, sensitizes people around what to expect when confronting a possible spirit child, and shapes sentiments and decisions. The spirit child model is not deterministic. Cultural models are not a script but a set of shared assumptions about the world with reference points that help people understand and generate meaning (Holland 1992, 68). Each individual's engagement with the spirit child model will differ, demonstrating the involvement of a range of conscious and unconscious desires, experiential realities, contradictions, and motivations (Strauss 1992). The diversity of responses to spirit children demonstrates not only how variations in circumstances affect families but also the diversity of models present across clans and individuals.

I do not want to reduce the spirit child to cognitive schema encoded in one particular location. Rather, a more holistic view acknowledges that the models are encoded across individual psychodynamics, people's bodily statuses and practices, intersubjective relations, forms of discourse, and social roles, structures, and institutions. When a family interprets a child as being for the bush, it is drawing on these domains and their intersections. To conclude, I identify some of the individual and family dynamics occurring around the identification of a spirit child. I begin with a discussion of "basic strangeness" (Piers 1978) followed by an exploration of the ways in which spirit children can become a disruptive embodiment, a scapegoat, and a target for aggressive impulses.

As noted earlier, families regard an infant, whether normal or abnormal, with a degree of ambivalence. Similarly, Fortes, in his research with the neighboring Tallensi, described the parents' task as conquering their ambivalence and identifying with their offspring. A parent must "feel them [children] to be so essentially apart of himself (or herself) as to cast out the destructive impulses" (Fortes 1987, 243). The experience of destructive impulses is not limited to Tallensi and Nankani families. Parental ambivalence, particularly simultaneous love and hate for a child, has been known to psychological and psychoanalytic theory for some time (Balint 1949; Parker 1995, 1). Under this theory, the strangeness or otherness Nankani families feel toward an infant is a starting point for any new family member.

On encountering a newborn or possible spirit child, family members might experience a degree of "basic strangeness"—a profound shock of otherness or misrecognition (Piers 1978; Scheper-Hughes 1992, 410). This misrecognition can be exacerbated when a child is born under unusual conditions or has an equivocal physical appearance. In these circumstances, family members might feel a lack of empathy, feel disconnected, or "turn off" and be unable to experience the infant as a human being (Piers 1978, 38). This form of detachment is likely one factor involved when some family members respond aggressively to a spirit child.

Among the Batswana, Livingston noted, deformities and aesthetically challenging bodies "pose problems for some people, parents especially, who experience deep negative feelings toward their children, for whom they are expected to experience unconditional love" (2005, 191–92). Karen Metzler noted that a child's physical condition and attractiveness influence the mother's ease in contact (1978, 173), and Hrdy observed that the sight of a defective newborn is "profoundly disturbing." While people in Western societies suppress these responses, the way people respond, Hrdy continued, has an innate component that is also dependent on resources (1999, 457). While Piers associated basic strangeness with a self-centered drive for survival brought on by poverty, basic strangeness, at least in some Nankani families, is also a reflection of the fact that some children do not fit into predetermined conceptual images of what an infant should be and what it should become. The embodiment and behavior of the spirit child cast it as an other that is separate from humanity.

Weiss's (1994, 1998) fieldwork in Israel found that an abnormal child's appearance influenced whether parents took it home from the hospital and whether they engaged with, neglected, or abandoned the child. She found that deviations from normal body images resulted in cognitive dissonance powerful enough to disrupt the social order. This resulted in stigmatization, rejection of the child as a nonperson, and parents referring to the child in a morally contaminated way, using terms such as *monster* or *devil* (Weiss 1998, 159). Much like spirit children, Weiss depicts families struggling with the identity of their children, wondering, for example, if a daughter is a guest or has the right to claim family membership (1994, 153).

Images of physical weakness and disability can represent concerns regarding social or experiential discontinuity and, importantly, the breakdown of generational succession (Jackson 1979, 126; 2002, 222). Spirit children are a sign of problematic or disordered social relations, in what Beidelman referred to as a "disruptive embodiment" (1993, 121). The disruptive embodiment of a spirit child not only foregrounds the breakdown of house-bush boundaries central to Nankani notions of family, humanness, and personhood, but it evokes the vigilantly guarded social and moral boundaries of the family. Indeed, moral concerns regarding taboos, sexuality, reproduction, pollution, and other products of family and social relations, as Gananath Obeyesekere observed, can be engendered on the child's body (1990, 73). This process is most apparent when a spirit child becomes a scapegoat.

Disruptive Embodiments, Vulnerability, and the Scapegoat

In the diagnosis and treatment of spirit children, Nankani families attempt to transform uncertainty and ambiguity by taking control of a potentially dangerous being and situation. Amid moral ambiguity and uncertainty, families focus on what is evident and visible—the abnormal child—to better understand what is occurring in the hidden realms. In this sense, a family's aggressive sentiments are less about the child than they are a response to other circumstances within the family, as previously described.

As an example, Azuma's father Azaare was drinking excessively, was argumentative, and was away from home too much, "going wherever he wants." A neighbor and fellow clan member, emphasizing his antisociality, said that Azaare had refused to take his younger brother to the hospital when he was seriously ill. "He told me it would be fine if his brother ended up in the earth," the neighbor said. Another man said that Azaare did not care if Azuma's mother, Abiiro, lived or died. "He will just get another one [wife]." What struck me most, however, was a fellow clan member's pointed critique, for he employed the very words widely used to explain the intentions of a spirit child. "He wants to destroy the family," he said.

Joe and Elijah later agreed when I suggested that perhaps the father was the true spirit child. From an interpretive vantage point, the actions and characteristics attributed to the spirit child are not ultimately about an "evil child" that has come into the family. While family members can identify a child as parricidal and consider it responsible for chaos and destruction, in fact these attributions come from within the adult who is interpreting the child's body and actions in terms of usurpation and disorder (Girard 1996, 232). This is also common elsewhere.[4]

Amid a crisis or uncertainty, the family identifies the spirit child as a target on which to project its hardships and uncertainties. In such cases, the spirit child emerges as a scapegoat, symbolic of, and guilty for, the family's misfortune and moral transgressions (Girard 2004). The expulsion of a scapegoat, or the ritual practice of sending the spirit child back to the bush, can effectively send the antisocial events, transgressions, and other associations back to their wild place of origin outside the family. Removing the scapegoat from the domestic sphere also helps remove guilt from the family (Anspach 2004, xxviii). Indeed, sacrifice, purification, and atonement are dominant themes present in the spirit child ritual. In some cases, the spirit child becomes an alibi, relieving the suffering of some family members, fostering unity, bringing events under control, and exonerating individual responsibility through ritual purification.

The scapegoat motif within the spirit child practice is similar to the Greek notion of *pharmakos* wherein, according to Jacques Derrida, a representative of an external threat comes to infect the inside of the city, or in this case the family, by breaking into it. However, in the case of the spirit child, the *pharmakos* is actually constituted from within the house. It is an evil both introjected and projected within the family. Through the ritual destruction of the *pharmakos*, "played out on the boundary line between inside and outside," or between the house and the bush, the identified problem simultaneously becomes the remedy (Derrida 1981, 133–34).

The confrontation of a spirit child brings forth a diverse set of sentiments and responses from family members, and there is no one interpretive script. Rather, a flexible cultural model, along with family circumstances and individual experiences, informs, in part, the larger space of vulnerability in which the spirit child dwells. The final chapter summarizes this space of vulnerability around spirit children and, in conclusion, demonstrates how family perceptions of a spirit child can be transformed as its circumstances improve.

Conclusion

Paul was impressive. Sitting down on a nearby rock still hot from the afternoon sun, he proceeded to play his *kɔlegɔ*—a traditional two-stringed guitar made from a large calabash shell—like an expert. He sang songs about spirit children, urging people not to kill them and to accept children with abnormalities. The topic was close to home.

Several years earlier, Paul's stepfather had accused him of being a spirit child. When Paul's mother was pregnant with him, they had married, and Paul, now around thirteen years old, grew up believing this man was his biological father. However, several years ago, Paul's stepfather began to treat him poorly. One day, he told Paul that he was not his child and did not belong among his children. The spirit child accusation came soon after.

Paul had no abnormalities. It was his unusual musical ability that some found suspicious. However, it seemed likely that Paul's stepfather was looking for an excuse to no longer support him. After being forced out of the house, Paul went to live with his maternal uncle.

Paul does not believe that spirit children exist. "It's likely that God made a mistake, not making one part complete," he said. "For me, in everything there are times that mistakes are made, so giving birth to a child with abnormalities is just natural."

Soon after Paul was kicked out of his house, rumors that he was a spirit spread. In response, he began to compose songs about spirit children. "Playing [the *kɔlegɔ*] is something that gives me wisdom," Paul stated, "and I also use it

Paul playing his *kɔlegɔ* (Stephen Fisher)

to teach people." Since AfriKids has been playing a role in helping bring spirit child awareness to his community, the accusations gradually declined. "The first year when I started, these people talked a lot about it," Paul said. "But over the last couple of years, I seldom hear such talk."

I asked how he felt about people calling him a spirit child.

"Very often I don't say anything in return," he said. "I don't mind them because I know all are deliberate attempts to stop me from what I am doing. I often think that this is something that shouldn't pain me." Occasionally his age mates tease him, but he seems to manage it well. A local primary school teacher explained to me that people are likely just jealous of Paul's talent.

Paul said his song lyrics explain "that deformities are not necessarily a spirit child, but from God's work. I compare the spirit child to a potter or modeler that uses clay; often they make mistakes or what they are modeling is not as accurate as they expected. I liken that to their perception of the spirit child."

"What do you dream for the future?" I asked.

"I really want to be a musician. I know that I will be a great future musician, a great musician in the whole of Ghana."

Paul represents a generation growing up in a context where spirit children are increasingly discussed in terms of their medical and physical condition and where people have improving access to maternal and child health services and a greater awareness of the causes of abnormalities. And there are more people like Paul, for example, using their skills to counter people's misconceptions.

Paul says that the key message in his songs explains that spirit children "could be great men in the future that could stand and help society." At the end of our interview, Paul picked up his kɔlegɔ and began playing a song that makes an appeal to the ancestors.

There Are No Spirit Children in Ghana

Mother where are you? Father where are you?
I am here. I am here.
Someone said that someone decided to kill somebody
A wife has given birth and they want to pick the child
Go 'round 'round 'round with whatever they want.

Father where are you? Mother where are you?
Who is it that's growing the okra?
Somebody is using tricks to kill the future leaders.
Somebody is choosing abnormal people to kill.

They are calling us dwarfs, they are calling us spirit children
They just want to make something up
Are we really spirit children?

Only human beings can decide
That yesterday's human is not today's human being
If a child's head is big
If a child's legs are unequal
If a child's hand is not straight
Then that child is in danger of being accused as a spirit.

Now we have understood it!
Father, we didn't know we were killing children.
We didn't know a child with a big head wasn't supposed to be killed
But now we know
We will kill no more.

Education has come
Now we know our left from our right

Now we are aware and we will no longer kill
There is no spirit child in Ghana.
I'm telling Ghanaians that there is no spirit child.

Father, if you go back to the ancestors, tell them that.
They should stop activities impeding progress today
We are now tired.
Father, you should go back and tell the world.

Father, go back and tell the people that there are no spirit children in Ghana.
Tell the people of Sirigu that they should kill no more.

Paul's generation is growing up within what Ghanaians frequently refer to as a "modern Ghana," which, from their perspective, no longer has room for practices like the spirit child. At the time of my research, the spirit child practice was already becoming less frequent. Older community members said that the spirit child practice was much more common when they were younger. A man in his late fifties recalled a number of spirit child deaths in the past.

> I live near the hill where they abandoned the spirit children. When I was a child, we would follow the animals as they grazed, watching over them. In those days, there were so many spirit children abandoned there. . . . These days it's no longer so, because of the medical treatment we have for them . . . and because the women attend antenatal care, these days when you go to the hill you rarely see any spirit children.

I accumulated similar accounts in which people said that only twenty years ago they would often encounter spirit children left near paths, in the forest, or by rock outcroppings. Many of the elders' accounts throughout this book, like the one quoted above, are based on their experiences before the availability of additional services and interventions or the restraining effects of institutions. Compared to my period of research, the spirit child practices of more than thirty years ago likely involved shorter periods of decision-making and help seeking due to limited maternal and child health services and greater food insecurity. Children and families were even more vulnerable than they are today, and consequently spirit child deaths occurred more frequently. AfriKids and community members report that there were no spirit child deaths in the eastern sections of the Kassena-Nankana Districts from 2010 to 2015. If deaths are occurring today, they are likely happening with greater secrecy and involve concoction men not known within the area.

A women's leader, speaking for the area around Sirigu in 2010, confirmed, "We haven't had records of spirit children over these few years, unlike the past. So, I believe that gradually it is vanishing in this community. The concoction men have been found and sensitized well. They accepted [the message] and threw away their practices. So, we don't hear about spirit children."

The concoction men's practices are not entirely gone. The concoction men I worked with now refer spirit children to AfriKids or medical services, and in 2007 they stopped using the concoction to kill.[1] Several do, however, maintain their *dongos* and conduct the rituals to send the spirits of children that have died for other reasons back to the bush. Now that the concoction men are in contact with each other, meeting several times per year, they regularly discuss techniques and cases. In 2010 they visited a school for children with intellectual disabilities in Tamale to learn more about their conditions.

Some elders believe that social and ecological changes in the region have driven the spirits away. Spirits are afraid to appear, they say, or have vanished due to deforestation and human encroachment in the bush, increased development, and changes associated with modernity. For instance, one elder said that spirits are not interested in the unfamiliar foods people are now eating, such as packaged spaghetti noodles, and have left.

The reduction in spirit child cases can be attributed to a range of public health interventions led by the NHRC and the Ghanaian Ministry of Health, particularly maternal and child health services, community health and immunization programs, vitamin supplementation, and family-planning services. AfriKids' provision of social services, education, and awareness programs provides families with alternatives and empowers many to question spirit child accusations. The Mother of Mercy Babies Home, an orphanage in Sirigu, offers families a place to take spirit children. Increasing rates of school attendance are also shaping people's understanding of illness and disability. Taken together, these changes have resulted in less tolerance of infanticide, particularly in village areas.

It is easy to identify people's attitudes and culture as responsible for infanticide and to target the removal of spirit child beliefs as the best way to induce change. However, the recent social and economic transformations and the availability of alternatives surpass efforts aimed at changing beliefs.[2] While culture plays a role, it is becoming increasingly difficult to blame it for the presence of the spirit child phenomenon and infanticide.

Despite these gains, further improvements in health infrastructure, child and maternal health services, and a range of other health-related domains are needed, particularly in rural areas. People still face limited employment opportunities and rely on labor migration. Subsistence agriculture and weather instability associated with climate change will continue to create periods of food insecurity. Most families have a limited capacity to confront emergencies and are often only one or two illnesses away from depleting their savings — whether in animals or cash. The changes made over the past two decades are significant, but they are tenuous.

It is important to note that this research presents a glimpse into one district. The spirit child phenomenon and related infanticide practices continue in other part of northern Ghana, the Volta Basin, and West Africa, predominantly in regions that are not subject to health and related development programs. Impoverished, rural, and isolated areas typically bear a significant burden of infanticide deaths, in part because, as we have seen, families often have a very limited set of choices. Perhaps some of the insights into family experiences herein will help emphasize that addressing child and maternal health and family well-being can have a significant impact in reducing family vulnerability and the limited choices that can generate the space in which infanticide occurs.

The Spirit Child as a Space of Vulnerability

I have shown that it is incomplete to reduce spirit child deaths to a single explanation and to characterize the spirit child phenomenon solely as an act of infanticide. Attending to Thomas Leatherman's "space of vulnerability," people's coping and decision-making practices are situated within the material conditions, economic strategies, and systems of meaning that are shaped by local, regional, and global histories and dynamics (2005, 48). Rather than considering a single set of spirit child determinants, this perspective offers a holistic framework in which we can examine the relationship that agency and meaning have with context and structure.

For the Nankani, I characterize the space of vulnerability in two ways: structural-contextual and phenomenological. The structural draws from a political-ecological position that links social and structural relations and their production to biological conditions. Leatherman characterized vulnerability as the local and historical intersections of one's risks of exposure to stress and one's risk of inadequate means with which to cope and recover.[3] In this definition, those with limited coping abilities or capacity to access essential resources will suffer the most. Indeed, poverty is central to producing vulnerable states, as are the structural and social inequalities that impinge on people's ability to meet their needs (Leatherman 2005, 50–51).

Second, a phenomenological orientation foregrounds people's experiences of vulnerable states and can emphasize intersubjective spaces and relational dynamics and the way structural and moral worlds are lived. One's own and others' states of vulnerability obligate a moral engagement (Hoffmaster 2006,

43), but this moral engagement need not be limited to caregiving. Vulnerable states can also elicit fearful or aggressive responses. In this case, for example, the vulnerable body, behavior, or misfortune associated with a suspected spirit child can evoke a sense of alterity in family members, which can result in caregiving or, in some cases, a shift in the family's attitude toward disengagement, fear, or aggression as the child becomes a cynosure for what is at stake. In other words, vulnerability can mobilize family members to engage in caretaking *or* it can destabilize the family and provoke othering responses. Framed in these two perspectives, factors shape a space of vulnerability in spirit child cases in at least three interrelated ways.

First, individual experiences and family histories of spirit children, the moral imagination, spirit-related discourses, and related cultural models shape one's interpretations of a vulnerable child and one's vulnerable family. The presence of vulnerability and abnormality may thus become entangled within concerns regarding marriage stability, patriarchal power relations, family conflict, intergenerational relations and continuity, and moral rupture. Accordingly, a spirit child can embody the issues most at stake within a family.

Second, the presence of a child with chronic illnesses or special needs places significant pressures on a family. When families say that a spirit child is destined to kill family members or destroy the house, this reality is not so farfetched. For a vulnerable family, a child with excessive needs can deplete limited resources, prevent the mother from working, and render the family more vulnerable to collapse, especially when future difficulties arise. A spirit child can also prevent the mother from having another child, furthering family concerns around intergenerational continuity.

Finally, structural contributors such as poverty, inequality, the colonial and postcolonial marginalization of the northern regions, food insecurity, limited access to medical services and education, and limited support for disabled children impinge on life chances and narrow the possibilities available to families and children.

In spirit child cases, the space of vulnerability model is not deterministic or predicative, and the way this space is constituted and how the realms intersect will differ for each family. However, understanding the potential ways in which cultural models and spirit discourse interact with, for example, limited disability resources and concerns about the origin of family conflict can render more holistic and sensitive understandings of infanticide.

Coming to the conclusion that a child is a spirit is often a last resort, a diagnosis born more of fear than of choice. In many cases, however, as circumstances change so, too, do the spaces of vulnerability and families' attitudes toward spirit children. Options and alternatives, ranging from medical treatment to empowerment, can ease suspicions and cast doubt on the spiritual status of a child. Azuma's case is one such example.

Azuma Returns Home

After our previous visit, Abiiro's husband and the other men in her family had met to discuss Azuma. The men discussed whether they should proceed with the concoction or accept AfriKids' offer to connect Abiiro and Azuma with help. At this point, Abiiro was still frustrated and unsure about Azuma, and my sense was that she was desperate for any sort of change. Soon after this meeting, Elijah and I returned to their house to find that the family had agreed that they should try any available treatment before giving the concoction. AfriKids took Abiiro and Azuma for a medical check and placed them in a feeding center for malnourished children and their mothers in Bolgatanga.

During their three-month stay at the center, Azuma and her mother were given food, a chance to rest, and an opportunity to participate in education programs with other women and children. Seven weeks after their arrival at the feeding center, Joe and I visited them. As we entered the building, Abiiro, beaming, uncharacteristically leapt up and ran to hug me. The swelling in her leg had diminished. She called for Azuma, who stood and walked unaided across the courtyard toward us. Both Azuma's and her mother's faces were rounded. I learned that Azuma had spoken her first words a few weeks earlier: "N'ma" (My Mother) and, quite appropriately, "Mam di" (My food). With medical care, good nutrition, and a chance for Abiiro to rest and focus on caring for herself and Azuma alone, they made rapid gains.

Azuma and Abiiro lived at the feeding center for three months. During that time, I took Ayisoba, the concoction man who also happened to be a fellow clan member and aware of her circumstances, to visit Azuma. Her transformation astonished him. On seeing her standing next to Abiiro unaided, he removed a handful of money from his pocket, ran over to Azuma, and, saying nothing, stuffed it into her fist as if he had lost a bet. After delivering a hearty laugh, he then turned to exclaim to me that wonderful things can happen.

A month after their return home, I stopped by Azuma's house for a visit. As I was walking up to their compound, I saw Azuma in the distance, running and playing with the other children. Her left eye still wandered, and there was still that layer of snot crusted on her upper lip, but it was cracked this time by a beaming smile.

"Do you still think that she might be a spirit child?" I asked Abiiro.

"That's not the case," she replied, glancing toward Azuma. "I have a different mind altogether. It was just some sickness. She's not a spirit child. There's no need to call the concoction man."

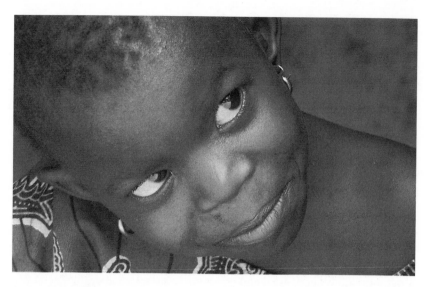

Azuma (Stephen Fisher)

The rest of her family agreed. In my periodic visits over the years, I watched Azuma grow and make gains developmentally. Although she lagged behind other children her age in speech and some cognitive abilities, she could complete small tasks around the house and family members were patient with her.

Nearly four years after the suspicions first emerged, Azuma's grandmother reflected on the past and the reasons why the family thought she was a spirit child. "The situation was getting worse and worse," she said. "All the things we did to help solve the problem were not doing anything. That made us believe she was a spirit child. We could not hear or understand her, but now she speaks and we understand. If a child speaks and you can't understand or you can't even hear her, you would obviously conclude that she was a spirit child. Under normal circumstances, we know how children develop. We expect them to learn from their parents; her situation was different. But as of now, we have come to understand that the situation has changed. Now she is a normal human being."

Similarly, a senior sister-in-law remarked, "Yes, I admitted that she was a spirit child years ago, but as of now, she is a normal child. She is our daughter."

Tensions between Abiiro's husband and the family seemed to have lessened. He is still rarely home, but few seemed to care. During my most recent visit with Abiiro, she had only positive things to say about Azuma. "She can eat well, play with her friends, and move around. Now I can also do other things to earn a living." And with no hesitation she added, "I love her so much."

NOTES

Introduction

1. For example, see Scrimshaw 1984.
2. See Lancy 2008; and Scheper-Hughes 1992.
3. See Allotey and Reidpath 2001; Amenga-Etego 2011, 36; Awedoba 2000; Cassiman 2006; and Howell 1997, 213.
4. "Ayisoba" and other pseudonyms are frequently used throughout the book, and some details have been changed to ensure privacy.

Chapter 1. Contextualizing Infanticide and Northern Ghana

1. See Shaw 2006, 256.
2. See the similarity of this definition to Susan Scrimshaw's (1984, 442).
3. See Porter and Gavin 2010, 99.
4. This was influenced in part by Michael Jackson's framing of an existential anthropology, in particular his emphasis on attending to the "critical moments" that define people's lives and the often ambiguous and irreducible periods that are existentially most imperative and at stake (2005, xxix).
5. See Gottlieb 2000 and Keller 2007 for work on an anthropology of infancy and Laughlin 1989 for a perinatal anthropology.
6. See chapter 3 for a description of such spirits.
7. See Bierlich 2007, which offers an extensive account of similar notions of illness causation.
8. For comparison, the under-five mortality rate in the United States is 7 deaths per 1,000 births. In Iceland and Finland, it is 2 deaths per 1,000 births.
9. Jónína Einarsdóttir (2004) offers a well-developed argument concerning parental investment and economic context.

Chapter 2. For the House

1. Thomas Beidelman (1993, 54) also details these domains.
2. See Fortes 1959.
3. See chapter 5.
4. Chapter 3 elaborates on women and spirits.
5. See Cassiman 2006 and Eguavoen 2008, 91.

6. See Knauft 2010, 39; and Lancy 2014 for descriptions of similar practices in other cultures.

7. See a similar description in Gottlieb 2004, 81–82.

8. See a similar description in Fortes 1987, 202.

9. Fortes also described neutral or good spirits (1987, 274).

Chapter 3. For the Bush

1. For example, see Fernandez 1966.

2. For examples of "snake children," see Dettwyler 1994; Gottlieb 2000a; and Sargent 1982.

3. The *dongo*, or horn, is the ritual object used to send the spirit child back to the bush. It consists of a cow horn filled with medicine and covered with chicken feathers from previous sacrifices to it. See chapter 6 for a full description.

4. The concept of moral imagination has been used by both Beidelman (1993) and Livingston (2005), and my use here closely matches their understandings.

5. Chapter 4 further develops the way this spirit discourse shapes concerns around the autonomy and behavior of women.

Chapter 4. Spirit Child Behavior and Causation

1. See Cassiman 2006 and Smith-Oka 2012.

2. Many thanks to Albert Awedoba (personal communication, 2013) for emphasizing this to me.

3. See Goody 1962, 391.

Chapter 5. Detection and Decision-Making

1. See chapter 6 for a description and analysis of the *dongo* and its powers.

2. See Denham 2015 for more details and an analysis of the divination process.

3. Chapter 8 offers details on running away and its consequences.

Chapter 6. Concoctions and Concoction Men

1. Bernhard Bierlich (2007) and Jon Kirby (1997) further elaborate on color distinctions for medicines in northern Ghana.

2. Jónína Einarsdóttir (2004, 2005) also remarks on the role of ants in Guinea-Bissau.

3. The LD_{50} of the root bark is 2.45 milligrams per kilogram for mice, and the LD_{100} is 3.4 to 3.8 milligrams per kilogram (Tessier, Bouguet, and Paris 1975, cited in Neuwinger 1996, 514).

Chapter 7. Causing Death and Prolonging Lives

1. See Denham et al. 2010 for more on the process of classifying all spirit child deaths as infanticide in demographic data.

2. Chapters 5 and 8 support this position.

3. See Brandt 1987 and Einarsdóttir 2009.

Chapter 8. Why Infanticide?

1. See chapter 5 for a discussion of decision-making.

2. Einarsdóttir (2004) and Nations and Rebhun (1988) offer similar observations on expressing maternal grief.

3. Chapter 5 details the process of gathering evidence.

4. For a similar example, see Weiss 1994, 267.

Conclusion

1. N'ma was likely the last known spirit child death that was intentionally facilitated in the area where this research occurred.

2. Ingstad (1995, 248) also discusses this process.

3. Leatherman draws on the work of Chambers (1989) and Watts and Bohle (1993) in his definition of *vulnerability*.

REFERENCES

Abu-Lughod, Lila. 1991. "Writing Against Culture." In *Recapturing Anthropology: Working in the Present*, edited by Richard G. Fox, 137–62. Santa Fe: School of American Research.

Adongo, Philip B., James F. Phillips, Beverly Kajihara, Clara Fayorsey, Cornelius Debpuur, and Fred N. Binka. 1997. "Cultural Factors Constraining the Introduction of Family Planning among the Kassena-Nankana of Northern Ghana." *Social Science and Medicine* 45 (12): 1789–1804.

Allen, Denise Roth. 2004. *Managing Motherhood, Managing Risk Fertility, and Danger in West Central Tanzania*. Ann Arbor: University of Michigan Press.

Allotey, Pascale, and Daniel Reidpath. 2001. "Establishing the Causes of Childhood Mortality in Ghana: The 'Spirit Child.'" *Social Science and Medicine* 52 (7): 1007–12.

Allman, Jean, and John Parker. 2005. *Tongnaab: History of a West African God*. Bloomington: Indiana University Press.

Amenga-Etego, Rose Mary. 2011. *Mending the Broken Pieces: Indigenous Religion and Sustainable Rural Development in Northern Ghana*. Trenton, NJ: Africa World Press.

Anspach, Mark R. 2004. "Introduction." In *Oedipus Unbound: Selected Writings on Rivalry and Desire*, edited by Mark R. Anspach, vii–liv. Stanford, CA: Stanford University Press.

Appel, Jacob M. 2011. "Toward a Psychodynamic Approach to Bioethics." *American Journal of Psychoanalysis* 71 (1): 58–66.

Awedoba, Albert. 2000. *An Introduction to Kasena Society and Culture through Their Proverbs*. New York: University Press of America.

Baiden, Frank, Abraham Hodgson, Martin Adjuik, Philip B. Adongo, Ayaga Bawah, and Fred N. Binka. 2006. "Trend and Causes of Neonatal Mortality in the Kassena-Nankana District of Northern Ghana, 1995–2002." *Tropical Medicine and International Health* 11 (4): 532–39.

Balikci, Asen. 1967. "Female Infanticide on the Arctic Coast." *Royal Anthropological Institute of Great Britain and Ireland* 2 (4): 615–25.

Balint, Alice. 1949. "Love for the Mother and Mother-Love." *International Journal of Psycho-Analysis* 30:251–59.

Bannerman-Richter, Gabriel. 1987. *Mmoetia: The Mysterious Little People*. Elk Grove, CA: Gabari.

Bastian, Misty. 2001. "The Demon Superstition: Abominable Twins and Mission Culture in Onitsha History." *Ethnology* 40 (1): 13–27.

Bechtold, Brigitte H., and Donna Cooper Graves. 2006. "Introduction: Towards an Understanding of the Infanticide Scholarship." In *Killing Infants: Studies in the World-wide Practice of Infanticide*, edited by Brigitte H. Bechtold and Donna Cooper Graves, 1–20. Lewiston, NY: Edwin Mellen.

———. 2010. "Introduction." In *An Encyclopedia of Infanticide*, edited by Brigitte H. Bechtold and Donna Cooper Graves, iii–xix. Lewiston, NY: Edwin Mellen.

Beidelman, Thomas O. 1993. *Moral Imagination in Kaguru Modes of Thought*. Washington, DC: Smithsonian Institution Press.

Bierlich, Bernhard. 2007. *The Problem of Money: African Agency and Western Medicine in Northern Ghana*. New York: Berghahn.

Binka, Fred N., Ayaga A. Bawah, James F. Phillips, Abraham Hodgson, Martin Adjuik, and Bruce MacLeod. 2007. "Rapid Achievement of the Child Survival Millennium Development Goal: Evidence from the Navrongo Experiment in Northern Ghana." *Tropical Medicine and International Health* 12 (5): 578–83.

Binka, Fred N., Alex Nazzar, and James F. Phillips. 1995. "The Navrongo Community Health and Family Planning Project." *Studies in Family Planning* 26 (3): 121–39.

Binka, Fred N., Pierre Ngom, James F. Phillips, Kubaje Adazu, and Bruce B. MacLeod. 1999. "Assessing Population Dynamics in a Rural African Society: The Navrongo Demographic Surveillance System." *Journal of Biosocial Science* 31:375–91.

Blench, Robert, ed. 2006. "Dagbani-English Dictionary." http://www.rogerblench .info/Language/Niger-Congo/Gur/Dagbani%20dictionary%20CD.pdf.

Brandt, Richard B. 1987. "Public Policy and Life and Death Decisions Regarding Defective Newborns." In *Euthanasia and the Newborn: Conflicts Regarding Saving Lives*, edited by R. C. McMillan, H. Tristram Engelhardt Jr., and S. F. Spicker, 191–208. Dordrecht: D. Reidel.

Briggs, Charles L. 2007. "Mediating Infanticide: Theorizing Relations between Narrative and Violence." *Cultural Anthropology* 22 (3): 315–56.

Briggs, Katharine M. 1976. *An Encyclopedia of Fairies, Hobgoblins, Brownies, Boogies, and Other Supernatural Creatures*. New York: Pantheon.

Bugos, Paul E., and Lorraine M. McCarthy. 1984. "Ayoreo Infanticide: A Case Study." In *Infanticide: Comparative and Evolutionary Perspectives*, 503–20. New Brunswick, NJ: Transaction.

Burkill, H. M. 1985. *The Useful Plants of West Tropical Africa*. Vol. 2. Kew: Royal Botanic Gardens.

Cannon, Walter B. 1942. "Voodoo Death." *American Anthropologist* 44 (2): 169–81.

Cardinall, Allan Wolsey. 1920. *The Natives of the Northern Territories of the Gold Coast: Their Customs, Religions, and Folklore*. New York: E. P. Dutton and Company.

Cassidy, Claire Monod. 1987. "World-View Conflict and Toddler Malnutrition: Change Agent Dilemmas." In *Child Survival*, edited by Nancy Scheper-Hughes, 293–324. Dordrecht: D. Reidel.

Cassiman, Ann. 2006. *Stirring Life: Women's Paths and Places among the Kasena of Northern Ghana*. Uppsala: Uppsala University Library.

Chambers, Robert. 1989. "Editorial Introduction: Vulnerability, Coping, and Policy." *Institute of Development Studies Bulletin* 20 (2): 1–7.

Comaroff, John, and Jean Comaroff. 2001. "On Personhood: An Anthropological Perspective from Africa." *Social Identities* 7 (2): 267–83.

Corti, Lillian. 1998. *The Myth of Medea and the Murder of Children*. London: Greenwood.

Daly, Martin, and Margo Wilson. 1984. "A Sociobiological Analysis of Human Infanticide." In *Infanticide: Comparative and Evolutionary Perspectives*, edited by Glenn Hausfater and Sara Blafer Hrdy, 487–502. New York: Aldine.

Das, Veena, and Ranendra K. Das. 2007. "How the Body Speaks: Illness and the Lifeworld among the Urban Poor." In *Subjectivity: Ethnographic Investigations*, edited by Joao Biehl, Byron Good, and Arthur Kleinman, 66–97. Berkeley: University of California Press.

Debpuur, Cornelius, James F. Phillips, Elizabeth F. Jackson, Alex Nazzar, Pierre Ngom, and Fred N. Binka. 2002. "The Impact of the Navrongo Project on Contraceptive Knowledge and Use, Reproductive Preferences, and Fertility." *Studies in Family Planning* 33 (2): 141–64.

deMause, Lloyd. 1974. *The History of Childhood*. New York: Harper and Row.

Denham, Aaron R. 2012. "Shifting Maternal Responsibilities and Trajectories of Blame in Northern Ghana." In *Risk, Reproduction, and Narratives of Experience*, edited by Lauren Fordyce and Aminata Maraesa, 173–90. Nashville, TN: Vanderbilt University Press.

———. 2015. "A Psychodynamic Phenomenology of Nankani Interpretive Divination and the Formation of Meaning." *Ethos* 43 (2): 109–34.

Denham, Aaron R., Philip B. Adongo, Nicole Freydberg, and Abraham Hodgson. 2010. "Chasing Spirits: Clarifying the Spirit Child Phenomenon and Infanticide in Northern Ghana." *Social Science and Medicine* 71 (3): 608–15.

Derrida, Jacques. 1981. *Dissimilation*. London: Continuum.

Dettwyler, Katherine. 1994. *Dancing Skeletons: Life and Death in West Africa*. Long Grove, IL: Waveland.

Devereux, George. 1948. "Mohave Indian Infanticide." *Psychoanalytic Review* 35 (2): 126–39.

———. 1967. *From Anxiety to Method in the Behavioral Sciences*. The Hague: Mouton.

———. 1969. "Normal and Abnormal: The Key Concepts of Ethnopsychiatry." In *Man and His Culture*, edited by Warner Muensternerger, 113–36. New York: Taplinger.

Devisch, Rene. 1999. "Sorcery and Fetish." In *Law of the Lifegivers: The Domestication of Desire*, edited by R. Devish and C. Brodeur, 51–91. Amsterdam: Harwood.

Dewey, John. 1934. *Art as Experience*. Carbondale: Southern Illinois University Press.

Donnan, Hastings, and Fiona Magowan. 2010. *The Anthropology of Sex*. Oxford: Berg.

Douglas, Mary. 1966. *Purity and Danger*. London: Routledge.

———. 1973. *Natural Symbols*. New York: Vintage.

Dowbiggin, Ian Robert. 2007. *A Concise History of Euthanasia: Life, Death, God, and Medicine*. Lanham, MD: Rowman and Littlefield.

Driscoll, Catherine. 2005. "Killing Babies: Hrdy on the Evolution of Infanticide." *Biology and Philosophy* 20 (2–3): 271–89.

Eguavoen, Irit. 2008. *The Political Ecology of Household Water in Northern Ghana*. Berlin: LIT Verlag Münster.

Einarsdóttir, Jónína. 2004. *Tired of Weeping: Mother Love, Child Death, and Poverty in Guinea-Bissau*. Madison: University of Wisconsin Press.

———. 2005. "Restoration of the Social Order through the Extension of Non-Human Children." In *Uncertainty: Ethnographic Studies of Illness, Risk and the Struggle for Control*, edited by Vibeke Steffen, Richard Jenkins, and Hanne Jessen, 31–52. Copenhagen: Museum Tusculanum Press.

———. 2006. "Child Survival in Affluence and Poverty: Ethics and Fieldwork Experiences from Iceland and Guinea-Bissau." *Field Methods* 18 (2): 189–204.

———. 2008. "The Classification of Newborn Children: Consequences for Survival." In *Disabled People and the Right to Life: The Protection and Violation of Disabled People's Most Basic Human Rights*, edited by Luke Clements and Janet Read, 249–64. London: Routledge.

———. 2009. "Emotional Experts: Parents' Views on End-of-Life Decisions for Preterm Infants in Iceland." *Medical Anthropological Quarterly* 23 (1): 34–50.

Elliot, Anthony. 2004. *Social Theory since Freud: Traversing Social Imaginaries*. London: Routledge.

Evans-Pritchard, Edward E. 1976. *Witchcraft, Oracles, and Magic among Azande*. Oxford: Oxford University Press.

Ferme, Mariane. 2001. *The Underneath of Things: Violence, History, and the Everyday in Sierra Leone*. Berkeley: University of California Press.

Fernandez, James W. 1966. "Principles of Opposition and Vitality in Fang Aesthetics." *Journal of Aesthetics and Art Criticism* 25 (1): 53–64.

Fesmire, Steven. 2003. *John Dewey and Moral Imagination: Pragmatism in Ethics*. Bloomington: Indiana University Press.

Finerman, Ruthbeth. 1995. "'Parental Incompetence' and 'Selective Neglect': Blaming the Victim in Child Survival." *Social Science and Medicine* 40 (1): 5–13.

Finkler, Kaja. 1994. "Sacred Healing and Biomedicine Compared." *Medical Anthropology Quarterly* 8 (2): 178–97.

Fletcher, Joseph. 1978. "Infanticide and the Ethics of Loving Concern. In *Infanticide and the Value of Life*, edited by Marvin Kohl, 13–22. Buffalo: Prometheus.

Fortes, Meyer. 1937. *Marriage Law among the Tallensi*. Accra: Government Printing Department.

———. 1945. *The Dynamics of Clanship among the Tallensi*. Oxford: Oxford University Press.

———. 1949. *The Dynamics of Kinship among the Tallensi*. Oxford: Oxford University Press.

———. 1959. *Oedipus and Job in West African Religion*. Cambridge: Cambridge University Press.

———. 1987. *Religion, Morality, and the Person: Essays on Tallensi Religion*. Cambridge: Cambridge University Press.

Fortes, Meyer, and Doris Mayer. 1966. "Psychosis and Social Change among the Tallensi of Northern Ghana." *Cahier d'Etudes Africaines* 6 (1): 5–40.

Foucault, Michel. 1972. *The Archaeology of Knowledge*. New York: Pantheon.

Gesundheit, Benjamin, Avraham Steinberg, Shimon Glick, Reuven Or, and Alan Jotkovitz. 2006. "Euthanasia: An Overview and the Jewish Perspective." *Cancer Investigation* 24 (6): 621–29.

Ghana Statistical Service. 2015. *Ghana Poverty Mapping Report*. Accra: Ghana Statistical Service.

Ginsburg, Faye, and Rayna Rapp. 1991. "The Politics of Reproduction." *Annual Review of Anthropology* 20:311–43.

Girard, René. 1996. *The Girard Reader*. New York: Crossroad.

———. 2004. *Oedipus Unbound: Selected Writings on Rivalry and Desire*. Edited by Mark R. Anspach. Stanford, CA: Stanford University Press.

Goody, Jack. 1962. *Death, Property, and the Ancestors*. Stanford, CA: Stanford University Press.

Gottlieb, Alma. 1992. *Under the Kapok Tree: Identity and Difference in Beng Thought*. Chicago: University of Chicago Press.

————. 2000a. "Luring Your Child into This Life: A Beng Path for Infant Care." In *A World of Babies: Imagined Childcare Guides for Seven Societies*, edited by Judy S. DeLoache and Alma Gottlieb, 55–89. Cambridge: Cambridge University Press.

————. 2000b. "Where Have All the Babies Gone? Toward an Anthropology of Infants (and Their Caretakers)." *Anthropological Quarterly* 73 (3): 121–32.

————. 2004. *The Afterlife Is Where We Come From*. Chicago: University of Chicago Press.

Gottlieb, Alma, and Philip Graham. 1993. *Parallel Worlds: An Anthropologist and Writer Encounter Africa*. New York: Crown.

Graburn, Nelson. 1987. "Severe Child Abuse among the Canadian Inuit." In *Child Survival*, edited by Nancy Scheper-Hughes, 211–25. Dordrecht: D. Reidel.

Hawkins, Sean. 2002. *Writing and Colonialism in Northern Ghana*. Toronto: University of Toronto Press.

Hill, Catherine, and Helen Ball. 1996. Abnormal Births and Other Ill Omens. *Human Nature* 7 (4): 381–401.

Hill, Kim R., and A. Magdalena Hurtado. 1996. *Ache Life History: The Ecology and Demography of a Foraging People*. New York: Aldine de Gruyter.

Hoffmaster, Barry. 2006. "What Does Vulnerability Mean?" *Hastings Center Report* 36 (2): 38–45.

Holland, Dorothy. 1992. "How Cultural Systems Become Desire: A Case Study of American Romance." In *Human Motives and Cultural Models*, edited by Roy D'Andrade and Claudia Strauss, 61–89. Cambridge: Cambridge University Press.

Hontela, Slavoj, and John R. Reddon. 1996. "Infanticide of Defective Newborns: An Old Midwife's Story." *Psychological Reports* 79 (3): 1275–78.

Howell, Allison. 1997. *The Religious Itinerary of a Ghanaian People: The Kasena and the Christian Gospel*. Berlin: Peter Lang.

Hrdy, Sara Blafer. 1999. *Mother Nature: Maternal Instincts and How They Shape the Human Species*. New York: Ballantine.

Hrdy, Sara Blafer, and Glenn Hausfater. 1984. "Introduction and Overview." In *Infanticide*, edited by Sara Blafer Hrdy and Glenn Hausfater, xiii–xv. New York: Aldine.

Ingham, John. 1996. *Psychological Anthropology Reconsidered*. Cambridge: Cambridge University Press.

Ingold, Tim. 2007. "Movement, Knowledge, and Description." In *Holistic Anthropology*, edited by David Parkin and Stanley Ulijaszek, 194–211. New York: Berghahn.

Ingstad, Benedicte. 1995. "Mpho ya Modimo—A Gift from God: Perspectives on 'Attitudes' toward Disabled Persons." In *Disability and Culture*, edited by Benedicte Ingstad and Susan Reynolds-Whyte, 246–63. Berkeley: University of California Press.

————. 2007. "Seeing Disability and Human Rights in the Local Context: Botswana Revisited." In *Disability in Local and Global Worlds*, edited by Benedicte Ingstad and Susan Reynolds-Whyte, 237–58. Berkeley: University of California Press.

Ingstad, Benedicte, and Susan Reynolds-Whyte. 1995. "Part Two: Social Contexts of Disability." In *Disability and Culture*, edited by Benedicte Ingstad and Susan Reynolds-Whyte, 137–39. Berkeley: University of California Press.

Jackson, Michael. 1979. "Prevented Successions: A Commentary upon a Kuranko Narrative." In *Fantasy and Symbol: Studies in Anthropological Interpretation*, edited by R. H. Hook, 95–131. London: Academic Press.

————. 1989. *Paths toward a Clearing: Radical Empiricism and Ethnographic Inquiry*. Bloomington: Indiana University Press.

————. 1998. *Minima Ethnographica: Intersubjectivity and the Anthropological Project.* Chicago: University of Chicago Press.

————. 2002. *Politics of Storytelling: Violence, Transgression, and Intersubjectivity.* Chicago: University of Chicago Press.

————. 2005. *Existential Anthropology.* New York: Berghahn.

————. 2007. *Excursions.* Durham, NC: Duke University Press.

Janzen, John M. 1978. *The Quest for Therapy: Medical Pluralism in Lower Zaire.* Berkeley: University of California Press.

Johnson, Allen W., and Douglass R. Price-Williams. 1996. *Oedipus Ubiquitous: The Family Complex in World Folk Literature.* Stanford, CA: Stanford University Press.

Johnson, Orna R. 1981. "The Socioeconomic Context of Child Abuse and Neglect in Native South America." In *Child Abuse and Neglect: Cross-Cultural Perspectives,* edited by Jill Korbin, 56–70. Berkeley: University of California Press.

Kapferer, Jean-Noel. 1987. *Rumors: Uses, Interpretations, and Images.* New Brunswick, NJ: Transaction.

Karp, Ivan. 1993. "Foreword." In *Moral Imagination in Kanguru Modes of Thought,* xi–xv. Washington, DC: Smithsonian Institution Press.

Keane, Webb. 2003. "Self-Interpretation, Agency, and the Objects of Anthropology: Reflections on a Genealogy." *Comparative Studies in Society and History* 45 (2): 222–48.

Keller, Heidi. 2007. *Cultures of Infancy.* Mahwah, NJ: Lawrence Erlbaum.

Kimball, A. Samuel. 2007. *The Infanticidal Logic of Evolution and Culture.* Newark: University of Delaware Press.

Kirby, Jon P. 1997. "White, Red, and Black: Colour Classification and Illness Management in Northern Ghana." *Social Science and Medicine* 44 (2): 215–30.

Kirmayer, Laurence J., and Norman Sartorius. 2007. "Cultural Models and Somatic Syndromes." *Psychosomatic Medicine* 69 (9): 832–40.

Kleinman, Arthur. 2006. *What Really Matters: Living a Moral Life amidst Uncertainty and Danger.* Oxford: Oxford University Press.

Knauft, Bruce. 2010. *The Gebusi: Lives Transformed in a Rainforest World.* 2nd ed. New York: McGraw-Hill.

Kohl, Marvin. 1975. "Voluntary Beneficent Euthanasia." In *Beneficent Euthanasia,* edited by Marvin Kohl, 130–41. Buffalo: Prometheus.

————. 1978. "Preface." In *Infanticide and the Value of Life,* edited by Marvin Kohl, 5–9. Buffalo: Prometheus.

Kropp-Dakubu, Mary Esther. 2009. *Parlons Farefari (Gurene).* Paris: L'Harmattan.

Lancy, David. 2008. *The Anthropology of Childhood: Cherubs, Chattel, and Changelings.* Cambridge: Cambridge University Press.

————. 2014. "'Babies Aren't Persons': A Survey of Delayed Personhood." In *Different Faces of Attachment: Cultural Variations of a Universal Human Need,* edited by Hiltrud Otto and Heidi Keller, 66–109. Cambridge: Cambridge University Press.

Larme, Anne C. 1997. "Health Care Allocation and Selective Neglect in Rural Peru." *Social Science and Medicine* 44 (11): 1711–23.

Laughlin, Charles D. 1989. "Pre- and Perinatal Anthropology: A Selective Review." *Pre- and Perinatal Psychology Journal* 3 (4): 261–96.

Leatherman, Thomas. 2005. "A Space of Vulnerability in Poverty and Health: Political-Ecology and Biocultural Analysis." *Ethos* 33 (1): 46–70.

Lerer, Leonard B. 1998. "Who Is the Rogue? Hunger, Death, and Circumstance in John Mampe Square." In *Small Wars: The Cultural Politics of Childhood,* edited by

Nancy Scheper-Hughes and Carolyn Sargent, 228–50. Berkeley: University of California Press.

Levinas, Emmanuel. 1998. *Entre Nous: Thinking-of-the-Other.* New York: Columbia University Press.

Levy, Robert, and Douglas Hollan. 1998. "Person-Centered Interviewing and Observation." In *Handbook of Methods in Cultural Anthropology,* 333–64. Lanham, MD: Rowman and Littlefield.

Livingston, Julie. 2005. *Debility and the Moral Imagination in Botswana.* Bloomington: Indiana University Press.

Lothian, Jason. 1996. *Children's Health in Ghana's North.* Ottawa, ON: Gemini News Service, International Development Research Centre.

Mauss, Marcel. 1938. "Une Catégorie de L'Esprit Humain: La Notion de Personne Celle de 'Moi.'" *Journal of the Royal Anthropological Institute* 68:263–81.

Mbembe, Achille. 2001. *On the Postcolony.* Berkeley: University of California Press.

McMahan, Jeff. 2001. *The Ethics of Killing.* Oxford: Oxford University Press.

Mendonsa, Eugene. 1982. *The Politics of Divination.* Berkeley: University of California Press.

Mensch, B. S., D. Bagah, W. H. Clark, and F. Binka. 1999. "The Changing Nature of Adolescence in the Kassena-Nankana District of Northern Ghana." *Studies in Family Planning* 30 (2): 95–111.

Metzler, Karen. 1978. "If There's Life, Make It Worth Living." In *Infanticide and the Value of Life,* edited by Marvin Kohl, 172–79. Buffalo: Prometheus.

Michalsen, Andrej, and Konrad Reinhart. 2006. "'Euthanasia': A Confusing Term, Abused under the Nazi Regime and Misused in Present End-of-Life Debate." *Intensive Care Medicine* 32:1304–10.

Miller, Barbara D. 1987. "Female Infanticide and Child Neglect in Rural North India." In *Child Survival,* edited by Nancy Scheper-Hughes, 95–112. Dordrecht: D. Reidel.

Mills, Samuel, John Williams, George Wak, and Abraham Hodgson. 2008. "Maternal Mortality Decline in the Kassena-Nankana District of Northern Ghana." *Maternal and Child Health Journal* 12 (5): 557–85.

Moore, Henrietta L. 2007. *The Subject of Anthropology: Gender, Symbolism, and Psychoanalysis.* Cambridge: Polity.

Morgan, Lynn M. 1998. "Ambiguities Lost: Fashioning the Fetus into a Child in Ecuador and the United States." In *Small Wars: The Cultural Politics of Childhood,* edited by Nancy Scheper-Hughes and Carolyn Sargent, 58–74. Berkeley: University of California Press.

Mudimbe, Valentin-Yves. 1988. *The Invention of Africa: Gnosis, Philosophy, and the Order of Knowledge.* Bloomington: Indiana University Press.

Nations, Marilyn K., and Linda-Anne Rebhun. 1988. "Angels with Wet Wings Won't Fly: Maternal Sentiment in Brazil and the Image of Neglect." *Culture, Medicine, and Psychiatry* 12:141–200.

Neuwinger, Hans Dieter. 1996. *African Ethnobotany: Poisons and Drugs.* London: Chapman & Hall.

Norwood, Frances. 2009. *The Maintenance of Life: Preventing Social Death through Euthanasia Talk and End-of-Life Care, Lessons from the Netherlands.* Durham, NC: Carolina Academic Press.

Obeyesekere, Gananath. 1990. *The Work of Culture: Symbolic Transformation in Psychoanalysis and Anthropology.* Chicago: University of Chicago Press.

Oduro, Abraham Rexford, George Wak, Daniel Azongo, Cornelius Debpuur, Peter Wontuo, Felix Kondayire, Paul Welaga, Ayaga Bawah, Alex Nazzar, John Williams, Abraham Hodgson, and Fred Binka. 2012. "Profile of the Navrongo Health and Demographic Surveillance System." *International Journal of Epidemiology* 41 (4): 968–76.

Olivier de Sardin, Jean-Pierre. 2005. *Anthropology and Development: Understanding Continuity and Social Change.* London: Zed.

Ortner, Sherry. 2006. *Anthropology and Social Theory: Culture, Power, and the Acting Subject.* Durham, NC: Duke University Press.

Parker, Rozsika. 1995. *Torn in Two: The Experience of Maternal Ambivalence.* London: Virago.

Parkin, David. 2007. "Introduction Emergence and Convergence." In *Holistic Anthropology*, edited by David Parkin and Stanley Ulijaszek, 1–20. New York: Berghahn.

Peek, Philip. 1991. "The Study of Divination, Present and Past." In *African Divination Systems: Ways of Knowing*, edited by Philip Peek, 1–22. Bloomington: Indiana University Press.

———. 2011. *Twins in African and Diaspora Cultures: Double Trouble, Twice Blessed.* Bloomington: Indiana University Press.

Piers, Maria. 1978. *Infanticide: Past and Present.* New York: W. W. Norton.

Pinto, Sarah. 2008. *Where There Is No Midwife: Birth and Loss in Rural India.* New York: Berghahn.

Piot, Charles. 1999. *Remotely Global: Village Modernity in West Africa.* Chicago: University of Chicago Press.

Porter, Theresa, and Helen Gavin. 2010. "Infanticide and Neonaticide: A Review of 40 Years of Research Literature on Incidence and Causes." *Trauma, Violence, and Abuse* 11 (3): 99–112.

Quinn, Naomi, and Dorothy Holland. 1987. "Culture and Cognition." In *Cultural Models in Language and Thought*, edited by Dorothy Holland and Naomi Quinn, 3–40. Cambridge: Cambridge University Press.

Rapp, Rayna, and Faye Ginsburg. 2001. "Enabling Disability: Rewriting Kinship, Reimagining Citizenship." *Public Culture* 13 (3): 533–56.

Rattray, Robert S. 1932. *The Tribes of the Ashanti Hinterland.* Oxford: Clarendon.

Resnick, Phillip J. 1969. "Child Murder by Parents: A Psychiatric Review of Filicide." *American Journal of Psychiatry* 126 (3): 149–63.

Reynolds-Whyte, Susan, and Benedicte Ingstad. 1995. "Disability and Culture: An Overview." In *Disability and Culture*, edited by Benedicte Ingstad and Susan Reynolds-Whyte, 3–32. Berkeley: University of California Press.

———. 2007. "Introduction: Disability Connections." In *Disability in Local and Global Worlds*, edited by Benedicte Ingstad and Susan Reynolds-Whyte, 1–29. Berkeley: University of California Press.

Ruddick, Sara. 1980. "Maternal Thinking." *Feminist Studies* 6:342–64.

Sahlins, Marshall. 2010. "The Whole Is a Part: Intercultural Politics of Order and Change." In *Experiments in Holism: Theory and Practice in Contemporary Anthropology*, edited by Ton Otto and Nils Bubandt, 102–26. West Sussex: Wiley-Blackwell.

Sargent, Carolyn. 1982. "Solitary Confinement: Birth Practices among the Bariba of the People's Republic of Benin." In *The Anthropology of Human Birth*, edited by Margarita Kay, 193–210. Philadelphia: P. A. Davis.

———. 1988. "Born to Die: Witchcraft and Infanticide in Bariba Culture." *Ethnology* 27 (1): 79–95.

Savulescu, Julian. 2013. "Abortion, Infanticide, and Allowing Babies to Die, 40 Years On." *Journal of Medical Ethics* 39:257–59.

Scheper-Hughes, Nancy. 1985. "Culture, Scarcity, and Maternal Thinking: Maternal Detachment and Infant Survival in a Brazilian Shantytown." *Ethos* 13 (4): 291–317.

———. 1987. Introduction: The Cultural Politics of Child Survival. In *Child Survival*, edited by Nancy Scheper-Hughes, 1–29. Dordrecht: D. Reidel.

———. 1988. Letter to the Editor. *Culture, Medicine and Psychiatry* 12:259–60.

———. 1992. *Death without Weeping: The Violence of Everyday Life in Brazil.* Berkeley: University of California Press.

Scheper-Hughes, Nancy, and Margaret M. Lock. 1987. "The Mindful Body: A Prolegomenon to Future Work in Medical Anthropology." *Medical Anthropology Quarterly* 1 (1): 6–41.

Schrire, Carmel, and William Lee Steiger. 1974. "A Matter of Life and Death: An Investigation into the Practice of Female Infanticide in the Arctic." *Man* 9 (2): 161–84.

Schwartz, Lita Linzer. 2000. *Endangered Children: Neonaticide, Infanticide, Filicide.* Boca Raton, FL: CRC.

Scott, Eleanor. 2001. "Killing the Female? Archaeological Narratives of Infanticide." In *Gender and the Archaeology of Death*, edited by Bettina Arnold and Nancy L. Wicker, 3–22. Lanham, MD: Alta Mira.

Scrimshaw, Susan C. M. 1984. "Infanticide in Human Populations: Societal and Individual Concerns." In *Infanticide*, edited by Sara Blafer Hrdy and Glenn Hausfater, 439–62. New York: Aldine.

Sen, Amartya. 1990. "More Than 100 Million Women Are Missing." *New York Review of Books* 37 (20): 61–66.

Shaw, Denise. 2006. "'What She Want to Go and Do That For?' Examining Infanticide in Toni Morrison's 'Beloved.'" In *Killing Infants: Studies in the Worldwide Practice of Infanticide*, edited by Brigitte H. Bechtold and Donna Cooper Graves, 255–80. Lewiston, NY: Edwin Mellen.

Shaw, Rosalind. 2000. "Toik Af, Lef Af: A Political Economy of Temme Techniques of Secrecy and Self." In *African Philosophy as Cultural Inquiry*, edited by Ivan Karp and D. A. Masolo, 25–49. Bloomington: Indiana University Press.

Shostak, Marjorie. 1981. *Nisa: The Life and Words of a !Kung Woman.* New York: Vintage.

Silver, Carole G. 1999. *Strange and Secret Peoples: Fairies and Victorian Consciousness.* Oxford: Oxford University Press.

Sklansky, Mark. 2001. "Neonatal Euthanasia: Moral Considerations and Criminal Liability." *Journal of Medical Ethics* 27:5–11.

Smith-Oka, Vania. 2012. "'They Don't Know Anything': How Medical Authority Constructs Perceptions of Reproductive Risk among Low-Income Mothers in Mexico." In *Risk, Reproduction, and Narratives of Experience*, edited by Lauren Fordyce and Aminata Maraesa, 103–22. Nashville, TN: Vanderbilt University Press.

Steckley, John. 2008. *White Lies about the Inuit.* Peterborough, Ontario: Broadview.

Stern, Donnel B. 2003. *Unformulated Experience: From Dissociation to Imagination in Psychoanalysis.* New York: Routledge.

Stoller, Paul. 1997. *Sensuous Scholarship.* Philadelphia: University of Pennsylvania Press.

Strauss, Claudia. 1992. "What Makes Tony Run? Schemas as Motives Reconsidered." In *Human Motives and Cultural Models*, edited by Roy D'Andrade and Claudia Strauss, 191–224. Cambridge: Cambridge University Press.

Stroeken, Koen. 2004. "In Search of the Real: The Healing Contingency of Sukuma Divination." In *Divination and Healing: Potent Vision*, edited by Michael Winkelman and Philip Peek, 29–54. Tucson: University of Arizona Press.

Sussman, Robert W., James M. Cheverud, and Thad Q. Bartlett. 1994. "Infant Killing as an Evolutionary Strategy: Reality or Myth." *Evolutionary Anthropology* 3 (5): 149–51.

Swain, Shurlee. 2006. "Infanticide, Savagery, and Civilization: The Australian Experience." In *Killing Infants: Studies in the Worldwide Practice of Infanticide*, edited by Brigitte H. Bechtold and Donna Cooper Graves, 85–106. Lewiston, NY: Edwin Mellen.

Tessier, A. M., A. Bouguet, and R. Paris. 1975. "Sur Quelques Euphorbiacees Toxiques Africaines." *Plantes Médicinales et Phytothérapie* 9:238–49.

Tobin, Jeffrey. 1997. "Savages, the Poor, and the Discourse of Hawaiian Infanticide." *Journal of the Polynesian Society* 106 (1): 65–92.

Tonah, Steve. 1994. "Agricultural Extension Services and Smallholder Farmers' Indebtedness in Northeastern Ghana." *Journal of Asian and African Studies* 29:119–28.

Traore, Aristide, Sylvin Ouedraogo, Adama Kabore, Hamidou H. Tamboura, and Pierre Guissoua. 2014. "The Acute Toxicity in Mice and the In Vitro Anthelminthic Effects on *Haemonchus contortus* of the Extracts from Three Plants (*Cassia sieberiana, Guiera senegalensis*, and *Sapium grahamii*) Used in Traditional Medicine in Burkina Faso." *Annals of Biological Research* 5 (2): 41–46.

Turner, Victor. 1967. *The Forest of Symbols: Aspects of Ndembu Ritual*. Ithaca, NY: Cornell University Press.

———. 1969. *The Ritual Process: Structure and Anti-Structure*. Chicago: Aldine.

Urban, Greg. 1996. *Metaphysical Community: The Interplay of the Senses and the Intellect*. Austin: University of Texas Press.

Van Hooff, Anton J. L. 2004. "Ancient Euthanasia: 'Good Death' and the Doctor in the Graeco-Roman World." *Social Science and Medicine* 58 (5): 975–85.

Verhagen, Eduard. 2013. "The Groningen Protocol for Newborn Euthanasia; Which Way Did the Slippery Slope Tilt?" *Journal of Medical Ethics* 39 (5): 293–95.

Verhagen, Eduard, and Pieter Sauer. 2005. "The Groningen Protocol: Euthanasia in Severely Ill Newborns." *New England Journal of Medicine* 352 (10): 959–62.

Waldram, James. 2004. *Revenge of Windigo: The Construction of the Mind and Mental Health of North American Aboriginal Peoples*. Toronto: University of Toronto Press.

Watts, Michael J., and Hans G. Bohle. 1993. "The Space of Vulnerability: The Causal Structure of Hunger and Famine." *Progress in Human Geography* 17 (1): 43–67.

Weir, Robert. 1984. *Selective Nontreatment of Handicapped Newborns*. Oxford: Oxford University Press.

Weiss, Meira. 1994. *Conditional Love: Parents' Attitudes toward Handicapped Children*. Westport, CT: Bergin and Garvey.

———. 1998. "Ethical Reflections: Taking a Walk on the Wild Side." In *Small Wars: The Cultural Politics of Childhood*, edited by Nancy Scheper-Hughes and Carolyn Sargent, 149–62. Berkeley: University of California Press.

———. 2007. "The Chosen Body and the Rejection of Disability in Israeli Society." In *Disability in Local and Global Worlds*, edited by Benedicte Ingstad and Susan Reynolds-Whyte, 107–27. Berkeley: University of California Press.

West, Harry. 2007. *Ethnographic Sorcery*. Chicago: University of Chicago Press.

White, Luise. 2000. *Speaking with Vampires: Rumor and History in Colonial Africa*. Berkeley: University of California Press.

Williamson, Laila. 1978. "Infanticide: An Anthropological Analysis." In *Infanticide and the Value of Life*, edited by Marvin Kohl, 61–75. Buffalo: Prometheus.

Zere, Eyob, Joses M. Kirigia, Sambe Duale, and James Akazili. 2012. "Inequities in Maternal and Child Health Outcomes and Interventions in Ghana." *BMC Public Health* 12:252.

Zigon, Jarret. 2008. *Morality: An Anthropological Perspective*. Oxford: Berg.

INDEX

Page numbers in italics indicate illustrations.

AFRICA AND THE DIASPORA
History, Politics, Culture

SERIES EDITORS

Thomas Spear
Neil Kodesh
Tejumola Olaniyan
Michael G. Schatzberg
James H. Sweet